JOURNEY TO THE HEART OF PACHAMAMA

ANN WINDES

Edited by Cynthia Damon

Edited by Cynthia Damon
Contributing editor and back jacket by Adell Shay
Cover designed by Angela Akers
Artwork by Meghan Fredrick
Author's photo by Kristen Hastings
Photos by the author

ISBN-10: 061566900X
ISBN-13: 9780615669007

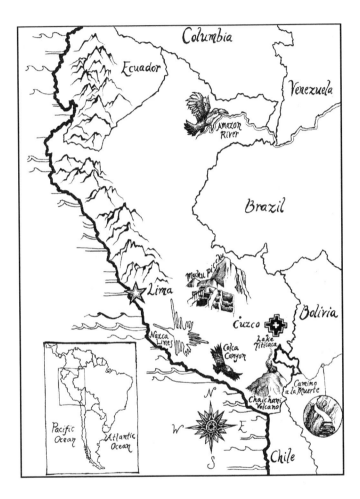

This book is dedicated to
The parental units, Seledonia, and Sam

ACKNOWLEDGEMENTS

Without sobriety, none of this would have been possible. For that I give thanks to my Divine Spirit, who has gracefully guided me along the path of recovery.

There are not enough words to express the gratitude I have for my editor, Cynthia Damon. She committed an unfathomable amount of time and effort into guiding, teaching, correcting, encouraging, and challenging me to be the best writer I could become. The transformation that took place from the first draft until the last page of this very book was due to her unwavering commitment to this story.

I would like to thank my parents, David and Tracey Windes, and Kathy and Joe Van Pelt for nourishing me with their love, faith and support. I'm grateful that they all put up with me during my difficult years.

Adell Shay was particularly invaluable in writing this book. I owe her my eternal gratitude for being a spiritual guide and for providing her wise counsel on many key chapters in the book.

A special thanks goes out to all my friends who invested themselves in this journey. Thank you, Saralyn

Smith, Alison Odekerken, mi hermana Lisa Windes, Aileen Willoughby, Gina Calescibetta, Marie Kuhn, and Bobbi Jo Thompson. Thanks to my dearest friend Carrie "Cockleshells" Fairbrother, who has been a cheerleader, a shoulder to cry on, and a staunch supporter in all my grandiose ideas.

Great thanks go to my mentor Dana Holman. Her gentle ways, humor, and uncanny ability to read chapters like they were *Masterpiece Theater* helped me through this journey. A heartfelt thanks also go to the women who surround me with their inspiration: Augusta Helmick, Katy Flatley, Lynne Waters, Karen Cleveland, Stephanie Beverly, Susan Condon, and Victoria Peters. I will always be grateful to my junior high English teacher Diane Dixon, who encouraged me to write and release the creativity within.

I raise my Shirley Temple to Captain Kylie Maguire, who saved my behind many times in Peru and was open to a serendipitous friendship that was instant, deep, and spirited. I am honored to have had the chance to put into writing her rescue story—I just hope I did it justice.

I'm indebted to Dr. Woods for fixing my back after the marathon stretches of writing. My gratitude goes to Principal Bowles for always giving me a high five and saying, "Go for it, kid!" whenever I had an idea that involved promoting my cause on campus.

Thank you Angela Akers for supporting my vision by creating a beautiful book cover. To Meghan Fredrick, a talented Palos Verdes High student who designed the llama and map pages at the beginning of this book. To Ally Oseas, another gifted PV student, who used her remarkable editing skills on the first draft of chapters.

My profound gratitude goes to all my students between the 2009 and 2012 school years who believed in my ideas and made possible so many of my goals with their donations and support. I'd like to send out a special thanks to Avery Durko, and Merit Milad who went above and beyond to help the cause. I have deep gratitude for the Liu family for agreeing to carry more than two hundred Christmas presents to Peru for the local kids in Clara's village.

And, of course, I could not forget to mention my loyal muse, Maya, my loving kitty who walked across the keyboard countless times, meowed when I typed for too long, licked my nose when I got excited about a chapter, and once dragged her soiled behind on freshly printed pages—probably offering her opinion on what I had just written.

Thank you to my dear neighbor Finn Nyberg who patiently listened to me read him chapters. Rest in peace my sweet friend—you were a light that brightened my life.

The person I am most indebted to is my Samisito, who has supported me through the humbling process of writing a book. He has been my rock, my late-night reader, and constant sounding board. I simply could not have written this without his love, patience, and loyalty. Gracias, Monchie, tú eres mi media naranja.

AUTHOR'S NOTE

This is a true story. I have recounted it as accurately as possible using my journal entries, blog posts, and subjective memory. Some names and details of individuals mentioned in this book have been changed to protect their privacy.

My references to recovery come from my personal journey in sobriety. I did my best to align with the traditions used by twelve-step programs and to adhere to the importance of the anonymity of those mentioned. This story is an example of one of the gifts of sobriety, and I am acutely aware that it all can be taken away in the blink of an eye. I was given a second chance, which is something I must remember every day.

Also, I'd like to mention my use of the word "God" in the book. I do not consider myself religious, but, to me, God defines the underlying loving spirit of all living things. My words are not intended to preach about believing in God, but instead to hopefully show an example of how having faith in the idea of a Universal Spirit can bring about miraculous experiences. Throughout the book, I interchange God with Divine

Spirit, Higher Power, the Source, the Force, the Universe, and Pachamama.

To me it is all the same.

It is all One.

We are all One.

THE HTO INDEX

The intense longing to share my life with some-one was becoming unbecomingly desperate. Why couldn't I seem to find a man who shared my interests and could be my partner in adventure? Even though there were over four million people in Los Angeles, it felt like I was fishing in a pool that was void of available quality men. Unfortunately, every bizarre and emotion-ally unstable bachelor within a hundred-mile radius was taking a bite at my lure.

Although I clung to a faith that there was truly someone out there who was undeniably compatible with me, being thirty-three, my loyalty to that child-hood fantasy was faltering. A tiny ember of love always remained lit inside, but I had nearly resigned myself to being an old cat-lady.

"You just need to dim your brights," a friend once told me. She said that maybe my personality was like someone who had left her headlights on high beam facing oncoming traffic. She explained that men were most likely daunted by the fact that I had played professional volleyball for over a decade, or by my indulgence in solo, risky adventures across the globe, or by the big whopper—being sober. Deep inside I knew there had to be a guy who could handle that total package and would love me for my high-beam personality and would not accept a dimmer version.

My parents had become exasperated that I seemed far from settling down, but they dealt with it playfully. Mom even gave me a shirt with a lady skeleton graphic surrounded by cats with the caption Still Waiting for The One. In turn, my father had invented the HTO index. A checklist cleverly linked to a mathematical formula he invented that would determine whether He's The One—or not. He knew I had an unhealthy habit of launching into false fantasies before I knew a man very well. Dad was only interested in hearing about a fella if he scored 90 percent or higher on the HTO index. Needless to say, Dad and I rarely spoke in detail about my love interests.

This sickening pattern of slipping into fantasy was easily facilitated through online dating sites. Captivating photos and faultless personal profiles allowed me to create idealized versions of who a guy might be; of course, once on the date, he never lived up to that expectation.

An endless succession of dreadful first dates via online sites left me feeling empty and hopeless; my girlfriends, however, remained entertained to no end. Many of the rendezvous are now amusing in hindsight, but after each letdown I felt disillusioned and was sure that a piece of the love coal burning within me had been extinguished.

I had the habit of deleting my profile directly following a catastrophic date, only to activate it again once I became inconsolably lonesome. The pages of my journals documented each and every dreadful date. I forced myself to reread them whenever I had the insane inspiration to reinstate my dating account.

* * *

• Never Been on a Date Jonathon: A superbly designed online profile enticed me, along with a dashing black-and-white portrait. Jonathon was tall, handsome, educated, played tennis, and was an avid reader. We spoke a few times on the phone, but I got the impression he might be reading questions he had prepared prior to the call. I did like, however, the idea that he was equipped to have a unique exchange and not just the typical question-and-answer interview session.

His presence was impressive, with elegantly styled mahogany hair and a polished smile visible from a distance. Jonathon's look was primed and precise with a white button-up shirt sprouting from a leather jacket, plus jeans and shiny dress shoes. The confident expression I noticed from a distance quickly transformed as he got closer, fear betraying him the second we sat down. An awkward silence loomed once I had introduced myself and he didn't do the same, but rather lowered his eyes to the ground and nervously wrung his hands.

"Actually, Ann, I have never been on a date before."

What?

Jonathon wiped his sweaty palms on his pant leg as he stuttered out a distressed explanation. "I have a phobia of people, but more specifically women. I'm actually in a support group, and we were advised to make a profile on Match.com to practice being social."

It was hard to believe that the thirty-five-year-old, good-looking man in front of me had never been on a date. *Ever.*

"It's easier to try to meet a woman through e-mail and on the phone because it's in a controlled environment. My psychiatrist has been coaching me ever since I chose your profile for my first attempt and has encouraged me to work up to this very moment right now."

Am I really his dating guinea pig? My optimism about the date was eclipsed as I realized this poor fella really needed me to be patient and kind with him. I lightened the mood by telling him a story of my travels to help get us through the discomfort. Then came his first practiced attempt at a compliment in a monotonous robotic voice.

"Ann. Your eyes sparkle like…the…stars…in… the…sky."

Oh boy. I feared for the good-bye stage of the date, which I figured would be one of the most intimidating parts for him. A hug? A wave? A kiss? A big kiss? A request for a future date? Or just a fist bump? I was thinking handshake.

His apprehension was obvious as he walked me to my car, and I sensed him getting tenser with every step.

Once we arrived at my car door, I turned to face him with my hand outstretched. With a ghostly pale face and on the verge of retching, he swiveled his back to me and…ran away. I could hear his fancy dress shoes clopping across the parking lot, his leather jacket flapping in the wind like wings.

• Oops, I Already Have a Girlfriend Andres: I kept going back to Andres's profile online but was in a phase of my Internet dating during which I didn't want to make the first move. He was Brazilian, built motorcycles from scratch, loved the outdoors and kite boarding. By chance one afternoon, I was thrilled to cross paths with him at a local coffee shop. The accidental meeting ended up in an invitation to mountain bike the following weekend. I skipped through the week with giddy anticipation.

Living only three blocks away, I rode to his house and threw my bike in his truck to head up to the hills of Palos Verdes. Being an avid bike rider most my life, I handled the rough terrain like a champ. Andres was obviously impressed when I took the corners with speed and challenged him on the uphills. We got to a clearing where he abruptly threw down his bike and strode over to me.

With a thick Brazilian accent he declared, "Oh, how I want to kiss you right now."

Really?

He paused and stepped back dramatically. "I am so torn! I feel shame, Ann, but I must admit, I *already* have a girlfriend. You must understand, I'm tired of her and I do not want her anymore. She cannot ride the bike like you do. I take many girls here on a bike to see if they can ride good for me. You did, and I *think* I want to be with you."

I felt sick to my stomach. *Hijo de puta!* "Why did you have a profile on Match.com if you already had a girlfriend?"

"Oh, Ann, you wouldn't understand."

Damn right, I didn't understand, and I was stuck way out in the hills with this jackass. "I am ready to go back," I fumed. "Now!"

When we returned to his house, he bluntly asked, "Do you always wear that style of clothing? It's just so *earthy*." Then Andres topped it off with, "It's not really *my* style."

Strapping on my helmet, I rode down the drive-way with plumes of angry steam blasting from my nose. Unexpectedly, a white Jetta screeched up the driveway, heading directly for me. I swerved, just barely missing a lamppost.

A crazed blonde flew out of the car and galloped toward me clumsily in her knee-high boots with jewelry a-jangling. It took me only a second to understand who *she* was.

Grabbing my shoulders, she shook me, screaming at the top of her lungs, "You fucking biiiiitch!"

Head-butting her heavily made-up face with my helmet was a solution, but I decided against it. In the old days, I would have thrown her ass down on the cement and given her a good thrashing, but, really, there was no reason to do that. It was odd, but a moment of peace and clarity came over me. So I stood my ground and stared her straight in the eyes.

"I didn't know," I said calmly. "I didn't know about you. Honestly. He just told me; that's why I'm leaving. Honey, you're raging on the wrong person. How about *we* join forces and beat the shit out of *him*?"

She exhaled as the steam fizzled out of her. We looked up the driveway, and Andres stood in the glow of an outdoor light watching the spectacle. I took the opportunity to jump back on my bike and take flight. Riding home in the middle of the empty street, I verbally vomited every explicative that heaved up from my being.

A week later, Andres called to leave an apology message in his distinctive accent, saying, "Well, what could I really do?" Then he had the huevos to ask, "So, Ann, what do ya say, how 'bout another bike ride this weekend?"

• Yorgos, the Greek George Clooney: While traveling Europe alone, I hopped a boat to Santorini, a volcanic island in the southern Aegean Sea. I dozed with the warm Greek sun streaming through the window. When I opened my eyes after a short nap, I discovered Yorgos, the Greek equivalent of George Clooney, sitting next to me.

Well, more like Clooney's distant cousin. He had a chiseled face, salt and pepper hair, and wore stylish island attire, which was all quite attractive except for his extremely hairy arms. He was charming, and his English was flawless. Giving me his business card, he invited me to call him to meet up for dinner.

When the boat docked, I emerged into complete chaos and stood off to the side with my bag, unsure of what to do next. There was supposed to be a pickup service from the villa I'd reserved, but no one had a sign with my name on it.

Suddenly, a sporty Fiat pulled up. The tinted window lowered to reveal Yorgos, with a big grin and his Ray-Bans dropped on his nose. "Hello, my beautiful, would you like a ride?"

"But of course," I replied.

He dropped me off and persuaded me to visit the Kamari Beach the following day, where he spent most of his time while in Santorini.

The next day, I rented a motor scooter and snorkel gear, then headed off to circumnavigate the island to explore the black, red, and white sand beaches of Santorini—each true to its name. My last stop was Kamari Beach, the most popular one with black sand and crystal-clear, deep-blue water. I lay back on one of the hundreds of lounge chairs with colorful umbrellas dotting the stretch of beach.

"Ann! My beautiful!" I heard just as I was getting settled in. I tried to hide my horror when I saw Yorgos strutting toward me. The sexy George Clooney lookalike had transformed into something entirely different. A thin, pale, and monstrously hairy man approached, like Chewbacca in *Star Wars*, but more like Hairbacca. Worst of all, he sported a bright yellow Speedo with hair sprouting out from all sides. He lowered his

Ray-Bans—his signature move—and winked. "What a coincidence!"

Yorgos lay on his side, hoisting his head up with his arm in an intended *GQ* pose. I was certainly jaded by growing up in Southern California where a guy would be heckled right off the beach if he wore a Speedo, let alone a yellow one. I attempted to swallow my judgment and enjoy him in what he considered culturally cool bathing attire.

"I dare you to go in the water," he taunted.

I agreed, feeling that nothing could be worse than lying next to him confidently displaying his furry physique. But then I considered the consequences: Yellow Speedo + water = transparent Speedo.

The water looked irresistible, and I felt instantly refreshed diving under the sparkling blue sea. While I tried to mermaid out in the deep like a true ocean nymph and keep my distance, he suddenly popped up before me like a sea monster from the depths, his body hair waving around like seaweed. He reached out and started tickling me through the water. I shrieked and pulled away, swimming to shore as if I were being pursued by a great white shark.

Scurrying up to my sarong, I lay back, out of breath. The *Jaws* shark-attack theme echoed in my mind: duh-dun, duh-dun, duh-dun. Yorgos pulled himself dramatically through the waist-deep water and then breached the surface. I looked the other way to avoid him glimpsing my fear, but an undeniable urge craned my head back. There in all its glory was his perfectly visible sea slug, moistly outlined by black squiggles, trapped behind the wet, yellow nylon. He pea-cocked himself up the beach and lay back in the sand in the same position as before, but now with a transparent Speedo.

Later, back at the villa, a young local boy knocked on my door and handed me a note. "My beautiful, please join me for dinner and dancing this evening. I will pick you up at eight." Disregarding my better judgment, I decided to go. Perhaps he deserved another chance since I had judged him on the quantity of his body hair and his customarily appropriate Greek beachwear.

We hit all the local spots, and he fed me an array of authentic Greek seaside delicacies. His disappoint-ment was obvious each time I declined his offer of an alcoholic drink.

"You are not allowed to leave the island with-out trying the wines of Santorini!" he'd protest. "The grapes are grown on volcanic soil, which gives the wine a unique mineral aftertaste."

"Believe me, Yorgos, that sounds amazing, but I don't drink," I'd say. "Please stop asking me!"

While I certainly would have been swigging down volcanic wine if I had visited Santorini a few years earlier, I knew how sobriety worked, and the number one rule was—obviously—don't drink. Yorgos didn't appreciate my abstinence and seemed to be get-ting more and more frustrated each time I refused a cocktail.

Later, we forged the steep cobblestone streets to the Taj Mahal, one of the busiest nightclubs in San-torini, where he knew a crew of locals. Being sober only a few years, I was still not at ease in drinking environments, especially when I didn't know anyone.

While sitting on one of the purple velvet sofas with oriental lanterns throwing silhouettes off our faces, he politely asked if he could kiss me. A potent blend of octopus, olives, and grappa rolled off his breath. Trying to make light of the situation, I attempted a Greek "No, thank you," "Ókhi efkharistó, Yorgos." He shrugged his shoulders, but I could see the wheels turning.

He invited me out to the dance floor, which brightened my mood since the DJ was playing funky Latin beats. After living for three years in Spain, I had picked up a distinct style of dancing that mixed flamenco—more specifically, the Sevillana style—with my own groove.

I was loosening up, really getting my rhythm going, when I noticed Yorgos observing me with a dark glare. Closing my eyes, I dropped into the music, twisting my hands above my head Sevillana-style, which visually is like picking imaginary fruit from a tree. I grabbed the corner of my dress, hitched it up to my thigh, and occasionally whipped my head quickly from side to side as done in Flamenco dancing.

A wave of enjoyment washed over my body, then Yorgos suddenly grasped my shoulder and shouted above the music, "Stop it!"

"Stop what?" I shouted back.

"Stop dancing like that!"

"What do you mean?"

He scowled overdramatically, demonstrating how I was dancing. "You dance like a bird!"

I was speechless. *A bird?*

"Actually, Ann, you're embarrassing me," he said. "I'm taking you back."

What? Are you serious? He needed to get rid of me so he could find someone else who would be willing to get alcoholically loosened up and then get busy Greco-Yeti style. Poor Yorgos had wasted all that charm, time, and money—all for a sober girl who danced like a bird.

• Mr. I Brought My Razor Bradley: Brad was a self-confident, hip yogi—with a sporty BMW convertible. Fascinated with flora and fauna, he stroked the leaves of every plant, flower, and tree within arm's reach, then inhaled the scent from his fingers and declared the plant's name, origin, and uses. After a month of getting together for yoga classes, hikes, foliage fondling, and beach picnics, I was beginning to feel optimistic about the relationship, except for one thing—the kissing. His kisses were unnatural, awkward, and didn't give me any sort of lightheaded delight, as kissing usually did.

He cocked his head far to one side, making a sideways oval with his mouth. If I tipped my head to meet his lips, he would abruptly switch to the other side, creating an even more difficult position. The few times we had kissed, both of us had pulled away with uncomfortable expressions, but never communicated about what we felt. Finally, after one more of our unromantic attempts at a kiss, he grabbed my shoulders and, with a look of disgust, snarled, "Good God, woman, your mustache is driving me crazy!"

My heart stopped and the blood drained out of my face. *No! Did he just say what I think he said?* Being a brunette, the dark hair on my upper lip had mortified me since the moment I was old enough to care. It began in junior high when a group of boys nicknamed me ATM—Ann the Man. My lip hair was not worthy of any award, but to this insecure young girl it became the focus of my obsession.

By high school, I bleached it and trimmed it, only to have one of my not-so-good friends call me out when were in front of cute boys. "Hey, guys, guess what? Ann bleaches her mustache!" Horrified, I always denied it, then raced home to analyze my lady 'stache from every angle.

As I got older and waxing became more common, I was diligent about it, but the upkeep for legs, bikini, and lip wax became an extravagant expenditure. So I took a break and went natural for a while. Seeing as how Brad was a self-proclaimed yogi, I figured he wouldn't mind. I was wrong.

With my greatest fear realized, I stood before him with tears welling up. Feeling like a frightened, unconfident little girl, my stomach turned and my mind went blank. I had yet to respond as Brad continued with his anti-mustache sentiments.

"I can't stand kissing you. Sorry, but it's driving me crazy, I have to turn my head all the way to the side just so it doesn't touch me."

Each of his words was like a humiliating slap that beat me into silent, lip-trembling shame.

"Oh, relax, Ann, don't get all emotional about it. Come on, now," he said patronizingly as he unzipped his backpack.

"Look here. I even brought you a razor. It's a really good electric one. So why don't you just go to the bathroom and take care of it—and then we'll be cool."

Although feeling a swell of boiling fury, I only had the capacity to squeak out, "Please leave."

Later, he e-mailed to let me know that I had overreacted, that his honesty was doing me a big favor, so I should have thanked him, not asked him to leave.

• Teary-Eyed Tony: The dating forces above were not ready to give me a break but rather planned to break me. Tony's profile was a dream. He was thirty-eight, played professional baseball in Italy, was a world traveler, meditated, liked to write, *and* was sober. The only thing was, there was no profile picture, which was almost always a bad sign. He had described himself to me over e-mail, so I took that into consideration.

I was a bit hesitant, but chose to ignore my intuition. He was shaping up to be a boy version of me! He claimed he would prefer not to talk on the phone but rather meet up for dinner directly since it was clear we already had a lot in common.

I was open to this suggestion since I had already tried every approach to the Internet dating dance. Since Tony seemed an ideal candidate already, I was grateful to forego my typical procedure of an initial coffee date and move right to dinner. This had backfired a few times previously, but I dismissed the data from my past experiences and agreed to the dinner date.

With eager anticipation of the big night, I told my dad that I had a good feeling about this one. I pulled up early to the Enterprise Fish Company in Santa Monica so I could meditate for a few minutes and ask selfishly to please let Tony be The One. The huge knot in my stomach tightened as the waiter guided me to the table where he waited. I slid in the seat across from a guy who could possibly be the man of my dreams.

However, the man sitting across from me did not look a thing like how he had described himself nor how I had imagined him. He was not thirty-eight, six feet tall, dark-haired, and in great shape, but more like fifty, five foot eight, bald, and overweight. I retreated back out of the seat before even saying hello.

"Wait!" he pleaded. "Please hear me out. I'm a good man, but no one will go out with me if I put up my real picture. Please, just give me a chance! We can have a nice dinner and then after you can decide whether you want to see me again or not."

I could feel a cold wind blowing out my faintly flickering love ember. I gritted my teeth with my hands fisted in my lap. I agreed to stay and convinced myself that if we really did have so much in common, it might be an entertaining meal.

I ordered a filet mignon and Tony asked for salmon and a pint of pale ale.

"Hey, there, Tony," I said, "I thought you were sober."

His eyes darted in panic, followed by a long silence. "Yeah," he finally said. "Well, actually, I have to something to admit."

With the next breath, he spewed his big confession. Tony had seen my profile online and fallen in love instantly. He came up with the bold idea of creating a new profile that matched mine entirely, combing through every word I wrote and inventing a Tony that I couldn't resist.

Once the food arrived, I had lost my appetite, but he had moved on to telling me his horrific life history. He was an untreated alcoholic, sex-aholic, and rageaholic. *Please tell me that means you're a big Rage Against the Machine fan*, I thought.

Just as the waiter brought the check, Tony choked up with emotion. He told me that his best friend Willy had died the week before. As the word "died" left his lips, a low moan escaped as he broke down sobbing. Sitting there awkwardly, I offered him a napkin when it suddenly hit me and I started to smile. *Ah-ha! I'm being punk'd!*

I swiveled my head around the restaurant with a big grin, looking for the cameras. All I saw were other patrons observing me apologetically, since I had a blubbering man at my table. There were no cameras.

"Why were you laughing?" he demanded between sniffles. He went on to explain, "Willy was the best dog a man could ask for! He was my best friend."

I sighed deeply. "Your *dog*? I'm sorry to hear that, Tony. Well, it's getting late, I'd better get going."

"Please let me walk you to your car," he begged.

"No, I don't think so," I said. "Good-bye, Tony."

He followed me out to the lobby of the restaurant. I turned to face him, putting up the palm of my hand.

"This is as far as you go," I asserted.

"Ann, I have something to ask you."

I raised my eyebrows expectantly.

"Will you please come home with me?"

I laughed aloud and shook my head. "*No way,* Tony."

Then the unimaginable happened. He abruptly leapt at me, wrapping his arms around my waist while straddling my thigh. Before I could tear him off me, I realized he was actually trying to dry hump my leg. *Thumpty-thump-thump*—he thrust himself upon me like a horny dog. I screamed, then viciously shook my leg and shoved him with all my strength, leaving him in a sniveling heap on the sidewalk.

Tony was most definitely *not* The One.

At that moment, I felt as if my childhood fantasy of finding true love had been snuffed out entirely. Resigning myself to a lonely existence, I was convinced that my destiny was to become an old-maid cat-lady. Would I ever find someone whom I could proudly pronounce to my dad that, yes, "He *is* The One"?

* * *

Perhaps what I needed was a good old-fashioned adventure to get myself out of the vicious and agonizing cycle of being single. It was a whole new ball game being single *and* sober. The guys I was meeting liked to drink and preferred a woman who did so too.

My problem was that I was still fishing in the same pond as before but expecting a different fish. What I needed was to get off the pity-pot about not finding love and do something to be of service to others. This was exactly what I was being taught in my twelve-step recovery program, although I had yet to do much that didn't just benefit me in the end.

Each year when winter rolls around, my inner voice starts barking into a megaphone, clearly proclaiming what it wants me to do over the summer months. Being a high school teacher facilitates June-to-September travel extravaganzas, and tutoring provides the extra dinero to make it happen. A few summers before, my inner adventure voice had stretched my physical and spiritual limits by pushing me to walk five hundred miles by myself on the Camino de Santiago trail across Spain.

Perhaps this summer it was time for me to seek an adventure on a humanitarian level, as opposed to one based on self-will and reckless abandonment. I had yet to figure out what that would actually look like, but I was certain it would provide the perfect opportunity to help release me from the bondage of my I'll-never-be-loved woes. At the rate I was going with the poor-me syndrome, I might just poor-me until I poured me a drink. So an adventure with an altruistic inspiration would have to be the solution.

2

THE ANTICIPATORY PHASE

A fter our school budget had been cut, I requested classroom supplies from my students in return for a few extra credit points. With the irresistible bonus-points offer on the table, more than one hundred fifty students brought in at least one item on my list, if not two, three, or more. The Expo markers, construction paper, crayons, pens, and everything else a teacher could dream of were stacked up in the back of my room. The flooding of materials was excessive, and I soon realized there was much more than I needed, even for the next few years!

It suddenly hit me that I had at my fingertips a community of people with more than enough and who had no problem providing what I'd requested. So a bold idea slithered into my head like a hefty python. It squeezed my brain until I conceded to its extravagant plan. The question was, how could I translate that into helping those who were really in need?

Like a string of firecrackers, thoughts popped off, one after the other. The game plan would be to find a deserving school in South America and mail them the surplus of supplies. Then I'd travel to the school over the summer to volunteer and assess how I could set up a system of connecting my classroom to theirs.

On a professional level, I had no real knowledge of Central or South America, since all my experiences with the Spanish language and culture were from the three years I'd spent playing volleyball in Spain after college. My accent is Castilian and every cultural factoid, experience, and story I contain is from my time in España.

I didn't major or minor in the language, so I had never achieved a balanced education on Spanish-speaking countries and their histories, civilizations, and customs. Although it was incredibly difficult, I was lucky to pass the proficiency tests that allowed me to be a Spanish teacher without a degree in the subject. This trip would be an invaluable opportunity to travel south to a few of these countries and continue my education, which would make me a more knowledgeable and well-rounded instructor.

For weeks, I tirelessly searched online for places to volunteer in America del Sur. Finally, I whittled down the list to Peru and eventually came across the website for a learning center in Cuzco. The photos and the mission statement for the school sent chills through my body and resonated in my heart. It spoke of an organic approach to teaching kids and the love and compassion for the forgotten children of Cuzco. The director of the school captivated me with his earthy good looks, creative spirit, and selfless nature.

Even the hand-drawn school logo was almost identical to the large tattoo of the planet earth on the center of my upper back. I had gotten my personal drawing inked into my skin when I was nineteen years old and full of foolishness and fantasy. At the time, I thought I could carry the world on my back. I figured I would be a hypocritical fool if I didn't travel the world after marking myself in such a dramatic fashion. It certainly motivated me to globetrot in my twenties, but I often pondered its significance for me in the present. It had lost its novelty and luster, and it didn't help when a stranger would ask, "Excuse me, what's the significance of the marble on your back?"

So, needless to say, I was delighted to recognize the logo as a sign for me to choose that school. Immediately, I e-mailed the administration to set up a start date and to request a list of items the school needed most. Even with no references on the legitimacy of this school, not knowing anyone personally, and not having any idea what I was getting myself into, I still decided that I was just going to trust that it was legitimate and would work out beautifully. Once I got there, I would evaluate what they needed and figure out how else I could be of service.

My main destination was Cuzco, Peru, but I would be flying in and out of Santiago, Chile, since a family friend had graciously offered his three-bedroom condo for a week. Once in Peru, I planned to spend two months teaching, coaching, singing, building, storytelling, and offering whatever other resources I had that the school could use. I was eager to find a way to support them for years to come through fundraisers with my students and to initiate a pen-pal correspondence program between schools.

Without delay, I requested more donations from students, family, and friends and then sent three twenty-five-pound boxes filled to the brim with school supplies, books, games, and toys. It was a Herculean effort to organize, but it filled me with joy and satisfaction to help a cause greater than I. It also facilitated a significant experience for my students as they selflessly volunteered time, energy, piles of classroom materials, and the money to send it all.

The first hitch in the plan came when I received an e-mail from the school explaining that the postal service had confiscated the boxes and we had two weeks to pay a $250 tax on *each* one. All my resources had been exhausted, and I had already fundraised far beyond my means just to pay for the boxes to be sent in the first place. The representative from the school also explained that if I chose not to pay the tax and wanted the boxes back, it would be $600 for the return shipping. It was a crippling setback, and I pondered not telling my students about it since raising $750 more to get the boxes out of purgatory seemed out of reach.

At this time, a friend put the book *Three Cups of Tea* in my hands and Greg Mortenson became my fearless role model. He was willing to go to absolutely any lengths to bring education to children in central Asia. Although recently exposed as not doing exactly what he claimed he had done, in my opinion, he still faced insurmountable challenges in pursuit of accomplishing his humanitarian crusades. When a door slammed in Mortenson's face, he found a window, or even just a wee little crack. Now I just had to find mine.

I sold the textbooks from my master's program on Amazon.com and peddled my excess jewelry and clothes on eBay, but I was still $500 short. I borrowed Mortenson's Pennies for Peace campaign and set up donation jars labeled Pennies for Peru throughout the classrooms at my school. It was a slow and painful process, and I quickly realized that I needed seventy-five thousand pennies in two weeks to reach my goal. I shared this process with my students, who became outraged and determined to find a solution to the box hostage situation.

"I bet those jerks will sell everything to get money for themselves!" one student shouted. "Maybe they'll give the stuff to their own kids' schools," said another hopefully. "It's not fair, how can they do that?" a third kid cried out.

There had to be a way to get the boxes out of limbo in the Peruvian postal jail and to their home with the children who needed them.

Oh, where, oh, where could my little window be?

* * *

After the time I would spend at the school in Cuzco, I planned to hire a local guide to take me on the Inca Trail to Machu Picchu. Two months was not enough time to reserve a ticket, as online sites indicated that there weren't any permits available for July or August allowing entry into the Incan natural wonder. Besides what I found on Internet descriptions, I had no idea what it really took to get to Machu Picchu, but I figured I could work some magic once I got there.

I found a peaceful place to sit in my backyard and meditated while imagining myself amidst the energy of the ancient ruins. I was a believer in the power of visualization and knew that the more I disciplined myself to do it, the more likely it was that my goal would be accomplished. It had been a fundamental tool when I'd played volleyball, so I figured I would transfer it to my goal of reaching Machu Picchu.

Prevention of and preparation for disease was one important factor I needed to be aware of, especially while working with the poor and hiking in the savage wilderness. I had my tetanus and hepatitis shots and pondered the value of getting injected with the series of rabies shots and the typhoid vaccination. Also, it was recommended I purchase malaria prevention and altitude sickness pills, along with a prescription for potential intestinal problems.

These chemical preventatives would literally introduce all kinds of poisons and toxins into my body while attempting to thwart viruses and diseases. I guess science has proven their legitimacy, but I preferred to use my backup inoculation system of employing visualization to mentally cover myself with an impenetrable veil of healthy protection.

I scanned the Internet for feedback on the malaria medication Lariam, which my doctor prescribed. Most of the online reviews from Lariam users and the side effects they experienced were brutal enough to convince me not to take it.

- "Feelings of impending doom, paranoia, fear of death, nightmares, night sweats, depression, nervous breakdown."
- "Zombie-like state, verbal response to questions but no physical movement, short-term memory loss."
- "Hair loss, rage, social problems, feelings of hopelessness, screaming in sleep."
- "Facial convulsions, loss of energy and motivation for one year after, hallucinations."
- "Suicidal depression, brain damage, paranoia, loss of contact with reality. *Hell.*"

Being a bald, facial-spasming zombie filled with rage and suicidal depression while traveling alone in a foreign country didn't sound appealing. My mom often says, "Anticipation is better than actualization," which most certainly applies to Internet dating, but the same could not be said for those possible side effects. The pre-dread of what *could* happen was a world apart from the reality of what all those descriptions *would* feel like, let alone the outcome of actually contracting malaria.

On the last day of school, I waded through the sea of emptied locker junk—papers, pens, rotten food, note cards, and ripped books—that scattered the halls. In the main office, I found a single white envelope in my mailbox with *Señorita Windes* written in cursive on the front.

Inside was a slip of paper that said, "My son hasn't stopped talking about what you are doing to help the school in Peru. We have never seen him so passionate about anything before, and it has really been bringing our family together. We believe in your cause and want to help get the boxes to the school." Behind the note were five crisp $100 bills.

My little window of opportunity had opened.

3

THE FINAL COUNTDOWN

*W*hat are you doing? nagged my inner voice. My insecurities were bubbling up like lava, burning my insides and smoldering my mind with doubt. *Why didn't I just choose a tropical island to bask in luxurious sunshine? Maybe engage in an Italian romance in Florence?* That sounded quite enticing as I sighed in resignation. *Who came up with this plan anyway? Was it my idea to travel to a third world country, alone, and give of myself unconditionally? Really?*

About a decade ago, I was an avid solo world traveler who sought out the wildest and riskiest debaucheries I could find. I'd held in high regard personal goals such as: Could I beat the record of pints downed by a female at the Hofbräuhaus in Munich? Could I sleep all night in a tree in Amsterdam to save money? Could I ski down an Austrian glacier in a whiteout without goggles? Could I swim naked down the icy Rhine River in Switzerland without being seen? Could I swan dive off the Alps on the highest bungee jump in the world, barefoot and in a bikini?

Who was that chica loca?

All of the dangerous choices and behaviors had led me to the depths of despair. On the outside, I was holding it together, thinking I had everyone fooled with my successful and entertaining external life. But on the inside, I had taken a one-way trip down into hell until the wicked flames licked my feet. The viciously relentless mental committee never gave me a moment of peace.

Once I'd reached an unbearable bottom, a divine intervention pulled the elevator doors open and led me out of personal imprisonment before I completely crashed and burned. It was as if a power greater than myself did for me what I couldn't do. I had no other option but to surrender after becoming bankrupt—mentally, spiritually, and physically. This led me to make a commitment to give up mind-altering substances and alcohol through a twelve-step program.

It was an extreme endeavor, but created space for a powerful relationship with my most authentic self. It was tedious and painful to clean out the dark nooks in the basement of my soul. Filthy, cavernous resentments blocked me from the sunlight of my true purpose, and a casual dusting was not going to do the trick. I needed a thorough cleansing, inside and out. I agonizingly peeled back my skin, shedding the layers of previous beliefs that were really just fictitious stories I had created about myself. Stories such as "I will *never* be good enough" or "I will *never* be truly loved" or "*No one* values what I have to say."

These false assumptions had radically obstructed my own growth and restricted my relationships with others. They were irrational lies that had cleverly wound themselves around me so tightly that they had become part of the primary fibers of my belief system. Even after cleaning up my life, I found that during times of weakness I still fell victim to believing those old false-hoods. I had to be vigilant all the time to stay healthy in mind and spirit.

Prior to my transformation, I used to exist in survival mode. I was afraid that if I gave away even the smallest bit of myself, I would be left empty and unable to self-preserve. It was an unfounded fear that ran my life and kept me from doing anything for anyone else unless it benefited me.

I ran away from the people who loved me by living alone in Europe for half a decade and searched for adrenaline rushes by taking extreme risks. My old lifestyle was thrilling and made me feel present and alive, but it lacked any sort of purpose besides serving my own needs. I had been desperate to find another way of living, and my twelve-step program showed me the way.

Over time, and with an enormous amount of effort, a renewed version of myself emerged, which was still different and often surprised me. I just had to ride on the good sense of my initial decision to travel to South America and ask the Higher Powers to guide me.

My feeling was that, this time, my traveling experience would be dramatically different if I could just keep my demons in check. Sometimes these demons manifested as dark thoughts that sounded almost like a cacophony of birds squawking incessantly in my mind. Other times I felt a surge of rage, as if there were a wolf caged up inside, ready to lash out at anyone who challenged me. Being fully aware of this, I sent out a strong prayer to keep me sane during the trip.

* * *

I tightly arranged my backpack with multipurpose items and messenger bag to carry my petite computer. When called for, I am a packing machine, fine-tuned to the smallest degree. My brain seemed to work in clarified slow motion when figuring out what would be needed. I relished new discoveries of convenience like Dr. Bronner's all-in-one wonder soap that with one droplet could wash everything from my hair to my clothes *and* smelled lavender-ly delightful.

I checked with AT&T for roaming charges on my cell phone and on the USB plug-in for my laptop, and they gave me the unintelligible answer that for every five-thousandth of a kilobyte I would be charged a fee. *What the hell is a five-thousandth of a kilobyte?* So it looked like Internet cafés would be my best bet or maybe hijacking Wi-Fi outside of hotels.

As for the phone, a pleasant fellow in international services told me that if I took out the SIM card of the cell phone, the Internet would be navigable on my phone without roaming charges worldwide. I wasn't sure that carrying excessive electronics would be the best idea anyway. Cell phone, iPod, laptop, USB plug-in, flash drive, camera, chunky converters and chargers? I would hardly have room for much else. It was time to prioritize.

When I picked up the typhoid pills, I was told to expect tarry stool and other such pleasantries. I also filled the prescription for altitude sickness pills but opted out of the tablets for potentially nasty intestinal bugs, which I would later regret. In the end, I turned down the expensive series of rabies shots, and I didn't purchase Lariam, the malaria prevention. I'd just avoid wild dogs and perhaps wouldn't take such a long trek in the Andes, which would reduce my time in the proximity of mosquitoes. I continuously sent out positive vibes and asked the powers that be to keep me healthy, safe, and mentally balanced.

The next day I would arrive in Santiago, Chile, at 5:00 a.m. and the adventure would begin…

4

MY OWN CHE

In line at LAX, I suspiciously eyed the metal box that would determine whether I could carry on my backpack or would have to check it. When backpacking, I take on a turtle-esque existence and feel naked if my backpack is detached from me for any period of time. Not to mention the risk factor of straps getting caught or material ripping, especially while going through the bowels of the South American airport luggage system. I hurled the pack off my back and slid it perfectly into the sample size of an overhead compartment. Content, I returned it to my back and strolled confidently to the gate.

On the circuitous flight from LA to Miami (in order to get to the west coast of South America?), my seat neighbor swirled the ice in his Jack Daniels and inquired about my destination. When I told him, he sighed deeply and after a long minute grimly warned me of a high possibility of getting knifed if I were to drink too many *pisco* sours.

"I presume you speak from experience," I replied.

"Yep," he said after a hearty gulp, "when I drink those lil' lemon demons, baaaaad things happen." He abruptly put on his headphones and said no more, sipping his Jack blankly.

"Thanks, I'll keep that in mind," I replied, smirking, knowing that if I had heard that warning during my prime I would have been sucking down one of those piscos the moment I stepped off the plane. I later discovered that pisco was actually Chile's undisputed national drink, made from the distilled wine of muscatel grapes, lemon, sugar, and frothy egg white. Some say the name was derived from the Quechua word *pisku*, which means "flying bird." I could just imagine my seat partner ingesting a pitcher of pisco and taking flight.

To pass the time on the journey from Miami to Santiago, I pulled out *Motorcycle Diaries*, the highly entertaining travel memoir of a young Ernesto "Che" Guevara, the outspoken, rebellious Argentinean turned infamous revolutionary. I was grateful to have a captivating novel to occupy my mind, but my seat was less than satisfactory. There seemed to be half the normal leg space, plus a large, cranky man bitterly stuffed into the window seat to my right.

I felt sweat prickle on my forehead, and my anxiety level rose to red alert with find-a-solution-now intensity. Scanning the plane, I plopped down in a three-seater and turned to see a handsome man smiling back at me at the other end of the row.

Ernesto was from Argentina, which seemed quite a serendipitous occurrence as the Che book lay cradled in my lap. We engaged in lively conversation for a few hours, and when the lights were turned off, I pulled out a book by the Chilean poet Pablo Neruda to gently lull me to sleep. Translating Neruda's highly descriptive and encrypted prose can be challenging, so I asked for Ernesto's assistance.

As I opened the book, a postcard from the Spanish town of Cordoba fell out. He picked it up and turned it over in his hand, smiling, and revealed that *he* was from Cordoba—in Argentina. We moved in closer. As the rest of the plane slept, a narrow cone of light shone down on us from above as we both leaned into the empty middle seat and read the passionate poetry, each providing our own romantic interpretation. After we had done our best to dissect the metaphors, he read it all the way through in a gentle, crisp whisper. *Now that's some fantastic in-flight entertainment!*

Upon landing, Ernesto invited me to join him and his friends at a cabin in Sierra Nevada for the week. I swallowed hard and thanked him for the invitation, suggesting we just exchange e-mails. "Perhaps another time," I reluctantly squeaked out. I couldn't allow myself to be distracted. No sexy foreign man or wild adventure would sidetrack me this time!

I exchanged money and paid the one hundred dollar "arrival tax" levied on all US, Canadian, Australian, and Mexican citizens, since our respective countries impose the same fee on Chilean citizens. Without a plan for transportation to the condo, I naively exited the frosted sliding glass doors at 5:00 a.m. Suddenly, I was thrust into a pandemonium of hollering drivers, with a number of them waving signs with hastily scrawled names. I imagined seeing a sign with my name on it, then being whisked off hassle-free to my final destination; unfortunately, that was far from reality.

I had yet to accustom myself to the exchange rate, nor did I know how I was going to get across town to the glorious three-bedroom condo awaiting me. Walrus-mustached, smoky-breathed men jockeyed for position to block my path and convince me they had the cheapest ride to Santiago City. Through the ruckus of haggling drivers, I was stopped dead in my tracks—mesmerized by two dazzling sapphire eyes staring at me. Tousled, dark brown hair and a brilliant smile lured and hooked me. He coolly leaned against a wall with a taxi sign in hand and reeled me in like a big dopey fish.

Leading me outside to a car, he swiftly passed me off to an older mustached man who sat smoking in the driver seat. I shook my head in resignation, giving them credit for ingenuity. It was such a relief to be on my way that I failed to recognize that nowhere on the car did it state that it was actually a taxi. I asked the chain-smoking fellow the price and he told me, "Forty-three thousand pesos."

Although the exchange rate was noted somewhere in my backpack, I was eager to get going, so I agreed to depart without calculation. I slid into the backseat, thankful and thrilled to finally be in Santiago. My eyes soaked up everything flying by: the cars, the names of exits, villages, and the glowing red numbers on a Chilean bank billboard.

Remembering the electric red numbers from the exchange booth, I realized that five hundred thirty-two

Chilean pesos equaled one dollar. A chill went through my body. Math was not my strong suit, but I could figure that this would be a pricey lesson. *Welcome to Chile*.

"Perdón señor," I said. "¿Cuánto tiempo hasta mi destino?" How long until my destination?

"No mucho más," he replied hesitantly.

I continued my inquiry. "The price you gave me is extremely high. Did I hear you correctly?"

Oh, yes, I'd heard him correctly, and there was nothing I could do about it. I had shifted from excitement to concern to fear. Indeed, I was being scammed and hopefully nothing worse. I was more furious with myself for being so gullible and unprepared, especially after so many years of solo travel during which I had gained an acute sense of self-security. I guess I had let my guard down in the presence of those blue eyes.

The driver had to call three people and asked four in the street how to get to my destination. Jumping out was always an option, but my backpack was in the trunk. My tough-girl persona calculated that I could probably take him if he tried something shady.

The thought did cross my mind that I was in the initial perilous stage that women fall victim to all over the world, being alone, trusting, and physically inferior. No matter how brave or strong I was, if the driver had devious intentions, my trip might have been over before it had even begun. Fortunately, he was seeking financial gain and nothing more.

After an hour and a half to drive fifteen miles without traffic, we arrived. He held my backpack hostage until I reluctantly paid his outrageous fee. Smoky gave me a salute as he pulled away, leaving me in the center of a cul-de-sac carpeted in enormous fall leaves. It was a breathtaking sight, and I tingled with gratitude that I was finally standing in front of my destination, a little more broke but in one piece.

I pulled out the key and introduced myself to the security guard who directed me to my new home for the next week. I could almost taste the luxurious relaxation on the horizon. Putting the key in the lock, I waited expectantly to hear the click and see the door swing open to welcoming comfort. But there was no click. The deadbolt was locked with a separate key. According to the security guard, the only person who could open it was the off-site manager, Don Rodrigo. Kicking myself, I wondered why I didn't take Ernesto's offer to join him at the cabin in Sierra Nevada.

After an hour, Don Rodrigo arrived to find me leaning on my backpack, shivering in the cold with an uncomfortably full bladder. He excused himself repeatedly, embarrassed that he had forgotten to unlock the deadbolt. When I described to him my taxi experience, he became noticeably upset that I had been taken advantage of by one of his countrymen. As it turned out, the *taxista* and his blue-eyed accomplice had charged me four times the real fare, and it should have only taken twenty minutes!

My pack had only been off my back for a minute when Don Rodrigo vowed he would not leave me until we went to the gigantic Hiper Lider supermarket so he could be certain that I had food for the next few days. More than anything I wanted to take off my shoes, relax, and deal with it later, but his gracious and fun-loving attitude made it impossible to turn down his invitation.

He cheerfully pushed the cart through the market, filling the basket with what he considered dietary necessities for a girl like myself. I insisted on the petite filets, but he would not hear of it and dropped a five-pound chunk of meat in the cart. A massive brick of soft Chilean cheese was also added, along with a four-foot bread flute, which I knew would transform into a rock-hard light saber in less than twenty-four hours. But Rodrigo was so sweet and beamingly proud of his national food products, I couldn't help but agree to his selections. I was thoroughly exhausted when he finally dropped me off with my Chilean meat hunk and cheese slab. It was only 10:00 a.m.

Later, after taking a profoundly deep nap and watching three back-to-back episodes of *CSI Miami* in Spanish, I got in gear and explored the neighborhood, where I delightfully discovered the local Starbucks. I felt a bit ashamed, but it was the only place where I could find Wi-Fi (pronounced "wee-fee" in Spanish). I had five days to explore Santiago before I would fly to Cuzco to start volunteering.

I sank into the comfy Starbucks armchair, green tea latte and oatmeal raisin cookie by my side, and boldly taunted my destiny, "What have you got for me, Santiago? Bring it on!"

5

LA COMIDA CHILENA

A few days later, I sat peacefully at the Half Moon Café with the combo meal of a frothy cappuccino and two small, warm, glazed croissants. I had discovered on the first night that my flat was across a bridge from South America's most "important" mall, Parque Arauco. So what makes a mall important? Quality? Girth? I had to admit, it was a labyrinth of stores that I didn't dare step foot into for fear of discovering distinctive purchases only available in South America.

Without an inch of free space in my backpack, I reluctantly curbed shopping urges, which held until I found the Feria Santa Lucia artisan market in the city center. I felt like a kid in a candy store with so many one-of-a-kind items that kept getting more irresistibly unique from one stall to the next.

I convinced myself it was necessary to purchase an antique fork bent into a bracelet with the prongs curled to swirls with a stunning lapis lazuli, which the vendor told me was mined out of the local Andes Mountains. I also could not defend against a temptation to buy a purple stitched shawl with delicate pink roses. Unconcerned that these two items were clearly nonessentials for volunteering, I still skipped down the aisles with giddy shopping adrenaline. This then led to the absurd idea of buying a suitcase to transport my future purchases back to the States and carry it along with my backpack.

Admiring the new fork-let on my wrist, I dug into another round of the combo meal in front of me. The Americanization of this important mall was intriguing with its TGI Friday's, Ruby Tuesday, Benihana, and, of course, the same Starbucks where I sat my first night. Fancying a taste of the local cuisine, I ventured to the downtown fish market.

Mustache-y men with fishy fingers and galoshes lured me in to see their odorous specimens: black and white glazed-eyed eels, mouths agape alongside squiggle squids and headless fish. The reason that the fish vendors hounded tourists seemed a mystery. Chile's coastline stretches for a staggering three hundred miles and seafood is their pride and joy, but what was I going to do, buy a three-foot mackerel and tuck it in my purse for later? *Sorry, guys, but I already have a five-pound slab of cow waiting at home.*

That night I attacked the hunk-o'-meat, sawing at it for ten minutes with a dull knife to cut off a thick slice. I figured I'd report back to Don Rodrigo on its unparalleled quality. Attempting to cook it up, flipping it pro-chef style, I accidentally launched it across the stove. It deposited itself down the crack between the stove and the counter into the hairy dust-ball crevice below. I gagged fishing it out with a wire hanger and decided to bypass the meat option. Instead, I dined on Don Rodrigo's patriotic cheese atop a piece of the tooth-chipping bread flute. Maybe I should have gotten a mackerel to go.

Later that day, I hiked up to Cerro Santa Lucia, which would have been more appropriately named Make-Out Mountain. I wasn't sure what was in the air, but every bench, cave-let, nook, and cranny hosted make-out sessions, *pura tongue lucha libre*.

I huffed and puffed to the top, feeling like I was invading everyone's privacy, but finally reached the stunning panoramic of Santiago City. The backdrop of the towering, snow-peaked Cordillera mountain range was impressive. I was told by an elderly local couple that we were all lucky to catch the clear view, since the same gorgeous mountains that are so inspiring cause the air to get trapped in the city due to their surrounding formation. This leaves Santiago thickly polluted with stagnant diesel fumes and dust that blanket the skyline, making it rare to catch the true beauty of the Andes.

I stood alone, feeling smitten with the regal mountains, as other couples celebrated their love atop the mount-amor. A gay couple from North Hollywood took my picture and then locked lips, unable to resist the romantic moment. Loneliness consumed me as a scruffy dog sat at my foot, panting, with his "red rocket" out. I petted his knotty forehead as he blinked at me affectionately and licked my hand.

Yeah, buddy, I'm looking for love too, I thought.

* * *

One unexpected feature of the town of Santiago was the abandoned dogs that ran wild in the streets. Perhaps I should have gotten the rabies shots after all. Once I turned down a desolate road to find a German shepherd in an aggressive stance, growling in my direction. "Wrong street. Sorry!" I said, quickly turning around and nervously hustled back to a main street.

The pooches were more plentiful than the pigeon population, and I swore I had seen over a dozen dead dogs, but it was hard to tell if they were canine corpses or just napping. I found myself obsessively checking their stomachs for respiratory movements. These *perros* circulated through town like citizens with their own etiquette and openly accepted conduct, including shameless public mating.

I sat in the lively Plaza de Armas to admire the colonial architecture and observe the packs of mongrels and how they intermingled with the masses. There seemed to be a hierarchy where the largest and most aggressive kept the others in line and continuously nipped and chased and barked at other packs. Sometimes fearless local men would hit a dog with a rolled-up newspaper if it got out of hand or shooed it away if it got too close to their card-table chess game.

A bench in the middle of the plaza became the best viewing position to watch the amusing K-9 circus. I happened to shift my eyes to a rottweiler just as he took liberties with a frisky mutt. The moment I turned from the indecent spectacle, I locked eyes with an old man who had been watching me—watch the dogs. He raised his eyebrows playfully and winked with a devilish smirk. Wanting to throw up in my mouth, I gathered my belongings in a huff, feeling dirty, and shamefully departed the plaza.

The craziest behavior from the dogs was their ferocious pursuit of the tires on moving cars. They chased cars, barking savagely, and snapped at quickly moving vehicles, nearly losing their paws in the process. I took videos with my camera, cracking up and gasping in disbelief while looking around at other passersby to see if anyone thought it to be as amusingly engaging as I did. The locals passed indifferently, as if it was the most normal occurrence on earth.

Perhaps the dogs were why I had yet to see any cyclists in town. I imagined it to be quite entertaining to watch a pack of feral ruffians chasing bicycle tires. Little did I know that such a cyclist was going to be me!

The dogs of Santiago owning the streets.

6

AMIGOS ACCIDENTALES

Dating in sobriety was a challenge, but the selfish and isolating person that I was prior to getting sober made it nearly impossible to date or even make friends. The biggest difference with my South American travels compared to my five-year European stint in my twenties was that I was actually making a clear and present effort at making friends.

My previous choice of lifestyle required me to be a stoically unapproachable woman of mystery who projected a don't-even-think-about-talking-to-me vibe. I'd taken on this persona for absurd reasons that made perfect sense at the time. First of all, I felt embarrassed at how Americans traveled internationally and didn't want to be pegged as being one. I would often pretend as if I didn't understand a language spoken to me, even if it was my own. I also quarantined myself off by writing intensely in journals, documenting my every experience, emotion, and perspective. It was just me, my journal, and my Walkman, plus a variety of mix tapes.

I found a tragically poetic journal entry from one of my travels that described my state quite succinctly, titled "Don't Talk to Me":

Japanese, German, and French conversations fill the lobby late at night.

Laughter echoes off the walls of this Swiss youth hostel.

People connect. Cultures blend.
I sit alone,
and watch *them*.
I hear English.
I don't engage.
There are five bunks to a room.
I lay on my back,
hands folded on my stomach,
and stare at the ceiling.
I sleep in my clothes.
I don't dream.
I wake in the same position.
I shower without soap
and dry off with a pillowcase.
I don't look in the mirror.
I brush my teeth with my finger.
I sneak in the cafeteria
and steal cornflakes and coffee.
I speak to no one.
No one speaks to me.
And I don't care.

The disturbingly lonely memories of what I used to be like flooded over me. It also triggered a forgotten dodgy experience of that particular youth hostel in Bern, Switzerland. Heroin addicts wandered freely and ironically in the park adjacent to the very conservative parliament. They would shoot up in public and in broad daylight, while simply being ignored.

One of the addicts' common hangouts was the park surrounding the hostel where I was staying, so all lodgers had a curfew of 10:00 p.m. for their own safety. This pissed me off because I was a pot-smoking nightwalker and liked to do what I wanted, when I wanted. No matter how late, what country I was in, or whether it was safe or not, I walked, smoked, and listened to my Walkman.

On that particular night, I snuck out and found a bench to sit on to listen to my tunes and zone out. I soon felt a presence and so removed my earphones to let my senses do the listening. I could hear snorting and rustling in the trees nearby. My heart raced as I froze, my ears straining for the next clue to make an appropriate reaction. Then I saw him—and wished I never did. It was an addict in his last-ditch effort to reach euphoric annihilation. With his filthy trousers around his ankles, he was shooting a syringe in the side of his male organ.

A chill ran through my body as I struggled to erase the image from my mind. I hurried back to the hostel, offended that my night gazing had been interrupted and my safety compromised by some desperate junkie. Never did I realize that I was essentially a junkie myself, doing the same thing but hiding it under a cloak of self-delusional social acceptability.

* * *

In Santiago, Don Rodrigo proved to be not just an apartment manager and enthusiastic grocery shopper but also a friend-finder. He was quite concerned that I wouldn't have a thing to do by myself for a week, so he set me up with Makarena, a writer and editor about my age. It felt like a blind date as I waited for a girl with a red scarf on the bench near the Pedro de Valdivia metro stop.

As I waited for her, I searched my guidebook for the mini-biography of señor Valdivia. He was the infamous Spaniard considered the conquistador of Chile. He established (or rather took) territory in Santiago, and, after a peaceful period in 1541, the local Indians attacked the new village to take their land back. Valdivia was not present at the time, so his fiercely brave female companion Inés de Suárez successfully led the defense of the town.

Of course, there was only one line about his woman but four pages and a metro stop after Valdivia. My interest was piqued, and my task for the day would be to find out more about the mysterious woman who defended a town from wild, vengeful Indians.

Makarena wore a hip swoop haircut, smoked cigarettes incessantly, and seemed genuinely pleased to chat with me. We sat at a smoky cafe sipping coffee, eating sandwich triangles with the crusts cut off, and talking about influential females in Chile. She told the inspirational story of Gabriela Mistral, who won the Nobel Prize in Literature in 1945 and whose face was on the five-thousand-peso bill.

Mistral was successful in her career as an educator and had achieved extraordinary accomplishment as a writer in spite of her gender and her culture. Makarena crisply recited from memory one of Mistral's poems, which I wrote down on a napkin to decipher later:

No magulles a la tierra; no aprietes a la olorosa,
Por el amor de ella abájate, huélela y dale la boca.

Do not trample the earth; do not crush a thing as sweet as this. For love of her, bend down, smell her, and eat her in a kiss.

I could relate my old self to the earth-trampling ignorant woman who thought the world was created as her personal playground. She thought to give nothing in return nor took time to appreciate the journey. This trip would be the perfect opportunity to live with gratitude and put positive energy back into the universal pot.

Makarena and I both shared an affinity for the writings of Isabel Allende and I was besieged with excitement upon hearing her recommendation to read *Inés of my Soul*, a work of historical fiction that recounted the astonishing life of Inés de Suárez. Makarena briefly recounted the story of the daring Spanish conquistadora who toiled to build the nation of Chile and whose vital role had too often been neglected by history.

I was also enlightened to the fact that in 2009, Chile had a female president. Prior to being president, Michelle Bachelet was quite a remarkable woman. She was a pediatrician, epidemiologist, and diligent student of military strategy. Not only that, she was a mother of three who spoke Spanish, English, German, and Portuguese. I had no doubt that this chance meeting with Makarena came with a higher purpose of inspiring me through these South American ladies who broke the barriers of being extraordinary and paved the way for women the world over.

Makarena generously advised me on the short story I was working on about walking the Camino de Santiago in Spain. She was the perfect serendipitous puzzle piece to help me move me forward in the process. I found that filling gaps in my day with writing was the perfect way to satisfy my creative impulses and to keep me from getting squirrelly. I carried my minicomputer everywhere and spontaneously typed whenever moved to do so.

I was exercising the writing muscle like never before. It was as if I had a companion in my writing persona, and I thoroughly enjoyed her company. When traveling alone, the hours in a day seemed to double, especially without a cell phone or any sort of agenda to keep me busy. Not to mention that I didn't have the routine and support of my twelve-step program. There was nothing like the meetings and all the members who listened, encouraged, shared wisdom, and, most importantly, buoyed me through every difficult situation I faced. I no longer had the desire to drink or smoke pot, but I found that my tools weren't sharpened for dealing with life from a spiritually balanced position.

I used to believe that being terminally lonely while gracefully sipping vast quantities of red wine made me an exceptional writer. My role models were the likes of Charles Bukowski, Jack Kerouac, and Hunter Thompson. All who, in my mind, glamorized the life of being an alcoholically inspired writer. I didn't publish a thing, had few friends, and focused my money and effort on isolating myself in distant lands while pursuing yet another glass of the local vino rojo.

At times, it was agonizingly difficult to write without a creative lubricant, but I was starting to tap into a vein of universal female strength that was gently guiding me along the journey. I could feel the gravitational pull of my being toward something great just upon the horizon.

* * *

After a few days of aimless wandering in Santiago, I was running out of things to do by myself, so I signed up for an all-day coastal adventure. This was where I met Oscar (new friend número dos), the van driver for the full-day trip to Valparaiso and Viña del Mar. He explained the history of the tremulous political past regarding Allende, "the good communist" and the estranged father of Isabel Allende. This put a whole new twist to the knowledge I was piecing together from Makarena.

Oscar venomously spoke of Pinochet, whom he labeled "the murderer." He explained how General Pinochet seized power on September 11, 1973, in a bloody military coup that toppled the Marxist government of President Salvador Allende. He did lead the country into an era of robust economic growth, but during his rule more than three thousand two hundred people were executed or disappeared and thousands more were tortured or exiled.

Oscar also captivated me with stories of the powerful Mapuche Indians in their ceaseless and honorable struggle with the conquistadors. He spoke discriminatorily of Peruvians and made some degrading remarks about "those" people trying to come to Chile. Despite his prejudices, I enjoyed his company and we conversed throughout the day.

The jolly tour guide, Claudio, confessed that he was cheating on his wife with…the Andes Mountains. He eyes glazed over and a small tear escaped as we drove toward the majestic, snow-capped beauties. Claudio pointed out that I was a very lucky girl because if I took the first two letters of my first name and the last three of my last, it spelled…*Andes*!

* * *

My third and least favorite new amigo was Carlo, a short, goateed accountant whom I met in town. He had quickly discovered my routine at the local coffee shop where I had been writing daily. Several times, he asked to share the table and chatted me up. It was a relief to engage in conversation, as most days had very little of it. He was a fine conversationalist and had a charming laugh.

On the fourth day, he invited me to accompany him to a *discoteca* to get a taste of the Santiago nightlife. Was this a date? I didn't think so, but perhaps he did. An invitation by an unknown person often involved a bit of risk, but Carlo seemed innocent enough. Just in case, I left his information with the security guard I had befriended in the apartment complex and took the metro to the Banqueado station.

I stood huddled under a streetlight as the clouds threatened rain. Finally, headlights flickered at me as Carlo pulled up in his tiny, dented car, the eighties hair band White Snake blasting from his cell phone since the car radio was broken.

The club had four levels of dance floors and various nooks that carouseled, revolving with patrons. There was a three-level pub hidden up a secret staircase and a movie theater playing old Chilean films on the top floor. I felt a little uncomfortable since I was wearing the same casual, multipurpose outfit that I had sported the past few days. The music unpredictably switched from Men at Work to DeBarge to the Beach Boys' "(Ba Ba Ba) Barbara Ann." I wanted to people-watch and gossip about the amusing dance floor occupants but realized that Carlo was actually one of them.

He kept urging me to dance and drink, preferably both, but the DJ was uninspiring and throwing back cocktails was not on my agenda. Carlo bought me a pisco sour despite my request for a soda and then got angry that it was going to waste. I recalled my airplane seat partner's warning and was incredibly relieved to be sober.

Carlo downed his drink and then mine. He kept complementing me at strange and awkward moments, edging his stool closer. In the old Ann days, I would have milked him for all the drinks I could consume, ditched him, and then found another hombre more to my liking to close down the bar with. But that was the old way, and now I was stuck with him, for some reason feeling obligated to be polite and remain in his company. The uncomfortability level steadily rose with Carlo as my mind devised an appropriate exit plan.

Before this escape scheme could be enacted, I decided to spice up our strained conversation by telling him about the large, mysterious, ancient coin I found on the wilderness trail in Spain. The story was one of my best, so it was quite surprising when he had no reaction. He looked at me with a blank expression, like, "Are you done now?" and then dove into his own story. A bit turned off, I refocused my attention, figuring it must be a whopper of a tale.

Giving it his best shot, he began to tell of a gypsy who used to trail him as he walked to work, cursing him and predicting his death. This happened daily, and each time he'd turn around she would vanish into thin air. I was pretending like I wasn't interested and scoffed a bit at the disappearing part, but I was listening.

He explained how one day he convinced his brother to witness it, and the same inexplicable vanishing act occurred. The gypsy shouted out that Carlo was going to die from a dog bone that had *already* lodged itself in his throat. He nervously fondled his own throat as he recounted the story.

Then one day when the gypsy had shouted her malediction yet again, he had actually felt an extra bone poking out of his throat! He described how he went to the doctor, who did an X-ray and actually found a dog bone. Before I could react to his story, he took my hand, clutching it tightly and pulling it to his neck to touch the mysterious canine bone lodged in his throat.

Just as my fingertips unwillingly grazed his throat, he jerked forward and barked ferociously in my face.

I screamed, startled, as he roared with uncontrollable laughter, nearly tipping back in his chair. "Wasn't that funny?" he inquired. "Ha! A good joke, no?"

Confident self-amusement spread across his face as he puckered up, leaned in, and requested "un beso?" Now it was my turn to laugh. I refused, pulling back uneasily as he became quiet with fury. Taylor Dane's "Tell it to My Heart" played in the background as he stood and firmly demanded, "Bailamos." He grabbed my hand aggressively and pulled me to the dance floor as the DJ mixed in New Edition's "Cool It Now."

It was then that I began calculating my escape route. I wasn't quite sure where I was in town, but I could certainly figure it out. Carlo glared at the floor with the look of an eight-year-old boy who didn't get what he wanted. But he was not eight, more like thirty-eight, and I didn't know what he was capable of. Carlo stepped from side to side, junior-high-dance style, gripping my hands tightly as I stood there like a statue.

Lock-jawed, with primal intensity in my eyes, I could feel the rage of my internal wolf pacing. "Me voy," I firmly declared with a growl. I'm going.

I yanked my hands out from his vice grip, weaved through the crowd, and headed toward the entrance. People were coming into the club sopping wet, closing umbrellas and shaking out leather jackets. I stopped in my tracks at the sidewalk. It was a full-fledged downpour like a Southern California girl had never seen before. Buckets and buckets of water dropped from the sky, filling the streets like rivers. There were hardly any cars around, let alone taxis, and I had no idea where the metro was.

Carlo slinked in behind me and with a smirk. "Would you like a ride home, my dear?"

In the car, he cackled like the devil as the appropriate song "Rock You Like a Hurricane" by the Scorpions howled away on his phone speaker. He hastily navigated through foggy windows and took the brunt of full-frontal waves. He seemed to be getting a sick pleasure out of seeing my fear. There was no hiding my terror as I prayed aloud the entire way. If we didn't die in a terrible auto accident, then who knew what he had planned?

Carlo finally pulled down a street I recognized, so I jumped out of the moving car into an oncoming water surge, waded through until I could move freely, then ran to the apartment. Racing up three flights of stairs, I nervously rattled my keys in the lock, then slumped against the inside of the door in a wet, defeated pile. I guess I had arrogantly asked Santiago City on that first day to "show me what you got." And it did.

I had a day to recover before I was to catch a flight to Lima, Peru, where I would stay for a day then head to Cuzco to start volunteering at the school. This time I would not make the foolish mistake of taunting the city upon my arrival.

7

IT'S ALL ABOUT
THE CHANGE

A taxi scooped me up at the crack of dawn to catch a 6:00 a.m. flight to Lima, Peru, from Santiago, Chile. Arranging for a prepaid service, which cost $20 as opposed to the $85 that I was charged upon my arrival, seemed like a good idea. On the plane, I slept from departure to arrival and by the time we landed, I was ready to roll.

Swine-flu-preventative surgical masks greeted me at every turn through the terminal. Just a few months prior, in April of 2009, the swine flu had swept the States and eventually killed over four thousand Americans by November 2009. I hadn't seen such a reaction to the devastating influenza in the American or Chilean airports, but Peru seemed to be taking some major preventative actions.

I wondered why my doctor had never mentioned it, but, knowing myself, I probably would have disregarded her advice anyway. Clearly, germs were more easily dispersed in public places, but were masks really necessary? I held my breath for long periods and imagined my impenetrable bubble of defense keeping me safe until I breached the exit doors to fresh air.

I was pleased to find that the travel agency I'd contacted had come through with a driver waiting with my name on a sign. The same agency set me up with a bare-minimum hotel in the "nice" (meaning less sketchy) neighborhood of Miraflores for one day. I deliberately chose the twenty-four hour layover so I could get a feel for the capital of Peru prior to volunteering in Cuzco.

I soon realized that blending in here would not be as easy as in Chile. Santiago had a very European city feel to it and its inhabitants have a "Euro" look. Since the late nineteenth century, Chilean culture has been nurtured by the arrival of a large group of immigrants, mainly Germans, British, French, and Italians.

Peru, on the other hand, has not been a primary destination for Europeans migrating south over the past few centuries and has therefore kept a purer bloodline linking to the indigenous races. Even after their culture was devastated by the Spanish conquistadors, many Peruvians have still maintained their heritage and ethnic appearance. It wasn't as evident in Lima, from what I could see, but I was told that as I continued my travels deeper into the interior of the country, it would become distinctively indigenous.

I still had a hard time shedding my belief that when traveling internationally it was far better to appear to be a native from any other country than the US. Over the past decade and a half of my time overseas, without fail, once my nationality was exposed, I would be unwillingly dragged into defending my president and our country's politics and explaining our interference in other countries' affairs.

Not being a person with strong political opinions, it was deeply unsettling that I could be hated simply for the country I was born in. Once a man in Spain spit on the ground at my feet and sneered in a strong accent, "Who does this George Bush (but pronounced "Boooosh") think he is?" Then he dramatically tossed his hands up and stared me down with profound animosity, waiting for a defense.

Another gentleman once ineptly shouted at me, "I hate your Bush!" I stifled a laugh and replied, "Yeah, I'm not a big fan of 'my' Bush either," but it didn't register with the irrational anti-American man who continued his rant.

Once I learned Spanish, it became much easier to just pretend I was from Spain. But while I was in the land of the Incas, the wisest choice was not to claim citizenship from the country that had slaughtered their ancestors.

I plotted out the main sights for one whirlwind afternoon in Lima, then took a taxi to the impressively restored colonial center. One of the top sights in Lima is the baroque-style Iglesia de San Francisco, a haunted Franciscan church and monastery. My guidebook told me it was originally constructed in 1546 and was one of the oldest in South America. It also served as the first official Catholic cemetery in Lima at a time when the dead were put in catacombs beneath the church.

I ducked my head to climb below into a claustrophobic passageway that opened into various dusty rooms where heaps of bones were piled up and organized by body part. The guide claimed there were over seventy thousand bodies in the subterranean burial chambers, which was determined after a team of archeologists counted each and every one. That thankless task could certainly qualify the bone-counters for an episode of *Dirty Jobs* on the Discovery Channel.

In one of the covert rooms was an immense geometric pattern of bones covering the ground, which seemed like the sinister work of the devil, whom I could envision carpeting the underworld. Unsettling spirits seemed to stalk me as I pursued the route to the exit. My breathing became restricted and my gag reflex kept triggering, but eventually I welcomed the fresh pollution of the vast metropolis above.

I soon discovered that getting change for big bills in Peru was a complicated and maddening issue. Not to mention that bills with any sort of rip, writing, fold, or crease or those that didn't snap crisply when yanked from both ends simultaneously would absolutely not be accepted. Unsuspecting tourists usually get duped into taking an unusable one by a sly vendor pawning off his useless currency collection.

I flagged a taxi to get back to Miraflores from the town center, and during the ride, the taxista asked if I had *sencillo*–simple. I didn't understand what he meant until he stopped at a gas station and ordered me to get *plata sencilla*, or simple silver, a.k.a change. I only had a fifty-sol bill, which was worth about seventeen dollars, far too big of a denomination for him to break for my fifteen-sol (five-dollar) ride.

The driver directed me to buy something at the gas station and bring him the simple silver; I hesitated, but I needed bottled water anyway. My change was two twenties, which was still going to be too big of a bill for the taxista, so I asked for simpler silver but was refused.

The driver then pulled into *another* station and demanded that I buy something else. This time I shook my head and I told *him* to go buy something. He tried to buy one dollar's worth of gas, but they hissed at him, so finally he went in and bought himself an Inca Cola so he could give me back change. It took longer to scavenge up change than the ride itself.

As the driver pulled up to my hotel, he informed me that the next day there was going to be a twenty-four hour transportation strike, so I'd better prepare myself. This certainly presented a challenge since my flight was to leave at 10:00 a.m. Upon getting out of the taxi, I heard a jingle in my pocket and realized there'd been enough plata sencilla in my pocket all along!

I had been warned over and over by taxi drivers, receptionists, customs officers, and waiters that I must be very careful in Peru. Although I wasn't sure exactly what I was being warned of, I took their advice nevertheless. I could have used a specific "watch out for short goateed accountants" warning in Chile. In Peru, I did get a sense of insecurity and felt guarded when strolling the streets alone, so I chose not take unnecessary risks.

I opted not to walk the five blocks into town, but rather ate dinner early during daylight and stayed in for the night. (The hotel had Wi-Fi—bonus!) My internal warning alarm went off when a guy asked me the time, even though he wore a watch. He then insisted on accompanying me wherever I was going, claiming it was unsafe for me to walk alone. Listening to my alarm, I ducked into an arcade, then cautiously found my way back, frequently looking over my shoulder.

There was something about being a woman traveling alone in a foreign country that used to give me a rush when there was potential for something dodgy to happen. My adrenaline charged and I felt like I was a secret ninja on a mission in life's video game. I had to get from point A to B, with no lives to spare. A good half a decade was spent playing this game, with which I got into some dangerous states of affairs.

Once upon a late night in Bournemouth, England, I left a pub alone and quite intoxicated. About halfway back to the cheap bed and breakfast where I was staying, I heard a shout from behind. It was a dark, empty street and a clearly inebriated man was waving at me to stop. "Hey, you!" he garbled. "Come back here, I wanna talk to youuuu!"

He looked like a dirtbag fresh off too many pints, so I gave him a cocky smirk, turned back around, and picked up my pace. It was clear he wanted to do more than just talk. His intensity increased as he inaudibly barked at me again and began stumble-jogging in my direction.

At the time, I was playing on the British Pro Beach Volleyball Tour and was in good physical condition. One might scoff at the outrageous notion of beach volleyball in England, but it did exist, although played on pebble grit beaches with many of the women competing in skirts. I also considered myself a semiprofessional boozer and had just left a pub where I had held my weight with a crew of beer-chugging, shot-taking blokes, so I had solid buzz-induced confidence.

"Catch me if you can, motherfucker!" I taunted, then started jogging to see what kind of pace his sturdy, blue-collared physique could keep. He was about a block behind and, after my challenge, as determined as ever. I took off down the street like a cheetah, jumping over curbs and uneven sidewalks while glancing over my shoulder ever so often.

I was far enough ahead that I slowed my pace and cautiously entered a fifty-yard-long tunnel that took the sidewalk through a hillside. I noticed he wasn't following me any longer, so I strolled along, grinning at my outwitting a nim-wit.

Just as I breached the other side of the tunnel, he leapt out from a bush above it with a feral growl, hooking his claws into my shirt. His sour breath nearly took me out as we came eye to bloodshot eye.

I squirmed, scratched, and finally twisted out from his paws to break into a terror-stricken run with him close on my tail. Not a soul strolled the darkened street, but, thankfully, I spotted the grimy picket fence of my bed and breakfast. Gauging the distance, I hopped it side-style, like an American cowgirl. As I fumbled in my pocket to find the key to the front door, he unhitched the latch on the gate, closing in on his prey.

Key in lock, me through door, deadbolt locked, *slam!* His hot nostrils steamed up two circles on the door's small window. I gave him the double middle finger through the glass and then headed up to my tiny room. Lying flat on my back, my heart bursting from my chest, I couldn't suppress the wicked smile on my face. *Victory.*

* * *

I was certainly grateful I didn't actively pursue those sorts of risky interactions any longer. A bottle of sparkling water, a bag of nuts, and a good park to people-watch was quite satisfactory to me these days. I positioned myself in the best spot for observing park-goers in the bustling and artsy Parque Miraflores, which was where I met Alex, a Brazilian superhuman adventure man.

His dark chocolate eyes gleamed with travel wisdom while he enchanted me with details from his current motorcycle journey. He had ridden from the northern coast of Brazil to the tippy bottom of South America, the Tierra del Fuego, and was currently making his way up the west coast of the continent heading to Canada!

Now that's an aventurero auténtico! My heart ached with the faint hope that maybe he'd ask me to hop on the back of his bike and join him. Would I go if he asked? Despite my new commitment to be of service to mankind, it just might be too incredible of an opportunity to pass up.

I doubted the offer had even crossed his mind. He was a man on a mission, but so was I. Pushing the silly fantasy to the side, I shook my jowls like a wet dog to focus on the present moment. Since it was after dark, Alex offered to walk me back to my hotel, where I was relieved to find a fax at the front desk verifying that, yes, someone would risk life and limb to pick me up at 10:00 a.m. for the airport.

I bid the great adventure man farewell, feeling inspired by his courageous determination, and hoped someday I would meet my own aventurero auténtico.

8

THE STRIKE

Sketchy drivers are common in countries such as Italy and Greece, but Peru seemed to be in a class all its own. The US Department of State travel website warned travelers in Peru that "inter-city bus travel is *very* dangerous. Armed robbers force passengers off buses and steal their belongings and also sometimes hold up inter-city buses at night. Bus accidents resulting in multiple deaths and injuries are common, and they are frequently attributed to excessive speed, poor bus maintenance, and driver fatigue."

Take El Camino de la Muerte. The Road of Death is a sixty-five-kilometer highway leading from La Paz, Peru to Coroico, Bolivia, and is legendary for its extreme danger. In 1995 it was christened as "the world's most dangerous road," since it was estimated that two to three hundred travelers were killed yearly on it. This particular highway took the grand prize, but I had heard that were many other roads with a similar degree of risk snaking all throughout Peru.

On my last morning in Lima, I found myself in the middle of the strike, which the transportation associations around the country had called for in response to a new law passed by the government. The law dramatically increased the fines for driving offenses such as speeding, drunk driving, or running a red light. Many people felt that the law was unjust because the fines were out of proportion to the public's salaries and those who had little income could never afford to pay them.

My version of common sense suggested one should not break the law and therefore not suffer the consequences. Instead, the public decided to create maddening chaos in protest. The hotel receptionist claimed it was the politicians and lawmakers who were gouging the indigenous people yet again. I was sure there were many layers to it, but anything that eliminated traffic and helped me safely cross the street seemed like a great idea.

Although the situation was a nuisance, it was also ingenious. During a transportation strike, everything comes to a halt. The positive side was that the usual constant drone of taxi traffic was replaced by a peaceful serenity, punctuated occasionally by the sound of a private vehicle or single taxi whose driver had decided to risk doing business that day. Most people just stayed home. Anyone who opened a business or operated a taxi ran the risk of encountering violence. Strikers punctured the tires of vehicles that were out on the roads and looted open shops and market stalls.

It was an immense relief not having cars on the road since crossing the street was like being in the classic video game Frogger. I was nearly run over even while in the crosswalk with the green right-of-way! Respect for pedestrians was apparently an American attitude. Little, smashed-up vehicles recklessly zoomed down the street, zigzagging, expelling black plumes, aggressively honking, "Don't even think about crossing!" It felt like drivers deliberately tried to run over pedestrians, and if I stuck my baby toe on the asphalt, *zoooom!* A car would appear out of nowhere, the driver's palm slamming on the horn, making me leap back and shake my fist in fury.

My last morning in Lima, I felt lighthearted and carefree strolling through an eerie sea mist called *la garúa* that swept through the empty streets. The moist, chilly air couldn't dampen my mood because in less than twenty-four hours, I would be at the school in Cuzco where no doubt they were eagerly awaiting my arrival.

9

SANTA ANA

A spectacular plane ride flew me over the snow-capped Andes that seemed to be at fingertip reach from the window. I could see how Claudio, the tour guide, had been so deeply enamored with them, as they did have a majestic personality. With a mixture of excitement and apprehension as the plane landed in Cuzco, I wondered what I might be getting myself into.

The taxi ride cost seventy-five cents and hurtled me through the Spanish arches with wooden balconies jutting over narrow, cobblestone streets. Women roamed in colorfully layered skirts with stovepipe hats and long, sleek, braided hair, babies strapped to their backs and fluffy lambs cradled in their arms. Some women led vibrantly decorated llamas with fluorescent ear tassels. Rainbow flags fluttered on every street corner, making me wonder if a gay pride parade was taking place, but the driver assured me it was the flag of Cuzco. It was a bizarre combination of the Spanish conquest and the ancient Inca civilization coexisting.

We passed by the Spanish-style church of Santo Domingo, which sat atop the ruins of Korichanca, the Temple of the Sun for the ancient Incas. Cuzco was a fully functional, profoundly Andean atmosphere laced with Catholic influence. There were also random examples of modernization, like cars, Internet shops, ATMs, and, of course, tourists. Cuzco was so dramatically different than Lima it felt as if I had been time-warped and Spanish conquistadors might come galloping along next to the taxi at any moment.

The Incan Empire, for all its greatness, only existed for about a century. In one of the great tragedies of history, the Incas were at the height of their power when Francisco Pizarro and his band of Spanish conquistadors arrived on horseback with firearms, neither of which the Incas had ever seen. Initially, they believed the horse and rider to be a single creature and were too stunned to resist.

Showing an uncanny ability to turn circumstances to his own advantage, Pizarro used deception and deviousness to gain a personal meeting with Atahualpa, the Inca ruler, whom he calmly assassinated. In the face of fierce resistance, Pizarro and his men seized Cuzco and sacked the city.

Although the Incas continued to fight for the next several years, their empire was decimated and Spanish rule had begun, with Lima the Spaniards' capital. As a Spanish teacher, I knew the general history of most Spanish-speaking countries, but what is taught in books is nothing compared to actually learning by engaging with locals.

The cab squeezed up an alley and stopped in front of a door that didn't seem like it would be the entrance to anything hospitable. The taxi departed with a farewell puff of black exhaust in my face, leaving me standing with my oversized backpack on a narrow sidewalk. Tentatively, I rang the bell, and after a few long minutes, a petite woman opened the rusted metal door.

The passageway opened into a courtyard where perhaps four families lived. From the outside, one would never believe an entire interior world existed. The woman guided me into the foyer and introduced me to Marisol, the lady of the house. I was shown my room, which had a grand view of the mountains and the garden below. I asked to be taken to the school, thinking they might *need* me, but Marisol told me to relax and drink some coca leaf tea since the altitude would probably affect me soon.

I was a bit nervous about the tea because of rumors that it was a drug in liquid form, but Marisol assured me the coca leaf itself was not a drug. I later discovered that the coca leaf was often chewed in a saliva-soaked ball to provide a mild stimulant and to help overcome altitude sickness. I followed her instructions and drank the tea, trying to unwind although I felt anxious to get to the school to make a good first impression. Perhaps I'd be treated like some sort of saint for all the supplies I'd sent to the school. *The name Santa Ana has a nice ring to it,* I thought.

As I sipped the earthy coca tea, Marisol kept me amused with stories about her family history and interesting factoids about Peru. She had experienced a lot in sixty-plus years as reflected in her soft blue eyes, a rarity for Peruvians. She told me about one of the extraordinary aspects of the Incan rule. They'd created an empire with the absence of a written language, horses, or the wheel. They had a remarkable way of keeping records by using a system of knotted string called *quipus*. They also built a royal road that extended over three thousand five hundred miles, which was longer than the longest Roman road.

Because the Incas controlled such an immense territory, they needed a way to communicate with all the corners of the empire and so designed a network of messengers by which important messages would be transported. These mail carriers, known as *chasquis*, were chosen from the strongest and fittest young men. They ran many miles a day to deliver messages and lived in huts, usually in groups, along the roads.

The Inca ruler living in Cuzco was also known to fancy a fish dinner, which had to be delivered in the same manner, all the way from the coastline. When a chasqui was spotted, another one would dash to meet him and run beside the incoming messenger, trying to listen to and memorize the message or pass off the goods. They would also hand off knotted quipus.

The exhausted runner would stay and rest while the other one continued on to the next relay station. In this way, messages could travel over fifty miles a day. The historical story made me feel quite pathetic for the constant longing I felt for my cell phone.

Another volunteer entered the large dining room and introduced herself as Helen, a Russian-American.

She had a cherubic face with wire-rimmed glasses and wore an oversized red sweater with patterns zigzagging down the front. She eagerly dug into the fanny pack cinching her mid-stomach and pulled out a town map. She offered to be my guide, which I gratefully accepted since I wanted to get a feel for the city's layout. (Of course, I secretly hoped to convince her to take me to the school at some point during the tour.) She was excessively talkative, but I was happy to have someone to converse with after going such a long stretch without much communication in English.

Helen had a wealth of knowledge about Peru and all its intriguing mysteries. She educated me about how the Andes Mountains split into two high-altitude plateaus and atop one of them was Lake Titicaca, the world's highest navigable lake where indigenous Indians lived on floating reed islands. Helen planned to visit that area of Peru after she fulfilled her commitment to the school.

She also told me of the enigmatic Nazca Lines in northern Peru, which consisted of enormous geometric designs and long lines crisscrossing the desert. When flying above, one can see the forms of a monkey, spider, hummingbird, and a killer whale. They have been linked to visiting aliens and astronomical calendars, but the most likely explanation was that they were created during rituals as offerings to the gods. It was believed that ancient shamans could fly once they entered the spirit world and could thus enjoy the designs in all their glory. I wondered if perhaps pisco sours contributed to their airborne abilities.

I insisted on visiting the school, but instead Helen brought me to the hostel, which housed most of the volunteers and the employees who ran the school. It was a colorful wonderland with hammocks and rainbow-painted balconies. Music blasted from a transistor radio, and a slew of foreign university students were splayed out on the ground smoking cigarettes.

I was immediately thankful I had opted to pay a bit more for my housing with Marisol, the mother of the guy who ran the school. Not only did her son manage the school, but also the hostel for volunteers, the restaurant that funded the school, and an organization to help incarcerated kids. I was chomping at the bit to meet this extraordinary one-man show.

Since I had attached a photo of myself in my most recent e-mail to the school, I thought someone might recognize me. However, after I tracked down the administrative assistant, it took a few reminders for her to even comprehend who I was.

"You know, me, Ann…the teacher who sent three large boxes of supplies," I said.

Her brow crinkled. "Ohhhh, yes," she said hesitantly. "Sí, I remember now."

I wasn't convinced, but it didn't matter if she knew who I was, it was the boss I was interested in.

"Is Javier here? I'd really like to meet him." Maybe he would greet with me with a little more gusto.

Admittedly, another reason I was eager to meet the big *jefe* was that ever since I'd seen his picture on the school website, I couldn't get him off my mind. The photos depicted a man with dark curly hair tucked into a colorful handmade beanie, inviting warm eyes, and earth-toned clothing. He seemed to have a glowing presence with an irresistible smile.

I was curious as to how much his good looks had actually influenced my decision to come, as I felt my little heart irresponsibly whirling into fantasy. Perhaps I would make such a difference at the school that Javier couldn't help but fall in love with me. So, naturally, I would have to move to Peru and run the school with him, both of us making our profound mark on the world.

"Stop!" I growled at my love-starved imagination. My mind had already weaved together my entire future with this man, whom I had yet to meet. I needed a reality check—and fast. I reminded myself sternly (yet unconvincingly) that I was there to selflessly volunteer, to set an example for my students, and to bring back an experience that would inspire them.

I smiled sweetly. "So…Javier, is he here?" I asked, while my mind enthusiastically whispered, *Tell him Santa Ana has arrived!*

IO

PERUVIAN ODDITIES

Attempting to identify the peculiarities of the Peruvian culture was infinitely entertaining. The customs, habits, and oddities of the local people were like potent and unusual ingredients. When mixed all together, it made up the uniquely flavorful recipe of Cuzco. The streets were filled with some sights that delighted, others that brought gut-wrenching tears. Scents that made the mouth water, others that made the stomach turn. Sounds that enchanted and those with the potential to drive one to insanity.

Every imaginable unnecessary item was available to buy on the streets. An indigenous woman in layered alpaca skirts sold bobby pins organized in neat rows on a sheet, while another peddled earring backings. A bright-eyed teenage girl held a roll of toilet paper, selling individual squares. On most corners sat traditionally clad women of indiscernible ages with piles of odd-looking produce. A blind man slammed the keys of an out-of-tune organ a few steps down from a blind guitar player. They seemed to be competing in volume and lack of pitch.

A man with glistening eyes and a leathery face stood patiently next to an immense orb of string. What circulated through his mind all day with scissors in one hand and the tail of the string in the other? Sincere delight spread through me the first time I saw him measuring off a piece for a customer.

In Cuzco, there seemed to be various modes of street vending. There were the people who sat on the sidewalk with vacant expressions and products displayed in front of them. There were those who relentlessly harassed with their supply slung on their backs. Then there were the vendors who actually created or prepared a product for a customer.

At the locals' market, there was a row of booths with women operating ancient sewing machines. Fresh-fruit smoothie ladies occupied the second row with their colorful produce piled up, blenders whizzing away making marvelous creations. I had already indulged in four smoothies since I arrived—until I shared with Marisol my delicious discovery.

"Ay, no, Ana!" she scolded. "Never, *ever* eat anything from that market, it's not safe for your foreign stomach!"

The market sold everything from roasted guinea pig on a stick—eyeballs included—to bags of coca leaves and hot dog waffles. A chubby, aproned woman sold warm, red corn juice from a large bucket—one glass at a time. The cup was "sanitized" for the next customer by dipping it in a dirty water bucket and then filled again.

Luckily, since I was staying at Marisol's house, all food and beverages were prepared with foreigners in mind and therefore as clean as could be.

I saw an old man with *three* colossal, wooden wall units on a cart, pulling it over bumpy cobblestones with a harness strapped across his forehead. Another fellow walked effortlessly with a dining room table on the crown of his head, not even supporting it with his hands. Llama-pulling women were decked out in brightly colored traditional dresses with babies slung on their backs, and forlorn-faced children carried adorable puppies and little lambs, asking, "Hey, laaadeee, foto?"

One particular street that I frequently walked hosted a succession of women claiming to be masseuses. They tugged on my sleeve relentlessly, asking, "Laaadeee, masaje? You want masaje therapéutico?" Boys no older than ten constantly pressured me to allow them to shine my shoes, even when I was wearing flip-flops. Everything illegal could be purchased in the alleys that branched off from the main plaza. "Hey, laaadeee, you want coca? Marijuana? Hashish? Pills? Sexo? Un niño?" *Excuse me?*

Even children were being sex-trafficked to tourists who apparently indulged. A fiercely just and maternal voice shouted from inside me that I should devise a scheme to rescue the enslaved niños who were stashed away, trembling in fear somewhere near that alley.

It was common to see buses stuffed to the brim with bodies pressed against the windows. Once I witnessed a woman holding her child out the window since he didn't fit within the confines of the bus. There always seemed to be a child in some awkward spot with his or her face squashed to the glass. If only the people of Los Angeles carpooled with such efficiency, perhaps the 405 freeway wouldn't be such a tangled web.

* * *

To get my laundry done, Marisol instructed me to take it to a blue door up the street and knock three times. The door squeaked open with just the tap of my knuckles. Adjusting to the dark room, I finally made out an ancient woman in the corner hunched over on a stool.

I stood uneasily with my laundry bag in hand and attempted to communicate in Spanish, quickly realizing she spoke only Quechua. She tapped the ground with a crooked finger, indicating where I was to set down the bag. Shuffling over to a shelf, she brought over a scale on which she hung my bag of soiled clothing. She pointed to the weight, three kilos, and held up four crooked fingers, indicating four soles, about a dollar twenty-five. *What a deal!*

I returned the next day, and the following, but she kept waving me away. Getting desperate for underwear, I had even gone to the local market, but could only find XXL granny-panties, which rose above my belly button and cupped my rear end like a diaper.

On the third day, I came back with great anticipation for clean clothes, but she waved me away yet again. My irritation level rose as I glared at her and pulled up my shirt, pointed at the wide waistband of the *abuela* underwear, and firmly declared, "No!" as I gave her thumbs-down. She had no clue what I was trying to say. I needed *my* underwear now!

She stared at me blankly and pointed at the ceiling. I looked up, not understanding the language of her movement. "No sol," she finally said. *Oh, OK, I got it*. It had been raining on and off and was blustery cold, so her nature-dependent washer/dryer combo was out of service until the sun shined again.

I woke up late the next morning to sunshine streaming in and immediately jumped out of bed and hurried up to the blue door, knocking three times. She let me in, nodded, then pulled back a weathered curtain to retrieve my clothes, which exposed her laundry facility. It was a dirt patch with a dripping water spigot, a piece of flat wood, a wire brush, a thin slice of soap, and wires strung from wall to wall.

She handed over my clothes, which were too brittle and stiff to fit back in the bag. My underwear felt like construction paper, and it seemed as if she had papier-mâchéd my socks.

Maybe the time had come to wear flip-flops and go commando.

11

ESCUELA ARCO IRIS

The next day I was finally granted entrance into the
school, still having yet to meet the revered Javier.
Helen brought me, talking nonstop as I nodded, smiling
politely, but I was lost in a daydream about seeing all the
school supplies I had sent being put to use.

I envisioned kids overjoyed at having new paint-
brushes and colors to stimulate creations beyond their
wildest imaginations. I fantasized about the felt animal
hats hanging on pegs for easy access to creative thinking. There would be twenty-five individual plastic boxes,
each divided with supplies so that each kid could have
his or her own. Stacks of construction paper would be
organized by color in tray files. And finally, the colorful windsock I had personally purchased for the school
would be fluttering in the breeze. My heart eagerly tingled to finally witness the results of all my hard work.

The outdoor metal gate was unlocked at 2:45 p.m.
as volunteers gathered and waited to be let in, all preparing for the mass influx of fifty to eighty kids. Right

away, I was astonished at the unsanitary conditions of even the entranceway. Various stages of decaying dog excrement, jagged, broken bricks, and random holes in the ground were just a few of the obstacles. Carefully making my way in, I had to duck under old-man underwear bowing from a clothesline. Archaic, abandoned passageways and adobe-walled enclosures had been converted to make a school. It was unlike anything I had seen.

There were two parts to the facility, Escuela Una and Escuela Dos. A third part was in the works, the Magic Garden. After passing through a rusty gate, I was introduced to the soon-to-be garden wonderland. It was a filthy, trash-ridden, walled-in stretch of dirt that could only be reached by climbing through a hole in a crumbling wall.

Apparently, six volunteers had already been working for weeks to clean the space out. I couldn't imagine it being any worse than it already was, but I was entertained at thinking I would see this garden to completion someday soon with its greenhouse, cages for animals, and grassy carpet for frolicking kids. Maybe Javier would put me in charge of the garden since I was positive I could figure out a more efficient way to whip that square of dirt into something magical.

In the southern hemisphere, the seasons are reversed, so the academic year in Peru begins in March and ends in December, with the summer months being January, February, and early March. While some areas of Peru have an *escuela inicial*, which is similar to kindergarten in the United States, most of the Peruvian school system is comprised of six-year primary schools followed by five-year secondary schools.

In the highlands of Peru, many students come from families that don't speak Spanish and are raised speaking Quechua or Aymara, languages from the Incan Empire. Since classes are conducted in Spanish, in many cases the students must become bilingual in order to study. Many of the poorest areas of Peru have a high illiteracy rate and often students come from families in which the parents are illiterate or do not understand Spanish. Younger students must turn to older students to help them with their homework or to help them practice their writing, as their parents are not able to assist with these tasks.

At Escuela Arco Iris, I soon discovered that they taught year-round, even during holidays, the summer months, and on Saturdays. It was more like an after-school program, but most of the kids attending came because it was free, fun, and their only opportunity to get educated.

A few of the "upper" lower-class students wore school uniforms, but the rest were a blend of homeless kids and those who walked down from the poverty-stricken mountain villages nearby. The routine for the afternoon started with the kids lining up to wash their faces and put on lotion. Due to the dry climate, much of their skin was scaly, and a few children were covered in dead, black skin that indiscriminately peeled off. The cleansing practice helped keep them healthy, plus they were learning about personal hygiene, of which many were not aware.

I wanted to jump right in and get involved, but it was a bit intimidating. I tried to familiarize myself with the place and soak it up so I could fit in as soon as possible. Most of the volunteers hugged and kissed each and every kid, which was surprising since many students had snotty noses and coughed and sneezed frequently. Two patios were divided similarly for School One and Two—three tiny classrooms with doors that opened into the mural-covered common area. Clearly, a lot of work had been put into making the dingy, crumbling location a colorful, alive place of learning. It was certainly living up to its Arco Iris name which translated to rainbow.

Even though I was an unfamiliar face, the kids clung to me and yanked on me relentlessly. I hugged them discriminately, depending on the quantity of mucus seeping, and decided that it would probably be better if I refrained from any physical contact.

I had expected to be formally shown around or at least have someone explain to me what was going on and what I should be doing. Everyone seemed to be involved in his or her own tasks and didn't take notice of me. I hugged the wall and attempted chitchat with a few bold, young girls who wanted to wear my jewelry.

It was then I remembered my school supplies and decorations as I eagerly scanned the patio. Nothing was noticeable yet, but I figured they must have been distributed inside the classrooms.

Since no one was finding it necessary to give me any responsibilities yet, I decided to unveil the whereabouts of all my donations. A dozen unsteady stairs hardly held my weight as I climbed up to a small room where the volunteers kept their belongings. There were a few shelves with supplies beneath a window that looked like it had been shattered decades ago. *Ah-ha!*

As I inspected more closely, it became clear that none of *my* materials were there. There were a dozen dirty mugs with broken stub crayons; a plastic crate of markers, half of them missing caps; a metal lunchbox of buttons; half-empty glue bottles; and paper that had been recycled two and three times. A colorfully painted trashcan was jammed with fabric scraps, masks, sticks, old clothes, feathers, and other odds and ends that blocked an old wooden door.

My heart started to race and sweat beaded on my forehead. Where were *my* supplies? Before I could continue my search, I heard the noise level outside raise a few octaves as the kids squealed with delight, rushing toward the front gate.

He was here—Javier.

His energy radiated and seemed to infect everyone within range. The kids cheered and ran to him like he was a movie star. Javier hugged and kissed every child, giving special attention to each one. He then caught my eye and headed over. He gave me the typical greeting, a kiss on each cheek and a very friendly hug.

A thrilling surge of excitement raced through my veins as an entire fantasy future flooded my mind. Smiling serenely, I disguised the movie that was playing in my imagination. He told me to observe and get the hang of things and to jump in where I felt necessary and we'd talk later about further responsibilities. Talk later? *But of course!*

I studied how the kids were divided into the *Tortugitas* (the "little turtles," aged five to seven) and the Pumas (aged eight to ten). The first two hours, the kids had three options: art, games, or time in the library where they got help with their schoolwork or chose books to read. I had sent over two dozen children's books in Spanish, so I was sure this was a good place to see my donations shelved.

Hunching over to keep from bumping my head in the windowless, musty library room, I headed to the bookcase with half a dozen kids in tow. Their curious faces watched as I eagerly fingered through the collection of ragged old books. Where were all my books? No *Cat in the Hat*, *Goodnight Moon*, *Where the Wild Things Are*, or other such enchanting treasures for a child's mind. Each book was numbered on the bind, so perhaps they hadn't had time to register all the books and integrate them.

Discouraged and uncomfortable, I perched on a miniature, uneven wooden stool and rotated, reading with four or five kids. Sometimes they read to me or I to them. The books were uninspiring and dry and most were above their level or way below.

Daniela, a desperately shy girl, clung to me, using my pant leg as a Kleenex. I gagged a bit, wanting to push her away as I envisioned the dread of knocking three times on the blue door for laundry services. Instead, I carefully detached her, handing her a balled-up tissue from my pocket.

I soon realized she had exceedingly poor vision as she sat in a corner with her back to the room and a book an inch from her face. I did a mock vision test for her, holding up fingers from a distance, and understood how bad it was. She finally confided in me that she had glasses but had been teased so relentlessly that she decided to never wear them again, even though the glasses had cost her parents a week's worth of wages.

I gave her a little pep talk, telling her that I too had glasses but didn't like to wear them. I told her it would be more comfortable for me if she wore hers too. She hugged me tightly and agreed to wear them. Digging into the secret candy supply in my pocket—for the kids, of course, not me—I handed her a few sweets.

Actually, I did have a wee bit of a problem with candy. While living in Spain, I'd indulged daily in a bag of gummies, which could be purchased on every corner or transportation stop. My hand would plunge into the bag of gummy bears, bunnies, coke bottles, or worms and then I'd go skipping on my merry way. Every day. I found flossing tedious and pointless since all my friends in Spain seemed to think I already had movie-star teeth.

When I returned to the States and visited my dentist after a three-year absence, he actually asked me, "Ann, have you been eating an excess of something *gummy*?" *Holy shit, he really nailed it!* He regretted telling me I had *eleven* cavities, mostly in between my teeth. Incredulously, I still can't seem to defy the gummy urge, but I floss more often, especially because my dental hygienist friend told me that I should only floss the teeth I wanted to keep.

* * *

Two hours later, music cackled from a cassette player, which the older kids responded to automatically by gathering in a large circle in the common patio, sitting cross-legged, impatiently waiting. Soon enough, the young ones marched in, giggly and squiggly, as the older ones chanted, "Tor...tu...gi...tas." Then, Javier, with passionate charisma, facilitated a one-hour discussion on his personally chosen subject.

"What do *you* want to be when you grow up?" he asked the circle of enthusiastic faces.

Hands squirted up as the kids eagerly wormed around, trying not to shout out for fear of reprimand from their intrepid leader. It started small, with most unable to think outside the box of what their parents did.

"A taxi driver!" one shouted.

"A farmer!" said another.

"To sell cheese at the market like *mi mamá!*" declared a young girl.

Javier nudged them into thinking bigger, and soon the circle was filled with big dreams of being astronauts, doctors, and, of course, a lot of future Javiers.

After the discussion circle, Javier asked me to take over guiding the older kids with their presentation on the Peruvian celebration Inti Raymi to honor the Sun God. This would be performed the following day at the school assembly. He explained how the volunteer who had been working with them had had an unacceptable meltdown in front of the kids. By now, I saw that interactions with Javier were short. There was no time for questions or discussion. I wanted to know *why* she'd had a meltdown, but I guessed I would just have to figure that out for myself.

He pointed to a room hastily built on a second level with a rickety balcony, broken and missing floorboards, and a staircase without a hand railing. Keeping my judgments to myself, I swallowed my opinion about the serious hazard of the stairs and how it would *never* be up to standard for children in the States.

"You will work in there for the next two hours," he explained in melodic Spanish. "There's a cardboard box inside that needs to be made into a llama for the Inti Raymi skit."

I started to inquire about the location of my materials, but he cut me off and firmly stated, "The children may not leave the room for any reason. Is that clear?"

"No problem," I replied confidently. "I'm a high school teacher and I know how to lay down the law when necessary."

I felt a rush of excitement to be given the responsibility of a class on the first day and the potential difference I could make right at my fingertips. I cautiously climbed the steep, splintered steps up to the room and peeked my head in the door.

Feral anarchy was in full swing as a dozen kids ran around like savage creatures, climbing on desks and screaming. I cautiously entered as one kid leaped out, yanking my hair to pull my face close enough for a snotty, sloppy kiss. Repulsed, I pulled back, not wanting to get infected with Peruvian supergerms. The uncontrollable shrieking ensued at an animalistic pitch, while a cluster of girls stuck their little hands in my shoulder bag. The large cardboard box in the corner was being crushed, punched through, and torn to bits by a group of boys.

"Profi!" one boy hollered, using the short version of professor. "Voy al baño," he said as he shot out the front door toward the bathroom.

"¡Yo también!" declared another, following him into the dark.

I gave chase, but they had already scampered into the night. I stood in the doorway, looking back in at the pandemonium, and sighed with Javier's warning echoing in my mind. This was way more than I'd bargained for.

With candy bribes in hand, I gained moderate order and encouraged the kids to explain what Inti Raymi represented to them. What I could gather was that it was a special event for the Inca Empire that was celebrated in abundance in Cuzco. It was the Festival of the Sun— or, as we say, the winter solstice—which was the shortest day of the year. The Incas took the time to study the natural environment and gain an understanding of the yearly calendar—the days, the years, and the seasons— which provided them the knowledge to develop a means to sustain themselves in those high altitudes for many years—before the Spaniards arrived, that is.

The Incas worked in harmony with the rhythms of Pachamama, the Mother Earth, and it was believed that it was this connection that ensured abundance of crops and health for the following days ahead. Evidently, Pachamama enjoyed sacrifices of fluffy white animals and therefore was offered the heart of a white llama during the ceremony. The last Inti Raymi with a real Inca emperor's presence was carried out in 1535, after which the Spanish Catholic church suppressed it. Some natives participated in similar ceremonies in the years after, but it was entirely prohibited in 1572 by the viceroy Francisco de Toledo, who claimed it was a pagan ceremony opposed to the Catholic faith.

The pack of crackers in my bag helped keep order, since the children were so undernourished. The self-proclaimed leader of the kids, Tomás, explained how they were to act out the llama sacrifice using the cardboard box as the furry beast, and, of course, *he* was going to be the Inca emperor.

I thought they were surely conning me, but when I checked with a volunteer down the balcony, she confirmed it to be true. Gazing over at the desecrated cardboard box, I checked my watch, which indicated I had just over an hour to complete the task.

Quickly, I devised a plan, divvied up responsibilities, pulled out my personal supply of markers, construction paper, glue, and kid scissors, and attempted to get the children on task with edible rewards.

By the time our session was over, a skit had been invented. The llama had almost risen from the dead, and, as a bonus, one of the boys had gotten his bangs chopped off at the scalp with the dull kid scissors, courtesy of Tomás. I was frazzled, dirty, and exhausted from trying to keep order in Spanish, not to mention hard of hearing from the kids' high-pitched screaming.

If it would work or not was no longer in my hands. Tomorrow would be the true test of whether I could show Javier that I was the real deal.

12

THE SLAUGHTER

Prior to the assembly, I had a few desperate minutes to add in new ideas during the final run-through. I had hardly slept the night before since I'd exhausted my mind with new skit designs that would impress Javier as well as the others. They would hardly believe how quickly I had whipped those niños into shape. I had spent the morning scouring Cuzco for a few inexpensive items that could be used as props and a replacement llama, since the cardboard one had prematurely expired.

The Tortugitas and Pumas sat in their respective rows on alligator- and snake-painted benches, all of them restlessly squirming, finding it nearly impossible to contain their excitement. Some of the children's parents lined the back walls, which was reassuring to see.

I considered what it felt like for ten-year-old Paula from my group. She was quiet as a mouse and wore a filthy red T-shirt a few sizes too small, her hair in a natty ponytail. Another volunteer had told me Paula lived on the streets because her parents had too many children to take care of. They had pushed many of them out of the house to fend for themselves. Had birth control not been introduced to Peru yet? How could a mother tell her own young daughter that she could no longer come home and needed to go fend for herself?

Shamefully, I recalled how I resented that my divorced parents would come to my childhood sporting events and sit on separate sides of the soccer field with their new spouses. Once the game was over, I'd stand in the middle of the field, not sure which set of parents to head toward first. I didn't see it as solid loving support from all sides but rather a cruel circumstance that I was stuck in and despised. With a wave of guilt about how I viewed my own youth, I eyed Paula as she craned her neck back to catch a longing glimpse of the parents present to support their son or daughter.

Javier had made it very clear that we were not to take pictures inside the school. I was dying to document the experience and was guilty of exactly what he was trying to avoid. If volunteers constantly took pictures, then most likely their intentions weren't focused around doing their best at helping the kids. He had given a speech about cheapening the children's lives and their innocent expressions by exploiting them as a "Look at me in Peru!" post on Facebook.

It was nearly impossible to resist snapping a shot of all these kids with their dirty faces and gleaming eyes, though. Feeling justified, I decided to risk it, certain that I'd use the images to gather support back in the States to help Arco Iris school. I snuck my camera out and held it low, aimed at the girls who shared the bench with me. While pretending to look the other way, I took the picture and came eye to eye with Javier, who glared at me as if I had committed a mortal sin. With a nervous smile, I tucked the camera back in my purse.

As Javier was getting the group settled, I noticed a little Tortugita on the ground in front of me using her pink wool cap to wipe up the puddle between her legs. She looked up at me unconcerned; I grabbed her hand anyway and whisked her off to the bathroom.

I was horrified to find a tiny room with a toilet overflowing with excrement and soiled paper all over the ground. Peruvian pipes are unable to handle toilet paper, so one must wipe and put it in the trashcan by the toilet—that was *if* there was a trashcan. This method was used no matter if it was número uno or número dos, which could cause some gaggingly stench-y bathrooms. This particular one also had a bathtub that was obviously used on occasion as a toilet. If I were she, I would have probably gone in my pants too.

Back at the patio, it was showtime. I distributed the props moments prior to the performance, hoping to avoid total destruction of the accessories. I covered one boy with a white sheet to act the part of the llama and gave him a red scarf to push out of a hole in the sheet once he was sacrificed. The boy who represented the high priest got a foil-covered cardboard dagger and was draped in a red cloth for the ceremonial robe.

Tomás was crowned the Incan emperor, and one of the girls wore a sun cutout mask, all of which I had stayed up late designing the night before. Each child had a three by five card with the words of the chant for the blessings to Apu Inti, the Sun God, written in large, clear letters. The emperor would ask the gods for the blessing of his crops, the priest would sacrifice the llama and offer the heart to the sun, and they would all chant the ceremonial blessing. The kids would then bow to thunderous applause and I would beam with pride. In theory, it was brilliant.

Standing anxiously to the side, I encouraged them to begin, since they stood frozen in front of the crowd. I urged Tomás to start with his lines about how important the harvest would be for his people. Then, in one alarming moment, I witnessed the wicked flicker in the emperor's eye. Tomás launched himself onto the llama-boy, along with the priest, who used his cardboard knife to repeatedly stab the poor guy on all fours wrapped up in the sheet. The dagger bent in half and was torn to foiled shreds as the boys piled up in a tangled mess of red and white cloth. The sun-girl pulled off the cardboard circle of rays and launched it in the audience like a Frisbee.

All the kids squealed with delight at the visually stimulating mayhem. I tried to step in, but it was like trying to separate a pack of rowdy dogs, which Javier responded to by walking up like Moses parting the Red Sea. One step in their direction with a stern look and the group stopped their roughhousing and sulked back to their benches.

My jaw was still unhinged in disbelief as Javier glanced at me with a disappointed look. My brow furrowed in frustration at not receiving the praise I had expected. The excuses shouted in my mind: *I only had one day! This was an impossible task! Come on! If you could only see the real skit I had planned!* I was starting to get an idea as to why the previous teacher had had a meltdown.

Unable to stop myself from criticizing and judging the other skits, I was left feeling empty and irritated. Javier pulled me aside and harshly chastised me for buying extra props that weren't from the "supply room." *Supply room? You mean that room full of old broken bits of what used to be supplies?* Before I could ask him where my donations were, he demanded to know if I had clandestinely given my group food the previous night. I was a bit dumbstruck at how he worded it.

"Sí," I said hesitantly, "I did."

"That's unacceptable!" he growled. "I am *the only one* who decides when and to whom food will be distributed! ¿Me comprendes?"

"Yeah, I understand you," I grumbled back.

He turned, put a smile back on, and hugged one of the kids tugging at his pant leg. Feeling numb, I let out a long, deep breath, groaning wearily at the niños surrounding me, begging for attention. All my efforts had been thwarted, I had done just about everything wrong, and I had failed at my only task.

At the end of the marathon assembly, the kids got a large glass of milky oatmeal and a vitamin before they left the school. For many, this was the only meal they would get in a day. Volunteers had to make sure the kids swallowed the vitamins as they often tucked them in their cheeks to sell later on the street. I couldn't imagine anyone buying a single, moist vitamin, but there must have been a market for it.

By the time I had hobbled out of the school over broken bricks in the pitch black, avoiding gaping ditches and dog poop, I was frozen to the bone and had a pounding headache. The mental and emotional impact of witnessing the children's distressing lives combined with the remarkable opportunity the school provided for them moved me to tears. Not to mention the fact that I hadn't accomplished anything I'd set out to do and had been scolded like a child.

Ducking my head under the low, metal door, I exited out onto the street. Many parents or older siblings were waiting out front to walk the kids home. I thought of the long line of SUVs back home that jockeyed for position to pick up their little tykes from school.

The girl with the pink pee-pee cap pulled it down over her ears and clung to her big sister's hand. I started to head down the hill back to Marisol's house when something caused me stop. I turned to look back up the hill. A lone figure in a red shirt was slowly walking up the street.

"Paula?" I shouted. She stopped and I ran up the hill to her. "Do you want me to walk you home?" I asked.

But before I finished my sentence, I realized my mistake. She didn't have a home to be walked to. *Where was she going?* I wanted to pick her up, wrap her in my arms, and tell her it would be OK. She was so young, so alone, and so sad.

I dug in my bag and gave her a four-pack of Oreos. For a moment, I hesitated, thinking of Javier's recent reprimand, but this had nothing to do with him; it was between Paula and me. A meek smile snuck out and her eyes lit up as she darted away into the chilly shadows like a stray dog that had discovered a meaty bone.

Dazed with emotion, I dug my fingers deep in my pockets, exhaled a frosty breath, and turned my face to the sky. A diamond-studded, black velvet carpet spread above me and sparkled and danced with stars that can only be seen at such altitudes. Gasping with awe, it felt as if God had winked at me, letting me know I was on the right path.

13

BESOS ENFERMOS

By the middle of the following week, twelve volunteers were left at Arco Iris, the number dropping from twenty. The hostel was like an infirmary, most residents tortured by crippling respiratory infections or intestinal bugs, leaving them painfully congested or vomitous. I had consistently ingested an array of vitamins but suspected it was only a matter of time before I, too, became afflicted. I could sense that my cape of visualized invincibility was not going to protect me against the powerful Peruvian mega-germs.

Apart from Marta, a middle-aged Spanish woman, I was one of the oldest and most educated volunteers. Marta had been at the school for a week using songs, unique art techniques, and twisty balloons to entertain and charm the kids. Since I'd learned Spanish in Spain, we both spoke with the same accent and slang, which provided us a sense of camaraderie.

I asked her in confidence what she thought of how the school was run. She shook her head, clucking her tongue. "¡Es un desastre! So, how long do you plan on staying?" she asked.

When I replied, "One or maybe even two months," her eyebrows rose suspiciously.

"Honestly, Ana, there is no way you will last that long," she said. "We are *real* teachers and know how to teach, but this place is so backward, and that Javier is a tyrant!"

My defenses immediately went up wanting to defend Javier. Plus, I felt an instant challenge to stubbornly show off my abilities by hanging in there, just to prove a point.

"Well, Marta, perhaps because I'm younger, I'll have more patience for this. I'm going to stay and do everything I can to help these kids. It's amazing what Javier is doing here, and I support it."

"Vale guapa, buena suerte," she said fatalistically with a smirk. "You've only been here a few days, right? You'll figure it out soon enough."

Unfortunately, my experience was with kids from families of high socio-economic background who had two college-graduate parents and an incredible motivation to succeed. The students typically drove Range Rovers and Mercedes, wore the newest designer fashions, and were experts on every imaginable electronic device.

This was exactly why my trip had such a significant purpose. If I could just bring a piece of Cuzco to my Palos Verdes students and help open their eyes to how people lived outside of their protective bubble, it would be worth whatever challenges I had to face.

During a volunteer meeting, Javier had vehemently demanded that everyone must kiss and hug each kid when he or she arrived at the school and give love continuously throughout the day. He explained how a lot of the children had never had any type of positive physical contact with adults and many were physically, mentally, and sexually abused. Javier insisted that providing love and affection was the foundation of the school.

But I'd soon discovered that once those love-less kids got a drop of it, for them it was like experiencing the cool waters of the ocean after a hot, landlocked existence. They could never get enough and found every sneaky way to be touching, clinging to, or hugged by the volunteers at all times.

This was exceptionally challenging; most of the kids reeked, had snotty noses, never covered their mouths to cough, and projectile-sneezed. Utterly torn about the amount of physical contact I was willing to give, I had started skirting around visibly sick kids, avoiding eye contact so they wouldn't climb up me like monkeys and wipe their mucus-smeared faces on mine. I admired Javier for his passion and selfless love, but I wasn't sure I could provide what he was ordering us to do.

Jennifer, a cute, blonde Californian girl, translated the volunteer meeting. Javier introduced her as the co-director of the school who had been there almost a year. She had originally planned to stay for only a few months but could not tear herself away from the children.

And Javier! I noticed how she gazed at him admiringly, batting her long lashes and laughing delicately.

Look at all that makeup! Come on! And how about those fancy leather boots? Who travels with those, especially to volunteer in a third world country? Jealousy possessed me as I picked up on a chemistry passing between them when she enthusiastically expressed Javier's passionate ideas in her own words. It suddenly became a very good possibility that she was living out *my fantasy!*

The meeting was long, especially after an entire afternoon at the school. I thought I might go insane if Javier launched another exhausting monologue about his philosophy of children's education, volunteering, or countless other topics under the sun. While I tried keeping up with him in my mind, my translation soon fell behind. Jennifer, on the other hand, communicated with grace and ease, all the while comporting a sweet smile of unfettered loyalty.

Javier closed the meeting with a round of applause for Jennifer, who'd be leaving the school at the end of the week to return to the States. *Now he has my attention.* Mascara tears streaked down her cheeks as she gave a heartfelt farewell speech. Javier closed the meeting and asked me to stay afterward so we could talk.

Ah-ha! Here's my chance to ask about the mysterious location of all my donations! He wrapped his arm around my shoulder and shuffled me over for a personal introduction to Jennifer. He then informed us both that I would be replacing her as co-director, starting the next day. My eyes gleamed in anticipation as my stomach twisted in delight and trepidation. While Javier seemed emotionless at this changing of the guard, Jennifer's eyes went cold, and she wiped her face of previous emotion.

"Oh, I see," she said. "You've already replaced me? Don't waste any time, do you, Javier?" She grabbed her shoulder bag, flipping her long blonde hair out of her face, and began laughing. "Ha! Good luck!" she said to me. "You have no idea what you are in for."

"Oh, Jennifer, don't forget," interrupted Javier. She stared coolly at him with one eyebrow arched. "The next two days you will be training Ana to do your job."

Jennifer and I locked eyes like territorial lionesses. She gave me one last eye roll and stormed out, slamming the screen door. I turned back to Javier, prepared to ask my burning question— but he had already crossed the room to welcome a new voluptuous Italian volunteer.

14

LA JEFA

Wrapped in a blanket and hiding out in my room at Marisol's, I felt excited with my new responsibility as *la jefa*—well, more like co-boss. I was doing my best to avoid the other volunteers, staying at the house since they were getting on my nerves by constantly asking me to translate their conversations to non-English speakers or Marisol. Anxious from holing up in my room, I snuck out once everyone was asleep for a single late-night cigarette.

After getting sober, I had picked up the habit, which soothed me on the occasions when I felt overwhelmed or restless. I typically had no resistance against the urge to smoke, even though I found it a disgusting habit. It was clear that when I made the choice to smoke it indicated that I was shrouded in fear or anxiety. Luckily, Peru sold cigarettes in mini-packs of four, which was handy when I only wanted to smoke one (or two). In the States, I would purchase a whole pack of "organic" cigarettes, pull out a few, and throw away the rest.

Bottom line, if cigarettes were around, I would smoke them, even if my rational mind didn't want to.

This kind of behavior always reminded me of my wise decision to eliminate drugs and alcohol from my life entirely. Although clean from mind-altering substances, it was as if my emotional maturity had been stunted from all the years of escaping how I felt. This left me vulnerable, sensitive, and often unable to deal with difficult circumstances. I had the habit of enduring an emotionally painful situation instead of communicating how I was really feeling.

The absence of my recovery program and the support it provided was taking its toll. Tracking down a twelve-step meeting in the Cuzco area was proving to be a complicated goose-chase involving many e-mails and unanswered phone calls to the Peruvian Central Office of Alcohol and Drug Recovery. Meetings were generally made up of a community of individuals who felt like I did and who lived life with a magnetic spirit of enthusiasm. No matter where I traveled in the world, there were meetings, often in English for foreigners. I just needed to talk to someone who could help me regain perspective and guide me back on track.

As I sat in the garden with a cigarette burning between my fingers, my mind spun like a hamster in a wheel. Was I becoming just another one of Javier's *special* assistants with *privileges*? Did he choose me to be La Jefa because I was qualified? Or because I planned to stay an extended period of time? Or was it because I could potentially become his *amiga especial* outside the school? Despite his narcissism, he was so enigmatic and breathtaking that I rejoiced at the idea of having more quality time with him.

The next day at Arco Iris, I anxiously sat in the discussion circle, waiting for Jennifer to arrive and show me the ropes. Daniela sat cross-legged in front of me with a big smile, wearing her glasses, as was I. The themed circle chats were starting to lose their charm, plus Javier sat on a staircase above the group so we'd have to look up at him. It seemed like another platform for him to have our undivided attention for his impassioned opinions.

The children clearly enjoyed these talks and were visibly stimulated to dig below the surface and think in an alternative and creative way—like Javier did. He then transitioned the discussion to the daily ritual of going over the rules with all the children for the benefit of the new kids, as well as many of the current ones who constantly forgot what the rules were and how to follow them.

Suddenly, Javier asked Antoinette, an eighteen-year-old French volunteer, to enter the middle of the circle. She had seemed shy and uncomfortable at the school, usually finding tasks that didn't involve interacting with the children. She had assisted me a few times with various groups of kids, but since she didn't speak Spanish, she usually just leaned against the back wall and observed.

So there she stood, hands jammed in her jacket pocket, dead center of the circle, staring apprehensively at Javier. He outstretched both arms to all the children.

"¡Niños! Every day I ask you to follow the rules, right?"

The kids all roared, "¡Sí!" in unison.

"What do you think about people who feel they don't have to follow the rules?"

Pausing for the question to sink in, Javier then asked a boy on the stair below, "How does that make you feel, Raul?"

"¡No es justo!" It's not fair, asserted the little boy. The others copied Raul, stomping their feet and pounding their fists on the cement, "¡No es justo, no es justo!"

"Well, Antoinette has not been following the rules, even though she has been here for three weeks!"

The kids booed. Fear and embarrassment flushed Antoinette's face as she looked back with pleading eyes to her French compatriots. Javier then asked for two kid volunteers to come out to the circle for a demonstration. Two girls with long dark braids skipped to the middle, looking expectantly at Javier.

"Valentina and Fabiola, please show our amiga Antoinette how we greet one another here at Arco Iris School."

The two girls lit up, knowing they could easily accomplish Javier's request. They greeted one another and then kissed each other's cheeks and hugged. My throat constricted and my palms began to perspire. Javier applauded and the others followed suit. Then he asked for two more volunteers. The bully, Tomás, from my group and little Raúl went to the middle.

"Now, will you two please show us all how Antoinette greets the students?"

What followed was a grossly overdramatic interpretation of Antoinette refusing to give affection at all, even when begged for by the kids. I could feel her pain as tears streaked down her face in disgrace.

"This is what I call *vergüenza social,*" declared Javier. Public shame.

I was appalled and completely turned off by this dramatic shift in his "love"-based philosophy. So my choice was either hug and kiss all the kids and surely get sick or avoid them and risk being humiliated in the vergüenza social.

* * *

Finally, Jennifer came gracefully gliding through the gate as the kids shouted her name, a few unable to resist breaking the rules of the circle to run and jump in her arms. She filled me in on the job requirements, however the topic of Javier was clearly out of bounds. I was dying to get the scoop on their relationship but was not bold enough to ask her straight out.

She seemed melancholy as she explained the different roles I would take on in her place. I would oversee the running of the Tortugitas School for the little ones, which involved many minute details. Her essential message was that the kids were unpredictable and the possibilities of what could happen were endless. I would just have to learn from experience and use my best judgment.

Jennifer seemed completely at home with the kids, giving out kisses and hugs indiscriminately. Worry knotted at the bottom of my stomach since I had almost no practice with young children, especially ones with scant training on how to follow instructions or listen to an adult respectfully. The little ones were at phase one of even grasping that there was a daily routine.

Jennifer then hit me with a sequence of other required responsibilities. Each exploded in my mind, progressively getting bigger and more dramatic, like a Fourth of July fireworks display. First and foremost, I was soon to be responsible for managing the Tortugitas School and taking on the youngest and most difficult group of kids as their personal instructor each afternoon.

Second, I would be translating the Friday never-ending Javier monologue meetings, like the one I had recently attended. On Saturdays, I would accompany Javier to the outskirts of town to take the kids on an excursion.

Saturday? I was happy to be selfless and volunteer myself Monday through Friday, but I had to draw the line with Saturday! Another thankless responsibility was to inform the constant stream of new volunteers of the rules and to make sure they followed them. *Really? Where was she when I arrived?*

Then came the intense firework finale extravaganza. Javier had decided that the new theme for the month was Hinduism. Last month was the Peruvian celebration of Inti Raymi, which clearly made sense, but Hinduism? So, for the next month I was to teach a dozen wild, undisciplined five-year-olds about Hinduism—*in Spanish*. Each week, Javier would decide the specific subject to be taught within the Hindu theme.

"But I don't know anything about Hinduism," I said with trepidation. "Hell, I don't even know how to say Hindu in Spanish!"

Jennifer rolled her eyes. "It's *hindú*." She continued, unconcerned with my reservations. "Next Monday will begin with the geography of the Hindu religion. *That* should be fun," she said with obvious sarcasm. "Then, at the end of the month will be the all-school performance. You'll need to design a skit for the kids to perform, but you already know about that, right? Didn't you do something special for the Inti Raymi presentation?"

I growled, not liking the shameful reminder of the botched llama sacrifice—especially coming from her.

"So this time it will all need to relate to Hinduism," she said with a grin. "Ana, you came just in time, thank you so much for relieving me of all these responsibilities."

Sighing deeply, I swallowed hard, unable to reply to her mockery.

"Oh, I almost forgot," she said, tossing me a ring with a single skeleton key. "This is to the door in the upstairs room. It's where Javier keeps all the extra materials."

15

¿DÓNDE ESTÁN LAS BOXES?

I couldn't sleep.

The key was in my possession.

Anxiously lying wide awake at the crack of dawn, I knew I'd have to wait until that afternoon to conclude my nerve-racking investigation. The hours painfully passed as I bit my nails to the nub and drank too much coca tea.

Finally, I headed to the school and waited impatiently at the main gate. One of Javier's administrative assistants eventually arrived with the key, but by the second metal barrier, it wouldn't work. The gate with the consistently stubborn lock stood nine feet high and was wedged between two tall adobe walls. The jamming of the key was a common occurrence, which kept people in or out for extended periods of time until someone with the magic touch could get it to turn.

Restlessly, I shifted from one foot to the other, determined to get to the supply room straightaway. The boxes had become like an extension of me, and knowing that they were being used for what I intended was crucial to my well-being. One of the students was able to get the gate to unlock as the congestion of kids and volunteers pushed through.

Rudely pressing my way through the crowd, I bee-lined for the stairs to the upper room when suddenly Javier's voice boomed from behind me with his jubilant greetings for all children. I cursed under my breath, knowing I was supposed to greet the kids near the entrance to disperse kisses and hugs. My subconscious reminded me of God winking at me through the stars the other night, so I surrendered to my obligation with a deep exhale.

An unfamiliar volunteer with a dark grimace stalked past the welcoming committee and headed up the stairwell to my original destination. Once the last little munchkin scurried in, I raced up the stairs, bursting with anticipation. Rearranging cups of broken crayons, the beady-eyed girl sat hunched over in a corner with a scowl. She was clearly not a happy camper, and it appeared as if she was battling being very, very sick. Her face was pocked with acne and dozens of clips made her hairdo spout in random directions.

As I fumbled with the archaic lock on the mystery door, she barked, "What do ya think you're doing?"

Her attitude gave me no desire to explain. "What does it look like I'm doing?" I retorted.

"Excuse me. *I'm* in charge of the supplies. *You* can't go in there."

"Listen here…" I paused, asking her name.

"Pamela."

"Listen here, Pamela, I don't give a shit what you are in charge of, I am going in this room whether you like it or not, plus *I* have the key!"

Pamela got up to block the door. Her nose that ran like a sieve, bloodshot eyes, and cough suggested some form of incurable virus.

"You're not allowed in there!" she chided.

Although I was teetering on the edge of no return with this girl, I decided on a new approach.

"So, if you are in charge of the supplies, do you know where the three large boxes are I sent from the States?"

"Just so you know," she explained, "it is not my choice to be up here, Javier made me do it because I freaked out on those little assholes." *Ah-ha, the meltdown girl in the flesh!*

With a contaminated exhale she pointed at the door. "And the boxes, yeah, they're in there."

"OK, then, so do you mind, Pamela?"

She acquiesced, retreating to her chair in the corner.

The door swung open, and there they were in all their glory. I wanted to wrap my arms around them like long-lost children. How beautiful the boxes were with all the artwork my Spanish classes had designed on each side. As I got closer, I saw that they were pretty banged up, but since they were still taped shut and shoved in a corner, it was evident that they had been unused.

Was Javier planning on selling the supplies to make a profit? What about the tax I had paid to extract the boxes from the post office? The kids hardly had any supplies to work with on a daily basis and not ten feet away there was a mini-Office Depot! I slowly made my way around the room and observed the extensive stock of goods that were shelved and organized by item, along with new books and used children's clothes. *What the hell is going on here?*

I closed the door to keep prying-eyes Pamela out of sight. With my blood pumping and my mind racing, I pulled out my pocketknife, sliced the top open on the nearest box, and granted myself the power to utilize my own supplies. I greedily snatched a pack of construction paper, a dozen small boxes of crayons, glue sticks, kid scissors, stickers, and a few children's books. Then I came across the large, beautiful rainbow windsock that I had ordered online. I was particularly excited to hang it up at the school so the kids could enjoy watching it dance in the wind, especially since its rainbow colors complemented the school's name. All my hoarding didn't even make a dent in the gold mine of goods.

But my conscience tugged at me.

You have no right to take anything. It is not up to you how they're used.

The demon inside me countered, *So what! These are mine and I'll take what I want!*

And so I did.

16

RULE-BREAKER

After two weeks in Cuzco, I was barely keeping my head above water. The combination of various disillusionments and difficult situations had spun me into a state of agitation and impatience. I wasn't enjoying the experience but knew that discomfort of such proportions had to be building my character. Annoyingly optimistic clichés stood to the side of my mind like stoic warriors reminding me that all painful experiences were touchstones for growth.

I walked the cobblestone streets aimlessly. Hopelessly, I shed tears as I puffed on consecutive cigarettes instead of my typical allotment of two. Finally, I reached an understanding of what was transpiring.

First of all, I was under the illusion that I had been making a profound impact on Arco Iris School from a distance. I recalled hearing the deep-voiced announcer in my mind: *All the way from the command center of her classroom in California, humanitarian and multitasker extraordinaire Señorita Windes magically whips up miracles to help the underprivileged children of the world!* I wondered if I had been more enamored with the *idea* of what I would be doing and what it sounded like to others than with actually doing it.

At the time I was putting together the donations and transferring money to Javier, I wondered why I was going through so much effort for a school that I had no personal connection with. Had I been blinded with the hope that since I was finally committing to "do good" on such a grand scale, then perhaps it would eradicate my selfish past and allow me to feel like I was a positive, contributing member of society? Now the prospect of redeeming myself was becoming further out of reach.

Even still, it was as if something greater than myself had been driving me, so I had kept taking the next indicated step. It had been a new sensation for me to even *attempt* to put together such a project. But I could see in retrospect that I obviously expected more than just an altruistic feeling. How ridiculous had I been arriving at the school referring to myself as "Ann, the teacher who sent the boxes," hoping that Javier would find my efforts to be heroic? Secretly, I thought I might be lauded as a noble superwoman, when in reality all my blood, sweat, and tears didn't even make a damn bit of difference.

It didn't take long for me to realize that my idea of co-director and Javier's intention for the position were two totally different concepts. Each day made it evident that he was completely resistant to new ideas, especially *my* ideas. It seemed as if he had no desire to find a more efficient way to run the school. When I would make a suggestion, he was either defensive that I was insulting his work, or he'd completely misinterpret me, even though my Spanish was clear.

Javier's purpose clearly benefited and enhanced the children's lives, but working for him was proving to be overly demanding. Back in the States, if disgruntled about a task or the behavior of a boss, I had appropriate avenues to voice my concern. At Arco Iris, I was donating my services, so being obligated to follow Javier's command without any democratic system of communication was unfamiliar and infuriating.

One day, I hung the rainbow windsock from an overhang on the patio. When Javier caught sight of it, he yanked it down crossly. "Who put this here?"

"I did," I said.

"Ana! *I* am in charge of putting up *all* decorations, not you!"

Really, Javier? I thought to myself with indignation. With running a bustling restaurant, overseeing a teen delinquents program, supervising the hostel, running the school, and his new idea of starting up a pizzeria, one would think he could at least allow his co-jefa to put up a windsock!

Breathe deeply. I thought *I* was the master multitasker, but this guy had me beat by a long shot. Bitterly, I tossed the windsock back into the storage room, certain that my vision for it would never be fulfilled.

With Javier's multiple endeavors, he was only capable of giving a fraction of his attention to each of his causes. This overextension triggered vast disorganization and gaping holes in how the school could be run most effectively. Maybe he thought that more children receiving a touch of assistance was better than a smaller group receiving more consistent and long-term support. I was of the opinion that the latter was better, but it was not my school to run and I had to keep myself in check. *I am not in charge. Surrender and get out of the way of God's work.*

My frustrations were intensified each time Javier reprimanded me for not strictly enforcing the procedures for volunteers. This was no easy undertaking with so much turnover and so many distinct languages, cultural differences, and intentions for volunteering. Being the regulator of Javier's commandments had to be the worst job at the school, which was actually a close second to cleaning poops out of the tub in the bathroom. Theoretically, I was supposed to be the model of all the school's policies so the new volunteers could emulate my example. But following rules had never been my strong suit.

The perfect example of my aversion to abiding by rules had taken place at the conservative and religious Pepperdine University in November of 1996. The summer before school began, I had bleached my dark brown hair to platinum as homage to the Gwen Stefani look of the mid-'90s. I was in a wild, punk-rock stage and took on the persona of going against the grain, which didn't vibe so well at the clean-cut institution nestled in the hills of Malibu. The volleyball coach informed me that I'd be jeopardizing my full-ride scholarship if I didn't conform to the look the school wanted for their players.

This twenty-year-old was not going to be told what to do. However, I resentfully dyed my hair back to its natural color, substituted passive-aggressive insolence, and got into even more trouble. Eventually, I was punished for not wearing the colorful bow that was supposed to bounce playfully atop my brown ponytail. Not to mention I was also told to lose the Bad Religion punk-rock hat I frequently wore low over my eyes, which the Pepperdine religious zealots seemed to take the wrong way.

My roommate freshman year covered up the Bad Religion stickers on my closet with her own that declared, "God is No Monkey Business!" Explaining that it was just a band and I wasn't calling her God *bad*, she'd still just smile serenely and say, "Ann, I pray for you every day."

Unable to conform, I was continuously punished by the coach each time I butted against the rules, but sometimes I was able to get away with my schemes. On one occasion, at the beginning of my freshman year, after being told not to eat sugar or junk food prior to games, I gorged on a one-pound bag of candy corn an hour before a match, certain that I wasn't going to play.

Suddenly, while watching the match from the bench, I heard the coach shout, "Windes! Front row, left front!" It was my first college match and it was in front of a stadium full of fans rooting for the opponent. Feeling a gurgle in my throat, I tucked my shirt in tightly to my shorts and pretended to wipe my face, but I was actually throwing up a waterfall of candy corn inside the front of my jersey. Once finished, I turned to my teammates, eager to play, and shouted with a grin, "Play ball!"

The entire game I competed unconcerned with candy-corn vomit sloshing around in the belly of my shirt.

Cushioned amongst green hills overlooking an ever-sparkling view of the Pacific Ocean, Pepperdine had chosen blue and orange for its school colors, which symbolized the sun setting over the water. These hues are definitely beautiful for a sunset, but not so much for school colors. Our uniforms tormented my punk rock style to no end, but worst of all were the matching bows: orange and blue polka dots, orange and blue stripes, solid orange, thin ones, thick ones, curly ones, and so many more. Stadium stairs became my mortal enemy as I tirelessly ran them as punishment for being bow-less or other such deviations from the system.

Unfortunately, occurring simultaneously to my dark rebellion, my stepmother was battling breast cancer. Being detached, selfish, and scared of what that meant for our family, I didn't quite know how to support her. I had not experienced any sort of sickness in the family before and had no tools to deal with it. Stuffing down my emotions, I kept my distance, which caused me deeper anger at myself and a profound sense of powerlessness laced with fear.

During one of my only visits to see her in the hospital, I saw a beautiful interaction between her and my father that really demonstrated the love between them. I was moved and decided then and there that I would shave my head to show her support. Although I was practically incapable of doing much else to show I cared, shaving my head was something I could do that also represented my tormented, angry self at the time.

Temporarily satisfied with my good deed, I gazed in the mirror at my newly bald head, a devilish twinkle in my eye. Brazenly sauntering into volleyball practice, I looked at my coach with a cocky expression that said, "Where ya gonna put the bow now, bitch?"

* * *

So, under Javier's tutelage, I was supposed to embody the rules as a shining example of Arco Iris volunteerism, even though I clearly did not follow them myself. Perhaps this was my innermost desire. If Javier had shadowed me, he would have witnessed the epitome of rule-bending at its worst. I had become accustomed to avoiding touching children unless he was watching, I took pictures on the sly, and I gave out food and candy as bribes to get the children to behave.

Javier's displeasure with all the volunteers and me was growing by the day. We apparently didn't have the same passion and seemingly selfless intentions as he. This was practically an impossible request for post-college foreigners who just wanted to spend a little time volunteering and picture-taking. Of course, there were exceptions; some volunteers were fully dedicated to the cause and often stayed for extensive periods of time, helping Javier in his efforts with unwavering selflessness that was beyond comprehension.

Originally, I had wanted to be *the one* who had the right amount of passion and dedication, which would complement his style of running the school and therefore validate my humble efforts. But I could see that I was not doing it "right." I wasn't pleasing him, and none of my efforts were being valued in the way I had hoped.

I constantly tried to figure out ways in which I could use my personal skill set for the good of the school. The older groups of kids, the Pumas, were in absolute chaos, and I knew this was where I could make a difference. A recent addition to the staff was a kindergarten teacher from Mexico who knew all sorts of techniques and activities to tame the little ones. If permitted, she could run the young school, freeing me up to permanently take over the Puma school. It made perfect sense and I was giddy with optimism that I could get back to the older kids who were more familiar to me.

It took two full days to get Javier to even acknowledge that I wanted to talk with him. He responded to my proposition with a flat rejection before I had even finished my first sentence. On my second attempt, he completely shut me down, furious that I would even consider bringing it up again.

Why would Javier resist smoothing out the kinks? Perhaps he was spread too thin year-round with a continuous cycle of international know-it-all volunteers and he was fed up with the relentless "do it better" suggestions. Perhaps it was my mistake to think that effective organization was a desired goal. I was only guessing, but whatever the reason, it was painful to watch and be a part of.

Accepting the challenging task of continuing to teach kindergarten-aged youngsters, I did my best to let go and try to understand that perhaps God had me in that position for a reason. It completely stressed me out to think about working with the young, difficult kids, especially because I didn't know *how* to do it. Jumping on a bus never to look back was starting to sound like a good option.

My demons taunted me: *Forget this! You've done your best, now let's go have some fun!*

My pride retorted, *No way! I'm here to make a difference and I will not give in!*

Being pulled in polar directions was tearing me in half.

17

CARNIVOROUS
CONUNDRUM

A long with the pressure from the school, my living situation was also proving to be quite draining. I ate typical Peruvian meals for breakfast, lunch, and dinner, which meant having rice, corn, or potatoes prepared in every imaginable way. More than eight hundred varieties of potato grow in Peru, and fifty-five types of corn, which is more than anywhere else on earth. The corn sprouts in every color under the sun, with my favorite being the robust, yellowish-white, and mildly sweet *choclo*. This variety has massive kernels and was often served with a square of soft cheese.

The full-time muchachas of the house shopped, cleaned, washed, ironed, and cooked daily. And when they cooked, they rarely, if ever, served meat. This left me in a crazed, carnivorous conundrum with the cavewoman compulsion for meat in my diet. I desperately ventured out to the only market I knew of in town but was disappointed to find an assortment of fly-infested strips of animal innards.

I asked to pet the cute guinea pigs, called *cuy* in Peru, but soon realized that they were about to be skewered and baked in the nearby adobe stove. It seemed like their little beady eyes were looking directly at me as they squealed, pleading for their lives.

The street vendors' kebabs were also sketchy, especially the *anticuchos* skewer—a bloody barbecued heart on a stick. *Ay, ya ya. ¡Carne, por favor!* The closest I got to eating meat was a *papa rellena*—a deep-fried, mashed potato stuffed with vegetables, egg, and a tiny sliver of what looked like beef. Lack of meat protein added to the other stresses, tempting the ravenous wolf pacing inside me.

Mealtimes were a big production at Marisol's, which created a very defined structure to everyone's day. A continental breakfast was set up in the morning, which luckily we could eat when we pleased. The standard bread in Peru was like a big, discus-shaped cow pie, lacking in taste and texture.

Marisol requested our attendance for lunch and dinner at the specifically designated times. She regally headed up the table for the second and third meals of the day, which served anywhere from three to seven volunteers. She talked constantly, and, for the most part, her narratives were entertaining Peruvian history, but two times a day, every day, was a bit much. Plus, every other story was a beamingly proud, motherly chronicle of Javier's altruistic life journey. I found it revealing how my own interest in these particular stories diminished as my disappointment in my volunteer experience also transformed.

To make matters worse, the other girls in the house only knew an elementary level of Spanish, so I had become the mealtime translator. This meant I had to listen intently to Marisol's tale, condense it, and then relay it to the girls. Often times, I'd inject my own twist on the story, just to keep myself amused. But then they wanted to respond or ask a question and would ask me, "How do you say _____ in Spanish?" Too soon and too often they'd give up and declare, "Oh, forget it, my Spanish is terrible. Ann, just tell Marisol for me."

The Russian volunteer, Helen, talked more than the señora and had a talent for laughing excessively when nothing was funny at all. She wanted so badly to be able to converse with the señora and would ask me with exaggerated enthusiasm, "What did she say?" after every one of Marisol's statements.

During the first few meals I sighed and translated with a gracious smile, fully aware that part of my recovery program embraced the concept of being patient, loving, and kind. Since I used to be incredibly antisocial and resented anyone who wanted something from me, I had to actively pursue the principal of contrary action in situations that I wanted to resist.

The girls needed me to translate in order to communicate with our hostess, so it became an unending opportunity for me to be of service, whether I wanted to or not. To make it easier on me and to help the girls learn, I requested that they all bring notepads and a pen to meals so they could write down any new word they asked me at the table. Helen was elated to discover I was a Spanish teacher and asked for private lessons in my free time. I politely suggested she sign up for Spanish classes in town, which, thankfully, she did.

Soon enough, with all my other compounding stresses it became more difficult for me to be of service. I quickly became resentful of the incessant translating, so I sat with a sullen, fuming face that said in every language, "If you ask me, 'How do you say _____?' one more time, my inner wolf may pounce and tear you to shreds!" Digging my fingernails into the underside of the dinner table, I could feel my demons circling, ready to take over.

My routine after an exhausting afternoon at the school was to eat dinner while half-heartedly translating, then sit in a broken chair in the enclosed garden and look up at the starry-domed sky. Often accompanying me was a husky with one blue and one yellow eye and a massive natty tail that swirled upward with a piece of poop dreadlocked on the end. Feeling profoundly alone, I was really in need of some affection, even from a stinky dog.

Little guinea pigs pleading to be released.

18

CAPITAN KYLIE

It was highly recommended that women not leave the house after dark without being in a group or taking a taxi to a specific destination. The streets were sketchier than anything I had experienced, and I felt very unsafe and vulnerable, even while walking at dusk. Even my alter ego—Secret Ninja—was afraid.

Luckily, Kylie, a new volunteer, had arrived, whom I got along with brilliantly and who was proving to be truly a blessing. She was an adventure femme fatale of magnificent proportions who had traveled the world over by herself and who captivated me with our first exchange. Kylie arrived just in the nick of time, since it was decided that Helen would move into my room.

I had nearly choked on a potato patty that night at dinner when Marisol made the announcement but then added that there was a new girl arriving who could also fill that spot. I was willing to take the unknown to the known, and I thanked my lucky stars that Kylie was a quality travel warriorette.

Still wary of the unfamiliar and sinister streets after dark, we remained cooped up in the house at night. Embarking on journeys through each of our lives, we sipped tea and exchanged books, jewelry, and traveling experiences. When wandering internationally, I had been known to lose my mind when I didn't have an emotionally safe home base, but with the addition of Kylie, and her new friendship, it seemed like everything would be just fine.

Kylie was a fascinating creature, who at twenty-six had been traveling for more than three years with just the belongings on her back. She was an earthy being with dark hair and sapphire eyes who wore natural colors and jewelry made of shells, seeds, and hemp. She always traveled with a small bag of her favorite whimsical jewelry, since it made her feel creative and womanly without taking up too much room. This was a brilliant discovery for me as I had always worn the same staple jewelry for simplified traveling. Just the addition of turquoise dangly earrings or a red beaded necklace really spiced up the monotonous neutrality of the few outfits that streamlined long-term travel.

Kylie had a stomach of steel and could eat just about anything without getting sick, which was a practical talent for gastronomical exploration in countries like Peru. The weight of her backpack was shocking and would have been heavy for someone twice her weight and height. She proudly showed me her tent, Pipa, named after a beach in Brazil where she had camped alone for the first time. She also carried a large, orange hammock, which she had purchased in a spontaneous act of retail therapy and had not used once, but still lugged around with her just in case.

Kylie was originally from Lennox Head, Australia, but had felt that restless itch for adventure and figured out a unique way to support her habit. She had nautical experience and felt at home on the sea, so was hired on vessels that needed service staff for long-distance sailing. She used this method to transport herself across the oceans to far-off destinations like Canada, Ireland, Greece, the Bahamas, and Spain.

Unique love interests had hooked her on various occasions, reeling Kylie into the possibility of remaining in a foreign destination. Inevitably, she would become disillusioned with the relationship and set sail yet again.

"When will I meet this guy?" she asked, throwing up her hands. "There has to be a bloke out there with the same traveling spirit. Waiting for him to find me is beyond a joke!"

"I hear ya, girlfriend, believe me, I get it!" I replied enthusiastically.

I then entertained Kylie with my many disastrous dating sagas. I told her of Jacob, an industrious mountain man who worked at a unique school in the back hills of Santa Barbara, California. The school was situated on more than two thousand acres of ranch property where the teachers and students were committed to living off the land.

Jacob and his trusty dog Duke lived in a crafty three-room tree house. He had running water, electricity, and decks on all sides of his nest tucked high in the branches. We'd met online and communicated for over six months prior to meeting. I was chomping at the bit to meet him, but he constantly had excuses as to why he was never available.

Jacob kept me hooked by writing amazing, long letters, challenging me to think like Leonardo da Vinci. But month after month, it became an elusive goal to actually meet Jacob in person. However, much to my eager delight, he eventually agreed to meet where he lived in the Los Padres National Forest.

My heart fluttered at the first sight of his dark hair, green eyes, and woodsy appeal. We hiked, had a picnic, and splashed around with Duke in a refreshing pond. I was in heaven. We climbed up to his tree-house living room and I felt the giddy anticipation that maybe a kiss was approaching. My wish came true as Jacob leaned in and gave me a good, hearty lip-lock, then abruptly pulled back and looked at me strangely.

"I need to be alone," he said flatly.

"What do you mean?" I asked, confused.

He didn't reply, but turned and walked out with Duke at his heels. Awkwardly, I sat on the sofa until eventually he came back in and pulled up a chair.

"I don't know what's wrong with me, Ann. You are so fun to be with, I love talking to you, and I feel like I *should* like you, but something just doesn't feel right."

All the excitement I had felt earlier in the day quickly drained out.

Cussing under his breath and smacking his own forehead, he finally said, "Geez! What's wrong with me? I don't know what it is, but when we kissed it felt so wrong."

Then it hit me. I hesitated at first, but then it just came out. "Maybe you're gay?"

Now it was his turn to pause. "I don't know. Maybe I am?" he said, seemingly surprised at this epiphany.

My heart fell into my stomach. I had just wasted six months living in fantasy about this guy. He had kept me at arm's length because that was safe for a troubled mountain man who had yet to come to grips with his internal yearnings. All it took was one kiss from me to know he was ready to embrace being gay.

Kylie roared with laughter at my dating trials and tribulations, appreciating every edge of the stabbing knife that cut away my faith in love.

After exchanging more of our dating horror stories, she told me her own whopper of a tale.

* * *

Kylie had flown to Greece and made her way to Crete in order to set sail on a thirty-nine-foot sloop, the *Samudra*, which was essentially an old, busted-up yacht. She joined Klaas, a seventy-two-year-old Dutch captain, and an Italian fellow, Giovanni, for the first leg of the trip to Sicily. Soon the three of them were ready to hoist the sails.

The first five days of the trip were smooth, but then the weather turned. The change in Mother Nature's temperament allowed Kylie the opportunity to get her sea legs by riding the swells and to gather the confidence to be at the helm of *Samudra* by herself. Giovanni, on the other hand, was not enjoying the rough seas and spent his time below deck getting sick. He insisted that Klaas pull the boat into port to let him off, but there were only steep cliffs off the coastline.

On the sixth day, Kylie woke up to begin her watch but looked out the porthole to find the ocean surging and vengeful. Her stomach knotted and she wondered if Klaas was going to make her take the helm with such little experience and in such terrible weather conditions. Breaching from the safety and false comfort beneath the deck, she was greeted by gale-force winds blasting her hair and salty water dousing her face. Kylie was shaken to see that the ocean's normal rhythm had been transformed to white incongruity.

Both men were on deck trying to handle the boat through the raging seas. Klaas was silent and serious, and Giovanni, sick and visibly terrified. Klaas ordered them to roll in the jib, but Giovanni forgot to release the line and it snapped. The sail went slack as hurricane winds violently whipped it back and forth until it was completely shredded.

The weather progressively got worse as the *Samudra* rocked and swayed at the mercy of the sea with the wind picking up even more strongly. Klaas remained silent, giving no more instructions, as Giovanni stayed below deck in hysterics and eventually called Mayday as night fell. *Arc Angelo*, a large cargo ship, was in range and pledged to stand by until help arrived.

Arc Angelo circled the small yacht all night, keeping it in its view. Kylie was slammed around the interior of the boat, trying to hold on to her sanity as Giovanni lost his entirely. With the ferocious, unpredictable storm and lack of visibility, the massive cargo ship nearly ran them over like a steamroller.

Things got even worse when Kylie remembered that Klaas was hypoglycemic and had been at the helm for hours without food or water. Finally, he held onto Kylie's shoulder with a weathered hand and pronounced in a defeated whisper, "I cannot go on."

The waves were colossal and the wind so strong Kylie felt like she'd be whisked away in a blink of an eye, becoming an insignificant speck bobbing in a surging, unforgiving liquid beast. With waves crashing ruthlessly on the deck, Kylie coaxed Klaas to the cabin below where Giovanni was already curled up in the fetal position.

She then made the daring decision to take the helm. Knowing that the *Samudra* was not being steered, she also knew it could turn and roll with the waves. If that happened, they could be demasted and the boat would take on water—and eventually sink. Captain Kylie took the helm and focused on riding the waves through the mottled spray and darkness, all while avoiding the cargo ship.

Without warning, the yacht's lights went out. Realizing that all the fuel had been expended chasing the lifelines, reality set in that the *Arc Angelo* would not be able to see the tiny boat. Kylie feared the worst as she sat by the crew hatch, clinging on for dear life, watching over Klaas and looking at Giovanni with disgust, as he did nothing to help.

In the morning, a large helicopter from Sicily arrived and was able to communicate with Giovanni in

Italian over what was left of the VHF radio. Klaas finally took the helm, but he had gone into a silent delirium, ever so often muttering that he was going down with the boat. The Italian rescue crew ordered them to dismantle the small dinghy and attach it to the *Samudra*, then jump in it.

The three of them stood at the stern as Giovanni untied the dinghy. They planned to count to three and jump, but the Italian abruptly leapt in first and pushed himself away, leaving Kylie and Klaas stranded on the boat. Kylie watched as the small, rubber-toy-like boat drifted further and further away until the line was taut.

The helicopter got a hold of the line and pulled Giovanni up as he frantically steadied himself in the flying dinghy. Suddenly, the line snapped and he was dropped back into the surging cauldron below. He eventually scrambled out of the boat in terror, swimming desperately after a harness that finally plucked him out of the sea and reeled him up into the helicopter like a slippery sea beast.

Over the radio in broken English, the rescuers instructed Kylie to tie a line around herself, connect it to Klaas's boat, and then jump into the wild water. Klaas grabbed her shoulders with a crazed flicker in his eyes and shouted, "What would your father think of you if you abandoned this boat?"

"I am not sure what your father would think of *you*, Klaas, but I know what mine would want me to do," she bellowed as she jumped.

She bobbed in the water like a miniscule cork, watching as the *Samudra* quickly faded into the distance. Kylie swam to the rescue line, placed the harness over her head, and buckled it with frozen, wet fingers. Feeling the tug, she was swiftly lifted out of the water.

Looking down, it was peacefully surreal as the *Samudra* faded into the waves and the immense cargo tanker became dwarfed by the infinite stretch of water. The thunderous copter propellers swirled above as Kylie was swung into the cabin.

Even after desperate coaxing, the rescue team was unable to convince the Dutch captain to leave his boat. The copter headed toward safety as Kylie solemnly watched the *Samudra* become smaller and smaller, until it was just another drop in the vast immensity of the ocean below.

* * *

After hearing Kylie's story, I was ready to bow and honor the Survivor Woman Goddess before me. It was comforting to know that in a sketchy place like Peru, if I was ever in danger, there was no doubt that Kylie would have my back and I hers. Little did I know that she was going to be called on to do just that.

Kylie and a stowaway on a bus ride to the Pisac ruins.

19

THE WOLF WITHIN

At the height of all my combined frustrations, someone at the school stole many coveted items from my purse. I was almost positive it was Pamela. Considering that she had been delegated to organize the donations instead of working with the children, this left her all afternoon with the volunteers' belongings.

I was in such a restless state, I wasn't sure how I was going to handle the theft. I could feel the wolf growling inside, clawing at the earth, ready to attack. Although I was not 100 percent certain that it was Pamela, the ominous energy that had been clouding my vision wanted to make her the culprit.

My identification, stamps, key to the señora's house, seventy dollars, and my treasured flash drive were all taken from my purse. *Anything but my flash drive!* The story about walking across Spain was stored on it, as well as the plans for Hinduism lessons in Spanish, not to mention photos, addresses, and more. The pilfering of the house key was a great loss to my freedom, since now I would have to ring the buzzer and wait.

Fury ravaged my being as blood vessels pulsated in my eyes. It was unconscionable for someone to pretend to selflessly help the poor while simultaneously committing acts of thievery. My wolf ears were flat back against my head; I would hunt her down and give Pamela what was coming to her!

The idea of the wolf had not been my creation. While some two hundred fifty miles into the pilgrimage across Spain, I had started having frequent nightmares about wolves. They stalked me with yellow eyes and growled through their sharp teeth and salivating jowls. Sleep was nearly impossible, as the wolf dreams progressively got worse. Soon enough it felt as if the actual spirit of a wolf had overtaken me as I plodded along the trail growling, lacking sleep and food. My body and mind were deteriorating quickly from the difficult journey.

While passing through a village known for its strong spiritual energy, an elderly farmer started chasing me with a pitchfork, shouting, "Leave here! We don't want your wicked wolf spirit here!" It stopped me in my tracks, and I paused, just in case I had misinterpreted his Spanish. But he said it again. My wicked wolf spirit. *How the hell did he know?* Although it sounded like a far-fetched fantasy when retold to others, I'd lived it and knew it had happened.

Part of the evolution of my journey in Spain was to come to terms with the darker side of my being. The lesson learned was that trying to *battle* my demons just helped them grow stronger. The key to expelling the darkness was not to fight it, but simply to invite more light.

Once I finished the long trek, I embraced the wolf aspect of my persona as if it actually existed. It no longer terrified me, but unfortunately, on the rare occasion when it chose to take hold of my psyche, it was hard to keep composed when the animalistic rage began to roar inside me.

* * *

Sleep was elusive as I writhed, sweating beneath layers of scratchy wool blankets. Nightmares of Pamela taunting me with my missing possessions infiltrated my restless mind. Clutching them in her hands, she cackled and ran away, always at a distance I could never reach. An endless percussion of early morning dog barks roused me back to the reality of my dilemma. Irritated, red-eyed, and with an emotional hangover, I bundled up and stepped out the front gate into the chilly alleyway.

The main street was scattered with street vendors, homeless wanderers, abandoned children, sickly dogs, and trash. I wandered without destination—solemn and lifeless. I came across a small figure in a red shirt digging in a trash pile where market vendors threw their food scraps at the end of the day. The child shooed off a ravenous dog and crouched down with a half-eaten cob of corn.

I moved closer. *Paula!* She abruptly dropped the corn and locked eyes for an eternity in a moment. Her deep stare lured me into her world, her fears, her sorrows, *her* life.

As quickly as we connected, she pulled her gaze away and darted down an alley. I pursued, calling her name, but was blinded by tears and devastation as my heart felt shredded to bits.

I used to think my childhood was difficult. I'd worn that suffering like a badge my entire life. The experiences that had "scarred" me were so insignificant compared to hers, but I carried them around like a backpack full of rocks.

Paula lived in survival mode every moment of her day. No little girl should have to live like that! What was going to happen to her? I slowly turned in a circle. In every direction, there were people who didn't have a warm place to sleep, food to eat, or the probability of a better future.

The selfish desires that had plagued me since I had first arrived in Peru suddenly waned in the face of such extreme deprivation. I couldn't help but think about all the ways in which I had wasted my time, energy, and heart space to obsess over things out of my control. I wanted *my* personal items back. *I* wanted the school to run my way. *I* wanted everyone to be grateful for the supplies *I* donated, and *I* wanted to speak and translate Spanish when *I* felt like it! Who the hell did *I* think I was?

Standing in the middle of the plaza, I was surrounded by the early morning bustle of people, yet I felt completely alone. Letting loose, I cried out like a mad woman—for Paula, for the hungry, for the poor, for the injustice of it all. So many people were suffering and here I was with a privileged lifestyle—and still I sulked because life was not arranging itself to suit my needs. All the time spent whining about not finding a man to love me, when as far as I knew Paula didn't have *anyone* to love her. Did Paula dream of a better life? Would she ever have the chance to change her circumstances?

The country I'd been serendipitously born in allowed me a whole distinct set of opportunities, which, most importantly, provided the freedom of choice. With enough grit and determination, anyone in the United States could choose his or her destiny and build a successful life. The Peruvians certainly had grit and determination. It was clearly evident by circling the plaza and drawing on my experiences thus far in Peru that this was not a universal liberty.

But in turn, this same society where I'd been raised manifested a diseased-like state of mind that infected me with the idea that I never had enough. It was as if there were a collective consciousness that persuaded one to believe that he or she was never going to be okay until a certain illusory goal had been reached.

But the catch was, once reached, there was always another new objective that lay ahead. I had lived my life ascending an infinite staircase of lofty goals with the idea that someday I would reach the summit and be eternally at peace with myself. It was exhausting to live in this fashion, but it was all I knew.

So what *was* my purpose in Peru? It didn't seem to be the school. What lesson was life trying to tell me that I was obviously not hearing? The universe had a funny way of shoving a huge, life-altering grenade down my throat to explode within if I wasn't getting the message it was trying to reveal to me. It typically blew to bits everything I felt I had ever known about anything to create space for a new understanding.

With a slight shift taking place in my consciousness, I dug my hands deep in my pockets and took a few slow, deep breaths. Thoughts, questions, and renewed hope swirled though my mind like the whirling dust piles in the plaza. If I wasn't pursuing a predetermined target, then what was I suppose to do with my time? How could I use my power of choice to serve someone beside myself?

A whisper of possibility lifted my spirits. I could hear an unmistakable, gentle voice in my head telling me to slow down and listen to the divine calling of my soul. With my busy brain in constant motion, I could understand why the message was having a hard time navigating its way to my heart.

20

THE TRUE TEACHER EMERGES

Unbelievably, my "stolen" items turned up in the storage room, either returned by Pamela or perhaps they had simply fallen out of my bag and someone had found them. I honestly didn't know which. The stormy sentiments cleared away as I jumped up and down, dancing a jig in raw, joyful emotion while cradling the flash drive in my palms.

Working with the youngsters had become a daily disaster. My stomach knotted up and my brain ached, which worsened progressively once I recognized that the kids could not even complete *one* of the activities I had planned. The responsibility was far beyond my expertise, and I saw little possibility for success. Resentment and resistance consumed me leading up to each afternoon with the kids, and my emotions swirled with the fear of failing yet again.

At five and six, these students were understandably a long way from being able to read or write. But even when I asked them to draw their favorite animal, only one kid could actually create it on paper. They didn't seem to have the capacity to transfer the mental image of an animal to physically drawing it. It was shocking to realize that many had never used a pen on paper before.

My already scaled-back lessons couldn't be any more simplistic, but the kids could still not perform the tasks I had planned. I couldn't predict in advance what they would be capable of doing. In time, I started to realize that children who lived in survival mode only had the capacity to learn what was directly useful to their reality.

By the end of the week, my emotional weaknesses and lack of training with the very young were glaring. I considered leaving the school to trek Machu Picchu instead of sticking to my initial commitment. It would be easier to just give in to my old, adventurous whims and leave this altruistic but challenging pursuit.

As painful as it might have been, I was in the process of shedding layer after layer of my preconceived beliefs of what it meant to be a teacher. I was evolving into a new version of myself as an educator, and so I just had to suit up, show up, and dig deep for the courage to stick it through.

I had a cushy job at Palos Verdes High School, California, where most of my students were motivated, disciplined, cared for, and had great hope for their futures. It was an ideal environment in which to teach, inspire, and set students up for success. I was very good at doing just that.

I realized that in Cuzco, the ball game was not just different…it wasn't a game at all. Most of the students were starving and many were homeless and abused. Worst of all, many had never felt what it was like to be loved and cherished. Even though my instructions failed most of the time, maybe the students needed my patience, love, humility, and generosity more than the ability to draw a llama.

* * *

Irresistible Nutter Butter cookies complemented my newly created happy-/sad-faced behavior chart. Even though Javier forbade it, I found this performance motivator to be necessary for classroom management. Most kids were suffering from malnutrition and would literally lick the table if a crumb dropped. I tried to ration the cookies to just one per student per class period because I understood that the repercussions of my actions could make it difficult for future volunteers. Not to mention other groups of kids might get wind of the cookie consumption in my class, which could result in a hurricane of jealousy. And…of course, there was the risk of Javier finding out and making an example of me in the humiliation circle, but that chance I was willing to take.

When a student was disobedient and got an unhappy face on the behavior chart, he or she was not to collect the cookie reward. The problem was, I couldn't comply with my own rule after seeing the face of a starving child watch the others gobble down their peanut butter cookies. I typically ended up giving everyone cookies unless they were all collectively naughty. Once the kids got to know me, they became deeply affected on the occasions that they disappointed me. It was as if I had gained their respect and they wanted to feel that same pride in themselves.

I stuck to my new methods and prayed to the universal energy of all the inspiring teachers to help me reach my potential. As the days passed, I dared to believe that the successes I was seeing were a sign that I was aligned with my divine destiny.

* * *

My simplified goal for the lesson on Indian geography was for the students to learn and collectively repeat, "The capital of India is New Delhi." I had also printed color-by-number maps of the world, with India enlarged, and had starred the capital. Not one child in the group could locate Peru on the map. I wrote the number one and colored yellow streaks next to it while handing out yellow crayons from my bag.

"OK, niños," I carefully explained, "now find the number one on your papers and color it yellow for the east region of India."

Returning to their unpredictable abilities, I had not foreseen that they would just scribble yellow all over the entire paper and the table. One little boy, Ramón, with goopy mucus permanently hanging from his nostril, bit the crayon in half and chewed it, adding a little extra nose slime for flavoring. Gathering the crayons, I made Ramón spit his out and wipe his nose with a napkin while I tried to hold back my gag reflex.

Giving up on the coloring exercise, I then tried to get them all to sit in a row so we could practice the capital of India statement, "La capital de India es Nueva Delhi." The goal for the Friday all-school show was for them to hold up colored maps, point to the capital, and repeat the selected phrase.

After fifteen frustrating minutes, they could only remember, "La capital…" It was clear that it was beyond their ability to memorize a sentence of that length that had no real significance for them.

Sitting on a rickety miniature chair, I felt stumped. Out of nowhere, a strong sensation blew through me and I suddenly knew what to do. First, I started making noises of animals one might find in India. The kids boisterously imitated me, squawking and flapping their wings, trumpeting while flipping an arm out like an elephant trunk, and tickling their own armpits while oooh-oooh-ing like monkeys. They sat at attention, eagerly waiting for the next sound.

I then switched it to repeat funny-sounding single words, then multiple words, and then sneakily added in my main objective for the lesson. "Laaaa caaapital!" I sang it out like an opera singer. They repeated in lively wonderment. Stomping my feet and hitting the table, I chanted "In-di-a" in three powerful syllables as they enthusiastically imitated me. They waited patiently, hungry for more playful repetition. I twirled around the room, singing and stomping my feet.

"La capital de India es…?"

Throwing up my hands and wearing a goofy expression, I'd say the phrase again. Finally, after a dozen rounds of repeating my question, one kid finally shouted, "Nueva Delhi!" They connected onto each other's hips in a train as I chanted, "La capital de India es…?" and they responded with, "Nueva Delhi!" Soon we were hopping and kicking our legs out while shouting the whole phrase effortlessly.

I dug into my handy bag of pilfered supplies and pulled out a pack of SpongeBob stickers. I asked if the kids knew of "EsponjaBob," and they cheered and ran around in circles releasing high-pitched shrieks of delight, which I presumed meant that they did. Putting a sticker with Bob expressing a distinctly exaggerated emotion on the top of each of their grimy paws, I encouraged them to say our designated phrase using the emotion of the sticker.

Wild emotions were freely expressed, like joy, sorrow, surprise, anger, or nervous Bob, depending on the image. By accident, I gave the hungry Bob sticker to Ramón, who improvised by eating the sticky square. Angry Bob caused them to crawl around like Bengal tigers, baring their teeth and roaring, "La capital de India es Nueva Delhi, raawwrrr!!" Sad Bob got them to shed fake tears, whining "Laaa capitaaaal"—sniff sniff—"de India es…boo-hoo…Nueva Delhi."

Overcome with joy and inspiration, I knelt down on my knees and put my arms out, welcoming them into my personal space for the first time. One boy clung to my stomach, the tiniest perched on my knees, Ramón hooked on my shoulders like a backpack, the girls kissed my cheeks, and others held my hands. The powerful impact of authentic love caused my chest to compress, taking my breath away.

I ducked my head to exit the windowless, dirt-floored cubby room at the end of the one and a half hour lesson. The refreshing night air swirled through my senses as a profound satisfaction tingled through me from head to toe. I heard my own voice proudly echo in my head, *I am teacher, hear me roar!*

* * *

The next afternoon, looking over my shoulder, I stealthily climbed up the stairs back to the secret supply room. I was surprised to find that one box of donations had been emptied, the materials distributed on the shelves but none transferred out to the kids. It felt deceitfully satisfying to secretly use *my* materials and was a huge relief to finally have something to use in the classroom.

Teaching the previous weeks with few supplies was the test I needed as a teacher to show me how to not hide behind supplements, props, and educational accessories. I was learning how to use them to highlight my ability as a teacher, but not to rely on them to do the job for me. I had to admit, though, a wild zing of pleasure raced through me as I grasped a brand-new dry-erase marker. Medium-sized dry-erase boards were mounted in every room, but only a few, nearly inkless markers were available for use.

As I sifted through the supplies, memories of the students who had donated them flooded over me. One boy had been so inspired he started his own organization to help the needy children in Peru for his senior project. He had put together all the plastic boxes filled with what he figured would be necessities for learning. Inside each was an initial pen-pal letter written by my students using the basic Spanish they'd learned in class. The walls of each oversized mailing box were colored with depictions of California, along with the messages my students wanted to share with the Cuzqueño kids. All that hard work just sat in a locked-up, dark room.

Perhaps it was simply a matter of perspective. I was really the only one who knew that those boxes were ignored. The kids at the school weren't even aware they existed, so they weren't missing anything. I had seen them play with a jump rope every single day, never tiring of it. *Was* ignorance bliss? As far as my Californian students knew, the Cuzco kids were rejoicing and romping around in delight with their new materials and games.

As I stood with my palms pressed upon the boxes, I absorbed all the hope my students had displayed of improving these children's lives. Glancing out the window, I could see the genuine joy bursting from the kids as they ran around chasing a piece of string.

I shook my head, laughing at myself. Maybe I was just the instrument for a higher authority that had worked through me. I had done my part, and now it was really not any of my business what happened from there. I resolved to not take any more for my personal use and understood that whatever their destiny was to be, the supplies belonged to the school—not to me.

I'd somehow equated being a good teacher with whether I could successful supply this school with what *I* thought they needed. If the kids had brand new supplies, then it verified that, yes, I had made the difference

I had set out to make. I was awakening to the idea that my purpose here did not have to do with what material things I donated, but rather that I just brought the best elements of me as a person, as a teacher, and as a loving human being. The kids didn't need new school supplies; they desperately needed someone to simply love them.

Suddenly, Pamela burst through the door. "Ah-ha! I caught you!"

I stood red-handed, holding a cloth sack filled with materials.

"Someone was stealing supplies from this room and I knew it had to be you!" she said, shaking her finger accusingly.

Was she calling *me* a thief? Pamela was lucky I was in a peaceful state because if that same incident had occurred a few days before, my wolf would have taken over and I might have tackled her in a blind fury. Instead, a clear awareness blanketed me in serenity.

I smiled and honestly explained my dilemma about the boxes and the conclusion I had just come to. It lifted the barrier between us and she immediately lit up, gushing about how much she'd enjoyed unloading one of the boxes because she saw how much care and attention was put into preparing it. "That must have been a lot of work, Ann! It's really cool what you've done."

Her response was music to my ears. She went on to explain that Javier received so many donations that he never had time to actually go through them. She then told me how she hadn't made any friends, was homesick, and then got really ill. She continued to push herself to work with the kids, but they didn't respect her and eventually wore her patience until she snapped.

Since she was required to stay at the school for a month to get credit for community college, she had been given the responsibility of organizing all of the donations ever since Javier had forbidden her to work directly with the kids. She was not sure if he sold the materials or used them, but she diligently went through and organized them by item. Rarely were there spare hands to actually do this work, so the donations just built up month after month and were never put to use.

She promised me that she would integrate some of my materials into the main supply room to help make the volunteers' jobs easier and for the kids to enjoy. Feeling deep compassion for Pamela, I gave her a big, warm hug and told her in all honesty that I felt grateful for her crossing my path, and that what she was doing at the school made a difference. Tears streaked down her face as she clung to me desperately and said, "I can't tell you how much that means to me. It's been a long time since someone has said that I mattered."

* * *

Crouching to exit the low metal door of the school, it hit me. For the first time since I had been at Arco Iris, I was concluding a day of teaching with spring in my step and joy in my heart.

Not wanting to return to Marisol's, I headed toward the path that led to the mountain behind the main plaza. After the arduous trek up, I stood beneath the towering white statue of El Cristo Blanco, the White Christ, his arms extending out as if he were embracing the city. I was alone except for a traditionally dressed man who leaned against a tree playing a Peruvian flute that added an authentic soundtrack to an already surreal moment.

Standing on the cliff's edge with the impressively sprawling city below, I stretched my arms before me, palms facing up, and gave thanks for being blessed with a renewed sense of faith that I was on the right path.

El Cristo Blanco.

21

JAVIER

Friday had arrived, which meant showtime! I headed over to the school in a nervous knot, but assured myself that this performance could not be as disastrous as the last. Prior to passing through the school gates, I had a pep talk with myself about being detached from the outcome. I had learned my lesson with the llama-sacrificing debauchery, so I kept it simple and tucked away my ego. I had given it my best, and now it was up to the kids to perform. I knew that they had learned a lot and had had a great time doing it—that was what mattered most.

We still had a whole school day to get through before the performance that night, but I had something up my sleeve to make it go by more quickly. Gathering a large group of kids in the library cubby, I divulged my secret. With the kids squirming at my feet, I slowly revealed the bright yellow cover of the children's classic *Jorge el Curioso, Curious George*, which I had recently "stolen" from the boxes in storage.

With the illustrated pages facing out in true kindergarten style, I read the playful tale in various voices and intonations. The kids' imaginations were visibly captivated as they giggled, their faces aglow with wonder. The innocent expressions of delight were worth any punishment I might get for reading to them from a non-Javier-sanctioned book.

Finally, it was time for the grand performance on Hinduism and the geography of India. The students settled in on the animal benches, parents squeezed in the back, and international volunteers mixed in amongst the kidlets. I took my position in the back corner, standing on a chair. Since my group was the youngest, they were slated to go first. Their faces watched me expectantly as I nodded my head that it was time to begin.

Ramón proudly marched out first, an honor he'd won for good behavior. The rest followed, grinning and holding up their personally designed scribbles of the flag of India, glued to a Popsicle stick. They lined up in front of the crowd, dropped their flags to the ground, and looked at me. One by one, I held up each of the five enlarged images of SpongeBob with his distinct expressions. In adorably animated voices the kids responded by reciting, "La capital de India es Nueva Delhi" for each image. The audience lit up in amusement with each new expression.

Then the eldest of the group, Diana, stepped out from the bunch and explained that they were going to do yoga poses common in India. Their dark brown eyes focused on me again. I held up my arms and wrapped them together until my hands pressed palm to palm.

They all mimicked me, unable to control their giggling. Continuing on, we did the next few yoga moves. Then one after the other, like dominos, they sat cross-legged on the ground—except for Diana, who stood and faced the crowd. She described that over the past week they had learned about a sound from India that symbolized the most profound concept of the Hindu people. She explained in her own simple way that *om* was not a word but a sound, which, like music, transcended the barriers of age, race, and culture. She invited the audience to join our group in a chant of the sacred om.

The kids closed their eyes and rested their hands on their crossed knees, thumbs and forefingers touching, and waited until they heard Diana start the "ommm-mmm." The spectators joined in and created a palpable vibration that wove a harmonious sound, penetrating each individual crowded inside the adobe walls. Once we had done three consecutively building sounds, the kids abruptly stood and put their hands in prayer position at their hearts and bowed.

A thunderous applause followed as the little ones finally broke their performance mode and jumped up and down in giddy elation. I pushed through the crowd to get to my munchkins and put my arms out, hugging each one with immense pride and pure joy. These kids just needed someone to believe in them, and I had almost missed out on the chance to create an opportunity for them to shine.

* * *

Later that night, during Javier's captivating and wild-gesturing speech to the volunteers, I scanned the facial expressions of the new group of girls who were enraptured with his passionate rhetoric. How many females visited his website and couldn't wait to see this guy in person? I gritted my teeth, diligently taking notes and translating as he went on and on and on with his mission statement.

Unlike Jennifer, who had so flawlessly translated before me, I found my mind wandering during his long diatribe and suddenly realized I had absolutely no idea what he had been saying for the previous ten minutes. So I improvised with my own helpful tips about what he expected from them on a daily basis, along with advice on how to most effectively work with the kids. Afterward, he walked around from girl to girl and kissed their cheeks, chatting them up, graciously thanking each one for coming to help his cause.

After the meeting, Javier invited everyone to meet up at the dance club Mama Africa for volunteer bonding. The discoteca was easy to find, he explained, since it was situated next to the only commercial fast-food joint in town—McDonalds. I knew exactly where it was because I had recently been a bit disturbed when I'd seen an indigenous teen in traditional clothing biting into a double cheeseburger.

I met up with Kylie at our designated bench in the Plaza de Armas, where she convinced me that it would be a good idea to go out and enjoy ourselves. She felt I definitely needed to loosen up, and getting out of the house on a Friday night would be good for us. I explained that being a sober alcoholic made it extremely challenging to be in a drinking environment. It was not enjoyable to be around drunken young foreigners if I wasn't partaking in the boozing too.

Staying out late was less desirable now that I didn't have the continuous consumption of drinks to keep me going or the alcohol-induced delusions to keep me occupied. More often than not, I longingly watched people drink and felt jealous that I couldn't partake. It was infuriating that I had not been disciplined enough with my drinking and therefore lost the privilege of ever getting to enjoy a cocktail as *normal* people did. It often took everything I had to keep from analyzing everyone's drinking intake around me.

I had no business being in a bar anyway, since I had heard countless times, "If you sit in the barber's chair enough times, you'll eventually get your hair cut." I knew that pretty soon, if I were around alcohol enough, a drink would start to sound extremely inviting, especially if I was struggling with something challenging in my life. I had to keep reminding myself, "A drink is not the solution, *it* is the problem."

Kylie nodded that she had heard me. "I'm not going to pretend that I know what that feels like, Ann. But you're a strong, disciplined woman, and I'm sure you'll find a way to enjoy the night. Let's get a cuppa coffee before we go and be mates and stick together tonight. Sound good?"

"Yeah, sounds good, amiga," I said, giving her a hug.

I knew it was necessary to let off some steam and have some fun, and, with Kylie by my side, I would feel comfortable and possibly even enjoy myself.

To wake up after the marathon day, we decided to get some Inka café, which was a combination of coca leaves and potently concentrated espresso. After consuming one cup, I realized that I had taken a one-way trip to the planet of caffeinated delirium as my eyes bulged and my heart thumped erratically. It felt scandalously thrilling to get a buzz, and I had been warned that this type of artificial boost could be a slippery slope if I became reliant on an external substance to alter my state of mind. But I rationalized its purpose.

Inside the club we met up with other volunteers, including Helen with her stomach fanny pack; Pamela, who was already at the bar taking shots; and Javier, who was surrounded by a harem of lady volunteers. The club was inundated with foreigners who had made this club their gringoland outpost.

I ordered my typical bar beverage, a Shirley Temple, which usually garnered a response from the bartender or anyone who heard me order it such as, "Oh, whoa, there, plan on getting crazy tonight, huh?" I had accumulated a variety of replies, which these days came out much more easily than when I was first sober, when I used to be mortified that someone would find out my dirty secret.

Now I would say such things as "You don't want to see what happens to me when I drink!" or "I've already consumed enough alcohol for three lifetimes, so I am taking it easy tonight." Once I had a drink like a Shirley Temple in hand, it looked alcoholic enough that it often kept nosy people at bay; I'd be persistently harassed if I held water or nothing at all.

Within moments, I had sized up the scene. Along the walls were local Peruvian men scoping out the foreign girls, probably waiting for them to get drunk enough to make a move. It was common knowledge that the foreign girls often hooked up with local Peruvian boys, but not customarily the other way around. The culture dictated that the local women remain in the home at night, so it was rare to see foreign guys with Peruvian women. The men, however, were free to roam and stay out late, preying on an international assortment of females and drinking the night away.

Chicha, the poor man's alcohol, was accessible to even the most impoverished individual. Corn, left to ferment in the hot Peruvian sun, eventually became a highly alcoholic brew. Nearly every morning, Kylie and I came across Peruvian men passed out in the most unlikely locations, like lying headfirst down a flight of stairs. Often times, these drunkards would be covered in vomit or had peed themselves or sported fresh, bloody wounds. Nighttime drunkenness was one of the reasons being a woman and walking late at night across town was a great risk.

Kylie and I squeezed together in a large sunken chair to observe our surroundings. Young and old Peruvian men hugged the wall, eyeing their victims for the night. The majority of volunteers were just shy of being of legal age but boisterously climbed up on the bar with drink in hand to dance, lip sync, and bounce their hands to the rhythm. The DJ was clearly skilled at whipping the foreign crowd into a frenzy.

Kylie and I were highly amused, especially when a mass influx of girls squealed and hit the dance floor within the first few beats of the theme song from *Grease*. The local creepers started to calculate their strategies. Through the crowd, I noticed Pamela, who was already being groped by a slimy, middle-aged man. Kylie held a freshly made pisco sour in her hand as we people-watched. She licked the fine white mustache of froth off her lips. "Mmmm, this shit is good! You've gotta try it."

"No, thanks, you know how it is for me."

She held it out to me. "Not even just one sip?"

"Ha! Yeah. No, not even just one sip. Remind me to tell you a story tomorrow about what happens to me when I take just one sip."

I couldn't help but keep tabs on all the girls I knew to make sure none of them left the club with their horny dancing partners. Being sober did provide me all sorts of opportunities that I never would have considered in my drinking days, like actually caring about the safety of others. During my heyday, drinking often put me in harm's way, but I didn't typically endanger the lives of my friends. Except for once.

Wendy and I had just absorbed an entire bottle of Patrón tequila at a concert when we met a few fine-looking fellows who invited us to join them as their special VIP guests at a club in Hollywood. While driving drunk to meet up with the guys, my voluptuous and provocatively dressed passenger passed out. Royally pissed that she was going to ruin our night by being a lush, I whipped up what I thought to be an ingenious idea. Just valet park her!

Without a second thought, I pulled up to the stand of parking attendants and handed over the keys, Wendy limply passed out in the passenger seat. When I returned four hours later, she was unharmed (as far as I knew) and still there. When she figured out what I had done, she refused to talk to me for a month, which was honestly the first moment I actually realized how careless and irresponsible I had been.

That was the kind of friend I was. Now I felt like I had some making up to do, whether it was for Wendy or any other girl who needed someone to look out for her.

Through the sweaty crowd, we could see Helen shaking her hips, having the time of her life. She caught my eye and headed over with a super-sized grin spread across her face. "Why aren't you dancing?" she asked. "This is soooo much fun!"

We decided to join Helen on the dance floor once the DJ started mixing in Latin tunes, which was more our style. Kylie could get a serious dance groove on, which stimulated me to release my Spanish-style "bird." I let out a deep sigh, undid my hair from its permanent ponytail, and let myself melt away into the music.

I found myself jumping up and down, shaking my hands at my sides, and singing the lyrics at the top of my lungs. Finally, for the first time since I had been in Peru, I felt relaxed and deeply satisfied that I was making a difference. Maybe it wasn't exactly how I'd envisioned it, but it was coming together. I had learned a whole series of lessons to finally teach me to get out of the way of the work of my Divine Spirit. Another layer of my selfishness and self-seeking had been peeled away, and now I could revel in the new sensation of what that actually meant.

Suddenly, the DJ mixed in "Suavemente" by Elvis Crespo, which, for anyone who dances salsa or any sort of Latin style, finds the body unable to resist the all-encompassing rhythms and beats. This is the kind of song during which my bird really takes flight. I hadn't noticed that Javier had been observing my dancing from the bar and was making a determined beeline toward me.

He said nothing but held my eyes with intensity, then took my hand and twirled me around, abruptly stopping my spin with his hand firmly on my waist. He grabbed my hips and synced his own with mine. The energy was strong and undeniable as we moved simultaneously and beautifully, as if we had choreographed the whole routine.

People near us stepped back to watch what was being created on the dance floor. Crisply, on the last beat, he arched me back to where my hair nearly swept the floor. He whipped me up from my semi backbend, leaving us face-to-face and breathless.

He looked deep in my eyes and gave me a sly smile, which felt like an invitation.

Wasn't this what I had dreamed of? Even though I had been disillusioned with him lately, he was enigmatic and irresistibly good-looking. Here was my chance.

22

JUST ONE BITE

Late Saturday morning, after our long night out, Kylie and I lounged on a café balcony overlooking the Plaza de Armas.

"So tell me! What happened with Javier last night?" Kylie asked.

Gleaming with excitement, I replied, "It was strange. One minute I was lost in his eyes, and the next instant a profound awareness surrounded me. It was love." I paused for the effect.

"Aw, come on! What happened?" Kylie begged.

"It was love," I repeated. "But not for him. It was love from the Universe. Almost like it was loving me so I wouldn't seek it out in Javier." Kylie nodded with understanding as I went on. "I'm not sure what my purpose is here, but it's not Javier. He might have been a lure that brought me here, but there's something bigger. I've just got to trust that there is someone out there for me. I know it, but it's clearly not him. Plus, there were so many red flags, seriously! I would have to be a complete idiot to ignore all that."

"Yeah, but sometimes we like to make guys out to be our ideal Prince Charming," added Kylie, "pushing aside all the warning signs, hoping one day all those behaviors just disappear and suddenly they'll be perfect once *we're* in their lives."

"No shit! I have done that so many times, and guess what? The same red flags were still there. Then I was resentful at the guy for the very behaviors he clearly had to begin with! It's time we commit to choosing a man for his authentic self and not what we hope he's going to be," I declared as we sealed our pledge with a high five.

"Ay, mate, you were going to tell me last night… something about not having a drink of my pisco?" Kylie prodded.

"Más café, por favor," I asked the waitress, getting ready to settle into my story.

In 1998, I was playing professional volleyball in a small town in Switzerland. I was the only paid player on the team, while the others paid to play. Their club fees covered my paycheck, which created an environment where my Swiss teammates acted as if they each owned a piece of me. They would gather at the end of each practice like a business meeting and designate the one girl who spoke a bit of broken English to tell me with a heavy accent, "Ann, today you were not worth it." Each time I heard this I would leave the gym and walk home crying inconsolably.

After a few months in the tiny Swiss village in the Alps, I was mentally and emotionally destroyed. Adding to my discomfort was my insecurity over my living arrangement. I had to share a flat with a thirty-year-old, non-English speaking man with crooked, gray teeth and a white-man Afro. I awoke one night to find him sitting by the side of my bed, his nest of hair haloing in the moonlight, watching me sleep. I wrote out a complaint in broken German and submitted it to the club president, but the team refused to move me. I would avoid my flatmate when I was at the apartment and lock myself in my room. This was one of the first situations in which not having a safe home base facilitated the beginning of a personal nuclear meltdown.

Not speaking the dialect, I felt isolated and unwelcome. My mental state was quickly deteriorating, and I had nothing to do all day but wait for practice in the evening, during which I would be harshly critiqued for every move I made. So I made friends with craggy, old Swiss men at the local bar. They got me as we shared pints and joked at my attempt to communicate in their language. Soon enough it was obvious that bar-speak broke all language barriers. This was where I felt the most comfortable and so logically spent most of my time there. I found that I was drinking earlier and earlier in the day, knowing I had to get rid of my buzz before I went to practice.

One day I was ecstatic to discover the local pot shop, which was in the back room of the "spiritual" store that sold incense and other such hippie items. After my first awkward interaction, I soon learned the protocol. I just had to say, "Ein düffsackli, bitte," one smelly sack, please. I'd then be handed a small bag of the chronic bud straight from Amsterdam. I was in ecstasy, knowing that with this discovery I would have endless hours of entertainment. The problem was, it was an expensive habit, and I was becoming reliant on it to get me through the harsh Swiss winter. If I didn't have some sort of buzz going on I was restless, and irritable.

One afternoon after a long, snowy trek across town, the storeowner offered me a Space Cake—on the house for being such a great customer. I didn't know how to ask in Swiss German what was in it, so I thanked him and tucked the precious cargo in my jacket pocket like it was a bar of gold. I rode my rickety pink bike through the snow-covered streets with a devious grin and a devil cackling inside.

It was already late afternoon by the time I returned home, and there were only a few hours before the volleyball match that night against our cross-town rival. They had a talented, professional Russian player, and in the local papers it was slated to be the biggest match of the season. The Russian versus the American, which local team had purchased the best foreigner? I was confident in my skills and knew that when it came down to game time, it was on. I could compete with the best of the best and had no doubt in my ability to perform under pressure.

I got back to my flat and unfolded the wax paper from the brownie-like Space Cake. My good sense told me it was too late in the day to experiment with this drug in edible form. *Just save it until tomorrow*, I told myself. *Go out there tonight and school the Russian girl and then celebrate—tomorrow!*

I had two hours until warm-ups on the court in a fishbowl gym where all the spectators sat above, overlooking the court below. Desperately bored, I occupied myself with a three thousand-piece ocean-scene puzzle, which was usually good for wasting away a few hours in a day. My eyes kept drifting over to the mind-altering treat on the shelf.

How 'bout just a lil' nibble? I thought.

Chastising myself for the foolish idea, I took a moment to reflect on what it had taken to actually get me to Switzerland. After playing Division I volleyball at Pepperdine, I was determined to continue competing, since I was certain that I was an unappreciated and gifted athlete. I soon discovered that no agent would pick me up since I was a mere five foot nine and had not earned any major volleyball honors in college. So I made up my mind to represent myself. I had just graduated with a public relations degree and what better than to market myself?

I was aware that most players toured with a group represented by an agent who arranged tryouts and vouched for the ability of the players. The teams typically covered the costs of all-star Americans who traveled around with an itinerary expertly arranged until a team made them a good offer. The agent made the deal, making sure the players were always taken care of. I knew that without a sports manager, it would be hard to convince a team that I was legit, but I had a plan.

In the late nineties, the Internet was just a shadow of what it is today, so much of the information about teams was very hard to come by. None of the clubs had websites, so I did months of research to track down teams that contracted foreign players. I wrote letters and had them translated at the Pepperdine language department, then sent them to fifty different teams all throughout Europe, with my message boldly stating, "Please give me a chance to try out for your team. Just give me a date and a time—and I will be there! I'll prove that you will want to offer me a contract to play for your team." Five teams responded, pretty much saying, "Alright, crazy American girl, go for it." And so I did.

I was a woman on a mission, traveling for two months with large maps marked up with each of my tryout destinations in Belgium, France, and Germany and two in Switzerland. I faced every challenge and hardship known to womankind due to my typical alcoholic debaucheries.

At each tryout, I showed up to a gym of people who had no idea who the hell I was. I had practiced various statements in each particular language so I could introduce myself, and then I'd just pick up a random ball and integrate myself into their practice. I did some of the most phenomenal playing of my career at these tryouts, but at the completion of each practice, the club owner would inevitably tell me, "Sie sind zu kurz" or "Vous êtes trop petite." You're too short.

"Excuse me?" I'd say. "Did you not just see my performance?"

It didn't matter. They would be able to find someone just as good as me, but who was six foot or taller. Head hanging low, I traveled to my last tryout in Switzerland, determined to find a way to convince them I could play big-league ball even though I was not an Amazon woman.

Upon entering the gym at my last tryout, the coach greeted me in High German, which I had studied for a semester in Heidelberg, Germany. "Du bist zuspieler?" Are you a setter?

I paused, knowing I was not a setter, but rather an outside hitter, the *aussenangreifer*. In American football terminology, a setter was more like the quarterback of a team and the outside hitter was the running back. I paused, knowing that the setter was pretty much the only player who could get away with being short—apart from the defensive specialist. But I wanted to be in the action at all times, and if I couldn't be an outside hitter, then setter would do.

"Ja, ich bin zuspieler." Why, yes, I am a setter. Miraculously, I pulled it off, and the coach, Hansjorg, took me to his office and had me look over the complicated contract in German. After a handshake and my signature, it was on. There were all kinds of loopholes in the contract that I was obviously unaware of since I was young, naïve, and acting as my own agent. One obvious glitch in the agreement was having tò share an apartment with a perverted Afro-creep who watched me sleep.

During the first tournament, I played to the best of my ability as a setter, but having never quarterbacked a team before, it was no easy task, especially when I could not communicate with the other girls, nor could I pronounce the long Swiss German words for the various sets I was supposed to flawlessly launch out to the hitters.

I was in over my head. During the second game of our first match, there was an off play and someone set me the ball. Up to this point, they had not even seen me attack the ball. I elevated and crushed the ball with everything I had. Coach Hansjorg called a time-out and told me I was no longer a zuspieler but now aussenangreifer. Game on!

I had been on the team for half of the season, and this greatly hyped Russian versus American game would be one of the biggest matches so far. I refocused on the puzzle pieces before me, then glanced again at the Space Cake.

Without hesitation, I broke off a piece and tossed it in my mouth. I swallowed, then pulled out of my mouth an odd-tasting fragment, which I soon realized was the stem of a magic mushroom. *Uh-oh*, I thought, devilishly laughing to myself. At that moment, I was defenseless against what I chose to do next. There was a lot on the line, but it did not make any bit of difference.

"What the hell," I said, and swallowed the entire piece of cake.

* * *

By the time I went to the gym for warm-ups, I still wasn't feeling much effect of the Space Cake apart from a slight buzz. I was cocky and anticipated a great match-up against the Russian. She had a beautiful doll-face and a long, lean body. Her lengthy blonde ponytail whipped around as she slammed balls to the ground during the hitting warm-up.

The crowd filled the sprawling seats above. The weathered faces of local villagers squeezed into the balcony, vying for the best position to view the much-publicized game. I could hear the mangy old-timers from the pub chanting, "Hop, Annie, hop, Annie!" *Hop* being the Swiss equivalent to "Come on!" or "Woo-hoo!" I waved at my personal cheering section while my teammates eyed me strangely, probably wondering why it was that I had an old-man fan club.

At first, the buzz worked to my advantage since the action seemed to take place in slow motion. It was starting to feel like *The Matrix*, when Keanu Reeves's character, Neo, avoided speeding bullets with ease, leaning from side to side, stealthily evading his assailants. I was set a ball in warm-up, which I watched slowly arc to me. I jumped and spanked it in front of the ten-foot line, bouncing it up to the crowd who cheered for *their* foreign player. I turned to the Russian, who was inspecting my abilities, and grinned arrogantly. *Bring it, Rusky!*

The whistle blew.

Game time.

The crowd's roar from above echoed off the gym walls. I had never noticed how warped the cheering fans sounded before. If the opposing team had good coaching, they could easily figure out a plan to shut me down, knowing I would be fed most of the balls. My own team wasn't always as quick to put together a strategy, even though I had tried many times to communicate a game plan with the stubborn Hansjorg.

I'd diligently translated into German detailed tactics for specific teams with the help of my geezer barbuddies, but Hans would become furious that I could be so bold as to tell him how to coach his team. "Du bist spielerein, ich bin der trainer!" You're the player, I'm the coach! I knew that if we didn't have a specific way to deal with this Russian, she would hammer balls over and around the block uninhibited.

During the middle of the first game, I was lost in thought, watching the beautiful Russian jump to hit the ball. The players on my team, who were instructed to block her angle attack, did not do so. There I stood, vulnerable in the open angle, unprepared for an attack to come my way.

Suddenly, life warped into real time as she athletically twisted her body midair and annihilated the ball in the angle, right where I was unprotected by the blockers. The ball rocketed off my chest, knocking me to the ground. The impact was so intense it felt like my lung had collapsed, and I couldn't catch my breath.

I lay on my back, gasping like a fish out of water. The crowd remained politely muted until I attempted to sit back up. Deafening roars filled the gym as the opposing team's fans cheered for *their* Russian, who had knocked the American on her ass.

It felt as if a switch had been flipped. I was whacked into a state of drug-induced disorientation and hallucination. The Russian snarled at me through the net, her features appearing to be grossly exaggerated—extra-large white teeth and a ponytail with a mind of its own. I turned to see Hansjorg, whose head looked like an overblown balloon, as he foamed at the mouth, furiously shouting at me.

I got back up and rearranged myself in the lineup. On the next play, I was set the ball, but my vision saw two. I carefully calculated how many steps I should take to approach the ball. Three? Four? Maybe even five steps? Stumbling, shuffling, and then awkwardly jumping up to swing, I missed the *real* ball entirely. The crowd gasped. Gazing up at the faces of local farming folk in the crowd, I pondered how out of place they looked at a volleyball match. Hansjorg called a time-out, screamed my name, and charged toward me with his eyes bulging.

"Ich bin krank," I pleaded desperately. I really was sick, but not the kind of sick they thought I might be. I ran to the locker room with my hand over my mouth in good drama-queen style. I stuck my finger down my throat to get the cake out of my system and dunked my face in cold water.

I passed my reflection in the mirror. My eyes were dilated, my heart erratic, my face wet and pale. I glared at my image. The rage and visceral loathing I felt for myself was all-consuming. "Fuck you!" I shouted at the girl staring back at me. The amount of courage, ego, and risk it took me to get a position on this team was nothing short of a miracle, and now I risked it all—and for what?

I could hear a girl on my team yelling in from the doorway to see if I was all right. I stared back at my reflection. "Now what are you going to do?" I shouted at myself as I violently slapped my own face and growled at the image I despised.

Cautiously, I cracked the locker room door and peeked out to the arena. No hallucinations entered my vision. My team was playing—and losing. I closed my eyes, calmly counted to ten, and then entered the stadium. All eyes shifted to my return to the competition as I heard a single "Hop, Annie!" reverberating around the fishbowl.

I clearly looked like I had gotten sick in the locker room, but Hansjorg substituted me back in anyway. Somehow, I focused every ounce of athletic ability to produce a performance that allowed us to come back from behind and win the match.

At the conclusion of the game my team was so grateful that I had played through my "sickness" that they lifted me up on their shoulders and carried me around the gym as the townsfolk crowded around their volleyball hero. They told me that on this day—I was worth it.

After the match, I forged through the snow-packed streets back to my flat, crying from the depth of my core. I was experiencing what alcoholics know as "incomprehensible demoralization." The gravity of my self-loathing was so intense that I could not stand my own presence.

Instead of pledging to give it all up for good after that incident, I went right to my supply of weed, grabbed a bottle of wine, and walked the freezing, desolate streets with my Walkman so I could escape—from myself.

* * *

I looked at Kylie to gauge her reaction.
"That's one hell of a story!" she gasped.

"Yeah, sometimes I need to tell those kinds of stories to remind myself that it was all or nothing for me. If I am going to make any kind of difference in the world, or find true love, it has to be a zero-tolerance policy. Total abstinence, nothing. I can never have one sip, one toke—or just one bite."

23

CHAOS

The next Monday, after a brief and awkward exchange with Javier, he announced, "Today, you are in charge."

He was a member on a committee that was meeting to discuss the prevention of spousal abuse, which affected nearly half the women living in Peru. Outside the major cities, the proportion goes up to sixty percent. At the domestic level, Peru adopted the Law for Protection from Family Violence in 1993.

The law, one of the first of its kind to be enacted in Latin America, was intended to ensure that victims of domestic violence had swift and effective access to protection and justice, but its impact has been practically nonexistent. In many cases, police, prosecutors, and judges from every region demonstrate an unwillingness to enforce these laws. The view of some law enforcement officials is that domestic violence is not a serious crime but rather a private problem to be dealt with by the woman herself.

I wondered what many of the schoolkids were witnessing at home. Quite a few of the boys were aggressive and lacked respect for girls at the school, including the foreign female volunteers. I then understood whom they might have been emulating—Papá. I had also seen quite a few native women taking care of their errands wearing black eyes and bruised faces.

Being in charge of the school for the day seemed exciting, until the gate slammed shut behind a waving Javier. It was as if every single niño knew within a millisecond that their omnipotent leader had departed. All love, kindness, and equality flew out the window as a hierarchy stacked on top of the homeless children who got pushed around by the kids in school uniforms. It was disturbing to witness this prejudice occur before my eyes as the "upper class" of third world poverty exploited those below.

Tania, a small girl from an impoverished village in the hills, was aggressively shoved from behind, causing her to chomp down on her own tongue. Blood gushed from her mouth, and she sobbed in obvious pain. A dramatic shift took place from the typical symphony of laughter, songs, and joyful children—sounds that Javier lovingly orchestrated like a no-nonsense magician. "You will treat others with love and equality or you are not welcome here" was his phrase of choice.

Many of the volunteers gathered around Tania, comforting her and giving her special treats. The other children transformed into jealous monsters seeing the excessive attention that she received.

On normal days, most volunteers, besides the highly capable ones, just stood around staring in disbelief at the mayhem on the verge of explosion—until Javier appeared. Then, suddenly, they began to scuttle about trying to look busy, kissing and hugging the kids. This I was absolutely guilty of myself. Now that he was absent and not around to publicly humiliate them, there was not much active supervision, just a lot of intravolunteer chatting as the kids rapidly unraveled.

Emily, from Wisconsin, committed a mortal sin by breaking the rule that prohibited volunteers from allowing students to use their phones. She let the bloody-tongued Tania call her mother. If the mamá decided to leave work and come to the school, she could lose half a day's pay or worse. This was possibly the money needed to feed her family.

Javier had explained that the parents frequently removed their kids from school for the most insignificant reasons since it was much more profitable to have them work the streets and bring in an income rather than get educated. It was part of the culture that was hard to work around.

Many parents who were not educated themselves could not grasp the long-term effects of schooling when their children's irresistibly photogenic faces could bring in five dollars in a few hours from tourists who took their picture in the city plaza. This was often the equivalent to what an adult made working a twelve-hour shift of manual labor. Javier wanted us to deal with all problems at the school and only involve the parents if absolutely necessary.

Surprising everyone, there was a loud a crash and then screams. Two girls had fallen through a rickety crocodile-painted bench. A long shaft of wood had stabbed one of the girls in the leg. Blood spilled onto the cement as the injured girl bawled hysterically, causing Tania to join in the cries of suffering. Total anarchy ensued.

Only a few of the volunteers spoke Spanish, so they were not of much assistance trying to gain control of the frenzied masses. As all this pandemonium was going on, Tania's mother arrived. She waited impatiently at the locked gate, shaking it violently, her face jammed between the bars like a deranged gorilla. She appeared to be a gritty, rough mountain woman who had come to crack skulls. My skull. I turned to the volunteer who had let Tania call her.

"She's all yours, Emily," I told her.

Terror flashed across her face as we both looked at the mother who was ready to scale the fence. Emily begged me with fear in her eyes, "Please, Ann, please! My Spanish is horrible, I don't know what to say. Oh my God, she's so mad!"

Once the gate was unlocked and then locked again behind Mother Bear, I handed Tania over and tried to find a way to explain what had happened. The mother's dialect was nearly indiscernible as she savagely chewed me out while I simultaneously tried to regulate the chaos underway. This never happened when Javier was here! Just when I started to crumble under the pressure, a spiritual quote struck me: "God *never* gives you more than you can handle."

Then the electricity blew. Besides the glimmer from a few stars in the sky, not a glint of light emanated from anywhere within the school. No emergency exit signs lit up, no backup generator went on, no flashlights or candles were to be found. The kids desperately rattled at the gate, trying to escape the confines of the school. Because of all the previous chaos, I was not sure who had the only key—which meant we were locked in. What if there were a fire or a real emergency? The key got passed around so much that no one knew who actually had it in his or her possession.

I felt my way through the narrow passageway, thinking about what a Peruvian fuse box might look like. I had no idea where to begin the search. *OK, God! You gave me too much to handle, now what?*

Then it hit me. I was clearly unable to find a solution through my own self-will. Therefore, the Universe *had* given me more than I could handle so that I would be forced to reach out to the great Source for guidance.

I slipped away from the kids yanking my pants, the grizzly mother stalking me, the blood-stained cement, the locked gate, and the electrical shortage. I headed to the bathroom. Its smell was on par with a construction-site outhouse that hadn't been emptied—ever. It was chokingly pungent, but certainly more pleasant of a place than standing amidst the insanity with no clue of what to do.

I closed my eyes and breathed deeply, gagging on my first breath but then finding my flow. I found a space of quiet in my mind, humbled myself, and asked my Divine Spirit to guide me. I took ten slow breaths, put my palms in prayer position at my chin, tipped my head, and said the serenity prayer:

God grant me the serenity to accept the things I cannot change,

(Like the uncontrollable incidents that happen while I am in charge.)

The courage to change the things I can,

(Like requesting the volunteers step up to find a way to calm the children.)

And the wisdom to know the difference.

(Like reminding myself that I am doing the best I can.)

Stepping back out, I took a deep, long sip of the fresh night air. As if on cue, the lights abruptly flickered back on. My mouth dropped as I stood for a moment in awe, then looked up to the stars and whispered, "Thank you."

Gently, I grabbed the hand of the first kid I saw and told her to take the hand of another. I directed the best Spanish-speaking volunteers to find the gate key and take the injured girl to the small medical facility down the street. Then I asked Kylie, who didn't speak much Spanish, to find a clever way to get rid of Mother Bear. She saluted me with a wink and a "Cheers, mate!"

A chain of kids followed along behind me, mechanically taking hands. The other volunteers caught on and mixed themselves between the children. Our efforts resulted in a circle of over seventy people, all of them following my lead. In a loud voice, I began the first line of "Twinkle, Twinkle, Little Star." Other volunteers joined in their respective languages, and the kids echoed with the Spanish version. All excess noise subsided, harmony and rhythm took over, and the kids swayed back and forth like wheat blowing in the breeze. At the last stanza, I sank to the ground, causing a chain reaction.

Pausing, I gazed around at the students who stared back, eager for my next move.

"Raise your hand if you have ever heard of meditation," I asked in Spanish. A few hands shot up. "Yes, Sonia?"

She stood. "It's when you sit by yourself and don't think of nothing."

"OK, good. Sonia, have you ever been able to not think of anything?"

"No."

The kids giggled. An ah-ha moment struck me.

"Which is one of the main countries where meditation is practiced?"

"Brazil!"

"United States!"

"Those are good guesses, anyone else?"

An arm shyly poked up. Then Paula, in her tattered red shirt and a sparkle in her eye said, "India."

"That's right!" I commended as the kids broke into thunderous applause. A genuine smile spread across Tania's face, exposing her tiny, rotted teeth.

Another raised hand had been patiently waiting. It was Tomás. I hesitated, afraid of ruining the atmosphere with one of his smart-ass comments.

"Yes, Tomás, is there something you'd like to add?"

He looked a bit nervous. "My grandfather is a shaman in the Amazon, and he taught me an *icaros*."

"Icaros?" I asked, unfamiliar with the term.

"There is a magical knowledge passed down through the generations of jungle healers. My grandfather uses a song that puts people into a trance or a meditative state. It's called icaros."

Pausing in amazement, I could hardly find words to respond. I had never seen Tomás act so maturely.

"I can do it. My grandfather taught me how, but the one in Spanish is not as powerful as in jungle Quechua."

"Go ahead, Tomás, do whichever you want," I said.

Tomás asked the kids to close their eyes and sit quietly. Remarkably, they did exactly as he requested. He then went on to belt out a song in a language I couldn't understand, with intermittent whistles. The kids seemed entranced, and I could see Kylie across the patio with her eyes closed too. Tomás must have said something to get the other kids to repeat after him because soon the other kids were also chiming in to his shaman jungle melody.

With a warm feeling spreading through my chest, I observed the energy of the patio where the kids sat in a circle. It felt like a tangible shift had taken place with the positivity, serenity, and love radiating from child to child.

The volunteers dispersed once the gate clunked shut behind the last student, and Kylie affectionately put her arm around me.

"Bloody hell, mate, that was a nightmare and a miracle all rolled into one!"

24

THE SHIT BIRDS

Early one Sunday morning, ear-shattering, heart-attack-inducing fireworks were ignited a block away from the señora's house. They commenced at 6:00 a.m., then at 6:30, and again at 7:00. On the first day of the explosions, I flew out of bed in a panic, ready to defend myself, thinking the house was under siege by a modern-day conquistador airstrike.

Noise-polluting grenades clattered the windows, knocked pictures off the walls, shook white paint chips from the ceiling, and sent dogs into a frenzy. It didn't end Sunday, but continued with a violently detonating trifecta of blasts each morning. When I asked señora Marisol about all the noise, she dismissively remarked, "Es algo con la iglesia." It's something with the church.

"Posiblemente," I nodded at the old woman and smirked at Kylie, declaring in English, "Yeah, right, what was God trying to say? Wake the hell up, fools!"

Kylie broke the upsetting news to me that she had decided to pursue another adventure instead of remaining in Cuzco at the Arco Iris School. She would move into a hostel near the town center until her planned departure. As with most hostels, she could leave all her extra travel gear in the storage area until her return and use that location as her home base.

I felt a wave of devastation, certain that she was the glue that was holding me together. Even after only a short period as roommates, it was clear we were made of the same free-spirited fibers and had connected on an indefinable soul-sister level. Being around her was like living in high-definition. Her awareness, spirituality, sense of humor, and creativity brought every situation to life. I could bounce all my wild ideas off her, as well as my harsh disillusionments.

But most importantly, she listened to me work through staying sober without a recovery support system. I was physically sober, but my emotional sobriety had been compromised. I was pretty sure I wasn't going to drink, but my old behaviors and character shortcomings had flown back and were roosting on my subconscious, crowding out my good sense.

The months prior to getting sober, it had actually felt like I was being mentally besieged by "shit birds." I could almost sense the emotional and spiritual decomposition taking place. I envisioned huge, black crows perched on my shoulders, squawking and taunting me, impregnating my mind with shit, all the while pecking away at my moral fiber. These internal voices criticized every step I took and judged every decision I made. Fear filled my empty vessel, consumed me with a feeling of insatiability, and persuaded me to believe I was a victim of life's circumstance.

The voices deemed me unlovable and convinced me that if I ever let anyone get close, they would see how flawed I actually was. Worst of all, I was certain that I would always be alone. At the time, I was oblivious that the voices were my alcoholism manifesting as mental torture. If I gave in and checked out, then the mental chatter miraculously vanished and left me with a moment of peace. This vicious cycle became the only solution, since I had no other tools to escape my mind's insanity. However, my only solution had become the problem.

After the Space Cake incident in Switzerland, I had found a "balance" to drugs and alcohol so they could still work for me in what I considered a positive way. They stimulated me, provided me a social lubricant, relaxed me, helped me be creative, and gave me courage; of course, sometimes I took it too far. But soon they stopped working in those ways, and I was consumed with escaping my mind with life or death desperation. The guilt and shame of what I was becoming was more than I could handle.

For so long, I had been such a disciplined athlete, but I could not be self-controlled enough to restrain from drinking or smoking pot. I would commit each morning to staying strong and not giving in to the obsession to drink. But inevitably, by the end of the day, I would find a reason to. The next day I would make the same commitment and truly believe in my resolution. However, I'd give in—again.

My next step had been to keep track of my drinking with spreadsheets, thinking I could outwit the addiction by keeping score each week of when I did or didn't give in. But it was impossible for me to beat the invisible entity that was relentlessly battling me—and winning.

I had been back in the US for three years after playing volleyball professionally for five years in Switzerland and Spain. I was competing on the American Pro Beach Volleyball Tour and was in school to get my teaching credential. On the outside, I appeared to be a disciplined, finely tuned machine, but if the shell of my exterior were unzipped, it would have revealed a sick individual who was rotting from the inside out.

Finally, I had to admit aloud that I had a problem I couldn't handle with my own self-will. I had to ask for help. Swallowing hard with tears waterfalling, I sincerely surrendered and turned myself over to a power greater than myself, a God of my understanding.

It was at that moment that silence echoed through my head with the crisp clarity of newborn peace. It was like someone had unexpectedly pressed the mute button during the most bloodied fight scene in *Gladiator*. The Shit Birds had disappeared—without a drink.

It was a sound I was not acquainted with. But I knew that if I followed the footsteps of the other women who had walked the path before me, I could experience a life beyond my wildest imagination. If I avoided mind-altering substances and worked a twelve-step program, there was a promise of new freedom, a shift in attitude, and an outlook on life that would bring peace and serenity. At the time, those words sounded empty and unrealistic, but if there was even the slightest chance that it was true, then I was willing to try.

After accumulating days, weeks, and months of sobriety, I naively thought that if I had eliminated the drugs and alcohol from my system, that it would also permanently rid me of the Shit Birds. Much to my dismay, I realized that they had roosted on a nearby tree with their beady eyes transfixed on me, waiting for a weak moment to come flying back.

If I didn't stay on guard and remain emotionally stable, then I was putting myself at risk. If I stopped trusting in my Higher Power and instead operated on my own self-will, it would be an open invitation for the birds to return, which, for someone like me, was just like taking the first sip. Then it would only be a matter of time before they entered my consciousness, and I would have no defense against the evil that infiltrated my mind—and I would have to do absolutely anything to escape it.

Without a doubt, if I took one drink, there would be more to follow, and soon I would be back to my old ways. I knew with the utmost certainty that I never wanted to live the way I did prior to getting sober, but sometimes the dark side lured me into thinking that it was never really *that* bad, and one drink would sure be nice.

When I get that squirrelly tug in my stomach, or I sense the crows getting restless in the distance, I dig urgently into my bag of distractions, searching for any way to get out of my funk. I employ various techniques to shift my mood, like taking a scalding-hot shower or eating sugar in any form. Indulging in a juicy cheeseburger with fries sometimes works, taking a nap, smoking a cigarette—or two, drinking a highly caffeinated beverage, shopping, or getting a massage. And if all those remedies don't work, *then* I employ prayer and meditation.

The mood-changer that almost always worked was doing something thoughtful for someone else—but this was hard to do when I was lodged in the thick of my own mind-muck. I was getting better at the praying and meditating, but I still often chose the other methods first since they were quick fixes. That was what I was accustomed to.

Anything linked to my recovery program was a breath of fresh air, but being in Cuzco made it difficult to stay plugged into that world. If only I could find a twelve-step meeting, I'd feel much more comfortable, but I had yet to receive a response from the Peruvian Central Office of Alcohol and Drug Recovery. Having a person like Kylie whom I trusted and felt safe with was vital to my staying sober.

Now Kylie was going to do what I most sincerely desired. Not only was she leaving the school and this town, but her chosen venture was to trek to Machu Picchu. Vile envy coursed through my veins as my mind cursed her: *Damn you! That's what I want to do! I don't want to stay here either!*

She explained how she couldn't adjust from the innocence, remoteness, and purity of the smaller and isolated parts of Peru to that of the intensity, desperation, and overwhelming density of Cuzco city. She went on to justify her reasoning, which I could hardly be present for since I was so wrapped up in how her decision affected me.

"Cuzco is a crazy place," she said. "The history is crazy, the tourism is crazy, the people are crazy, not to mention geographically and energetically it's like nothing else. On top of that, I feel slapped with a profound feeling of disappointment, unmet expectations, twisted experiences, and the unwelcoming feeling of the volunteer organization. The fusion of all these elements is so pronounced. I feel a separation between the locals and the tourists. I cherish our new friendship so deeply, but this is not a place I want to be any longer."

I completely understood her attitude, especially about not feeling welcome. It was as if the locals survived on tourism but at the same time despised it. Even Marisol seemed resentful of opening her house up to foreigners. I seriously considered throwing all my volunteer plans out the window to join her on a dynamic-duo adventure.

After our conversation, Kylie headed to the Internet shop in town to attempt communication with a guy from her previous travels in Chile. I shoved my head under a pillow and yelled and cried until my voice was hoarse and my sheets tearstained. She had put into words what I was feeling, and now I wanted to ride her coattails to the magical location I had visualized.

Then I thought of little Paula digging in the trash, Daniela and her glasses, Tomás and his icaro song, and my whole motley crew of kids whom I had now come to truly care for. I couldn't leave. Not now, anyway.

But I could make my living situation more tolerable. I was at a crossroads, since I had paid in two-week intervals to stay at Marisol's house and by Friday my time would be up. My new roommate was to be Tamika, a nineteen-year-old, six-foot-tall, big-boned girl from New York. Up to this point, she had occupied a single room, which was now going to be filled with a husband and wife. Marisol informed me she would be moved to my room once Kylie departed. At least it wasn't going to be Helen, but I was far from thrilled at learning about this new arrangement.

Tamika was sweetly shy, but had become excruciatingly homesick, and on top of that had gotten very ill. For the previous five days, Tamika had submerged herself in tears and germs in the only single room in the house besides Marisol's. During her first week, she had been placed in Javier's social vergüenza circle, and ever since she had shut down emotionally and physically. She rarely went outside, which probably had something to do with her black skin, which was a rarity in Peru. The kids at the school kept trying to rub her color off.

Tamika's height and weight made her nearly twice the size of the average Peruvian. Probably not helping her case any were her rainbow-ringed tights, short jean skirt, and braided hair sprouting outward from her scalp with colorful, plastic-balled rubber bands knotted at the ends. She was like a gigantic black Rainbow Brite doll that caused everyone within a hundred feet to stop and stare in shocked disbelief at the kaleidoscopic girl.

* * *

Communicating with Javier during school hours was futile, so I had to find another way to make my request. I was told that he never checked e-mail. He did carry a cell phone, but never listened to his voice mail. I didn't have a phone, but was determined to find one. I asked Marisol if I could use her home line or cell, but she shook her head, clucking her tongue in annoyance, and explained that phone use was not part of the housing contract. She directed me to go down the main street to find one.

An entrepreneurial female stood on the corner with a collection of cell phones on ropes hanging from her arm. To use one, I had to pay ten soles in advance and stand next to her on a two-foot phone leash attached to her elbow. The purpose of my call came from finally working up the courage to request that Javier integrate the Spanish children's books from the donations boxes into the mini-library. Day after day, I had read the same blend of books that did nothing to inspire the kids.

I felt foolishly nervous as the phone rang and rang. Finally, he answered, and as I took a big breath to spit out my rehearsed speech in Spanish, he told me to call back in fifteen minutes. I growled and paid the lady for each attempted phone call, along with the completed one, and stepped back to wait. Fifteen minutes later, I placed the call again. Busy. Five minutes later, he answered in a huff.

"¿Qué quieres, Ana?" What do you want, Ann? Thrown off by his rudeness, I awkwardly attempted my request when the woman with the phone started walking away—pulling me with her. She handed another one of her phones-on-a-rope to a man who stood face-to-face with me and proceeded to shout into his receiver, nearly touching me with his wild gestures.

Through the maddening distractions, I eventually articulated something having to do with books and the library, to which Javier responded with an exasperated sigh, "Ana, I don't have time to think about books!"

"Yes, I know. You don't have to, I'll take care of it! Please just let me add to the library the books I mailed to you. The kids are bored with the ones that are there now."

"What are you saying? That the kids are bored at my school?"

"No, no, that's not what I meant."

"Do you think I don't know what I'm doing?"

"No, Javier, what I was trying to say was…"

But before I could finish, he told me with finality, "¡No te precupes de eso!" Don't worry about it! And then he hung up.

I could feel a fury surging in my gut—and the Shit Birds cawing in the distance.

25

EMPLOYEE OF THE MONTH?

Since walking was my main mode of transportation in Cuzco, I spent a lot of time in the streets. It was a good way to release steam, plus solutions, responses, and ideas for my next course of action revealed themselves.

After my exchange with Javier, my brain felt like the teacups at Disneyland. Individual scenarios spun wildly as the foundation of my sanity whirled simultaneously. It made me sick to my stomach. The walking distracted me from my own worries since it exposed new and unique characteristics of the city.

But one thing always remained consistent in my observations—the contented resignation of the street vendors. Why couldn't I just do my job with that same attitude? Surprisingly, most didn't appear bored as they stood docile and enduring while marketing their products and services—day after day after day.

Why did they look so serene? Were they bored senseless and therefore had peacefully acquiesced? The sale of a few pieces of string or a handful of bobby pins was the income that put food on the table that night. There seemed to be a lack of stress, even though they lived hand-to-mouth. That would certainly be nerve-racking to me. But at least from what I could see, it seemed as if it were not even a part of their emotional spectrum.

As for me, my mind is always thinking, so a monotonous job requiring no directed thought would be torturous. Even during my meditation practice, I often slip into making to-do lists or swirling into the bottom-less abyss of my think tank. Is my brain so bloated with useless facts and worries that it just spins and spins itself into a perpetual restless state?

I was no stranger to menial labor and on one such occasion had experienced a degree of physical repetition that could approximate a monotonous Peruvian job. To occupy myself during the off hours of playing volleyball in Switzerland, I'd put the word out that I wanted a day job. Eventually I found a position at a pharmaceutical packing plant in a village a far train ride away.

Greta, a matronly woman with a sorrowful sag to her face, handed me the work uniform: a white, thigh-length coat and an ego-deflating shower cap to tuck my hair into, box cutters and a small white spatula. Being unable to communicate in Greta's regional dialect, I followed her like an obedient puppy to the long assembly-line table where I sat on a high metal stool for the next eight hours. Accordion music laced with static crackled from an old-fashioned radio as I joined the Swiss work robots who frowned at me suspiciously.

Near my stool were more than fifty enormous boxes stacked along the wall, each filled with hundreds of incorrectly packaged cases of cough syrup—all missing the dosage spoon. Greta demonstrated how to cut open a box and pull four cartons of syrup out at a time, take the plastic band off them, use the mini-spatula to pop their lids open, and take a spoon from the huge crate to my right and insert it in each box, then carefully close the tops, slip the plastic back on, and push them to the side. She made a wide sweeping gesture toward the mountain of boxes and grunted before walking away.

On the first day, I chattered anxiously in a mixture of English, German, and bits of Swiss German to the nonresponsive faces of the others while relying heavily on animated expressions and mime-like gestures. Nasty vending-machine espresso soured my belly but launched me into caffeinated singing sessions, causing me to belt out songs while carefully placing spoons alongside the syrup bottles.

At the end of the first day, I convinced myself that it wasn't going to be *that* bad. At least I would be making a bundle of Swiss francs an hour. Most importantly, a job would keep me busy so I wouldn't spend all afternoon getting liquored up at the local pub until the start of volleyball practice.

By the end of the first week, the fabric of my sanity had begun to unravel. Hours were spent systematically planning out how I would use the money I was earning. I followed that think-marathon by translating into German future conversations I planned on having with my team or the coach.

Then I unspooled my memory and analyzed every thread of my life. I walked myself through every house I had lived in, visited every room, opened every drawer. I recalled every birthday party, every pet, my favorite outfits, every vacation, every friend, every teacher, the cologne of every boyfriend, every book I had cherished as a child, every volleyball match, every heartbreak, every *everything* until I had absolutely nothing else to think about.

With my brain exhausted from such dissection, my new entertainment came from getting the cold, expressionless workers to interact with me. It seemed inconceivable that most were in their twilight years and had spent the majority of their lives cooped up in the dark factory doing mindless tasks. Swiss workers seemed despondent and long-suffering, whereas the Peruvians had light in their eyes and appeared to be at peace within the confines of repetition.

After the second week in the Swiss workshop, I had lost a bit of my spark, but nothing close to the lack-luster Greta who was on a dreary thirty-two-year streak at the assembly line. It was hard to imagine maintaining any sort of enthusiasm for life after a daily workload such as hers. I felt sorry for Greta yet respected her stoic dedication.

Being a competitive person, I found my task challenging, but not impossible. After each enormous box had received its spoons, I would celebrate by doing the moonwalk while making Michael Jackson noises, dancing the robot, or running in place with high knees while cheering for myself. The other employees watched in mild fascination, and, most definitely, at some point, they must have asked one another, "Who the hell *is* that girl?"

I practiced their dialect by counting how many boxes I had completed in one day and how many remained. After getting Greta's permission to fine-tune the radio station, I attempted to dance jigs to the traditional Swiss alpine tunes and even once convinced Greta to sing a song from her village. My distorted mind figured that once Operation Syrup Spoon was complete, it was quite possible that I would get a promotion or perhaps even an award for being the most inspirational worker.

By the end of the first month and with two boxes left, my back was destroyed from perching on the metal stool eight hours a day, and I was on the verge of stomping the radio to its electrical death. I could hardly gag down another cup of the concentrated espresso, but I still drank it anyway—every hour on the hour. My hands were painfully sliced up from the box-cutting and aggravated by the frigid winter weather.

Face wilted, eyes dull, I periodically screamed at the top of my lungs like a lunatic, made animal grunting sounds, or whimper-cried. I had resorted to smoking pot on my thirty-minute lunch break since I was desperate not to be alone with the jaws of my mind for so many hours. If I was high, then there were numerous ways to distract myself for the last few hours of the day. *So much for staying sober during the daytime.*

Eager anticipation lifted me as I spooned the last few four-packs of syrup in the final box. With a grin, I chanted in German to the other employees, "Ja! Guckt mal zu! Guckt mal zu! Nur noch einmal!" Look here! Look here! Only one more!

Plastic slip off. Open. Open. Open. Open. Spoon. Spoon Spoon. Spoon. Close. Close. Close. Close. Plastic on. Push to the side.

"Ja, ich bin fertig! Ich bin fertig!" I'm finished! I let out a celebratory scream, cheered with my arms up to the heavens, took a few victory laps, and gave each worker a high five. I jumped on an elevated platform and punched the air like Rocky Balboa, shouting, "I did it! I'm done!" The other employees observed me in amusement as old Greta shook her head, stifling a smile, and picked up the factory telephone.

After a brief exchange, she said something to the other workers in their dialect. Immediate laughter echoed through the warehouse, which was highly uncharacteristic for the gloomy lot. Delirious pleasure raced through my body from the reaction of the others. Finally, I had gotten them to lighten up and laugh for once. They all watched as I stood in my white coat and goofy shower cap wondering when the boss would come and congratulate me.

Hidden smiles were tucked in their faces as a distant beeping sound moved in closer. The plastic slats hanging over the warehouse door parted and a tractor entered in reverse. Once in the room, it swiveled to face the group, revealing a wooden platform on its forklift. It was loaded with two hundred more boxes of cough syrup.

Upon the realization of what that really meant, my face transformed from elation to chin-trembling defeat. "I can't do it," I sobbed. The grandmotherly Greta put her arm around me, whispering indiscernible Swiss words of comfort while guiding me back to my stool.

My throat constricted and my eyes filled with tears. I yanked the shower cap off, pushed past the plastic flaps, and heaved open the metal door to the snowy Swiss winter. Flopping face first into a bank of snow, I bawled until Greta sent someone to come get me.

My stool was waiting, and Greta brought me a cup of espresso as the first box was placed before me, yet again, of the cough syrup.

Plastic slip off. Open. Open. Open. Open. Spoon. Spoon Spoon. Spoon. Close. Close. Close. Close. Plastic on. Push to the side.

I quit the next day and swapped the metal stool for a bar stool with my good ol' gray-haired buddies at the local pub.

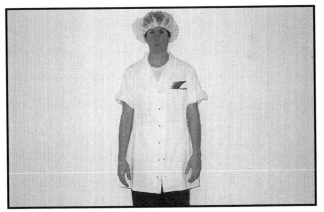

Not the employee of the month.

26

CRAZY KITE

On Kylie's last day in Cuzco, we traversed the city to sit atop our secret rock. We were soon to discover it was a national moment and were ordered to remove our rear ends from damaging it. During our time together, Kylie and I had continuously sought out nooks of peace sans urban chaos, which allowed us to breathe and let down our guard. The incessant harassment by street merchants was exasperating, coupled with the suffocation of being trapped in the compactness and grit of impoverished city living.

Typically, I brought along Crazy Kite, my high-flying friend who loved playing in the fresh Peruvian air. Crazy Kite was a loyal travel companion and truly had a personality of her own. Crazy liked to dive-bomb, hitting targets on the ground without any of my assistance. It was indiscriminate antagonism on her part, infinitely entertaining yet risky for anyone in range.

She once dove from the clouds and smashed herself directly on the head of my friend's dog that was standing still in the middle of a wide-open field. That friend happened to be my party buddy Wendy, the gal I had so inconsiderately valet-parked. Her boxer, Stanley, looked around, dazed and unable to identify his attacker, only to be pegged a second time on the crown of his head. The kite swooped back up in the sky, giggling and shimmying in the sunlight.

On another occasion, I took a guy to the beach to introduce him to Crazy Kite. He was not the playful type and mocked me when I insisted that she had a personality. He paid no mind to my warning that she liked to dive-bomb. After a few minutes of showing off, the kite suddenly plunged out of the sky and crashed right on his head. I nearly fell to the sand laughing. My date didn't find it as funny as I did and stormed off the beach—never to call me again. Guess he wasn't The One.

With Crazy Kite stashed in my daypack, Kylie and I ventured off to unearth the curious nooks of Cuzco. She was a brilliant photographer, which motivated us to wander without destination on missions to find unique settings where she could capture life through the "Kylie lens." Already we had discovered an eerie passageway, a pigeon-crowned statue, a passed-out drunkard, a globular cloud, a tethered alpaca with fluorescent ear tassels, and street dogs mating in a trash pile. Often, she froze images of me leaping from anything elevated, throwing my arms up in delight. She came up with new ways for me to master this airborne pose, which produced infinite hours of amusement reviewing the series of comical aerial expressions and confused background spectators.

Kylie also helped me work through the decision to leave Marisol's house, since she could relate to how stifling it was for independent women like ourselves. Marisol was particular in that she would not allow volunteers in the kitchen, so we never had the freedom to prepare our own meals or drinks. We had become comfortable staying out late at unique lounge bars and coffee shops near Plaza de Armas. If we lost track of time, we had to hustle back, usually to find Marisol perched on a wicker sofa in silent scorn, waiting.

Kylie also understood the importance of peaceful sleep and that the ritualistic, daybreak fireworks extravaganza had become too much to bear. She had witnessed how tedious and exhausting it was for me to be the mealtime translator, especially now that the stories were starting to repeat themselves each time a new volunteer arrived. Kylie had utilized my interpreting services but was respectful and thoughtful with her requests, unlike *some* people.

That evening at another meatless dinner, Helen sweetly asked, "Ann, could you please translate for me?"

I gazed at her blankly and nodded my head, waiting for yet another of her pointless inquiries.

"I would like to know which are Marisol's favorite milk products."

I paused, furrowed my brow, and tightly pursed my lips.

Fiery irritation burned my brain. "Ya know what, Helen?" I snapped. "You've just abused your translating privileges."

Getting up from the table, I stormed off in an irrational rage, Kylie's laughter trailing me down the hall.

Even though I still had a day left in my two-week contract, I jumped the gun and moved out early. Kylie's chosen hostel wasn't appealing to me, so I slung on my hefty pack and headed out to the streets without a predetermined destination. This new sovereignty also meant freedom to eat meat of my own free will. Without a strict mealtime regimen, I could gorge at the tourist restaurants that served a more international cuisine. *Carne, here I come!*

One of Kylie's photos of an alley jump.

27

ROCKET MAN

The new place of residence had to meet a few requirements. I must have my own quiet room, a private bathroom with a hot shower—preferably blistering hot—and a comfortable common area, and it had to be on a street where I wouldn't be assaulted by street vendors and beggars each time I arrived or departed. There were hundreds of hostels scattered throughout Cuzco, but the tough part was finding one that would provide a safe sanctuary for me to recharge so I could bring my best me to school each day.

Some places were as cheap as five dollars a night all the way up to astronomical rates at five-star hotels. I needed something inexpensive that wasn't too low-quality where I could stay for up to a month or longer and not break my bank account.

The possibilities were endless, but it was exhausting going through my cycle of questions and then getting all sorts of dubious replies. Soon it was evident that most receptionists said what they assumed I wanted to hear, whether it was true or not. They desired my money, and they were willing to say whatever it took to get it. Many of the rooms were grossly unsanitary and often there was an extra charge for being a single occupant.

"¿Agua caliente?" I would ask.

"¡Sí, sí, claro que sí!" Yes, of course!

Requesting to test the water, I was once shown a "shower" with a trickle of ice water dribbling from a rusted pipe jutting out of the wall at chest level. To my utter dismay, I discovered that at most hostels, guests had to be buzzed in the front door and didn't have the freedom to come and go with ease. I wandered up and down the streets getting more and more discouraged.

I headed up the Hatun Rumiyoc, or Big Stone Street, one of the many passageways tourists navigated to reach the district of San Blas. It was always clogged with tourists posing in front of the twelve-angled stone, the local symbol of Cuzqueño pride. The extraordinary polygonal rock was part of an astonishing structure with its walls forming a complex jigsaw. This method of masterful masonry, without mortar, had become symbolic of the skill of Incan architects.

These days there was almost always a vigilant guard to keep people from defacing the wall. Even in my most rebellious days, I never once felt the urge to carve my name into anything, especially a work of art or natural formation. It is inconceivable how many people actually destroy precious artifacts of historical and cultural value to immortalize their existence.

During the peak hours stood an uncharacteristically gigantic Peruvian man dressed as an Incan warrior with gold head plates, a loincloth, staff, and an emotionless gaze. I would have liked to have seen him catch a graffiti delinquent so he could unleash his Incan fury. No doubt, it was building after silently standing there all day while thousands of holiday-makers took pictures with him alongside the unphotogenic rock.

I squeezed past the monster Inca and the tourist congestion, making my way up the snaking, cobbled streets to the neighborhood of the artists. I was told it was a hippie hangout and an artists' retreat that was simple, humble, and very beautiful.

I passed open workshops with artisans showcasing their chosen crafts. There were weavers, sculptors, and specialized painters designing endless images of rosy-cheeked virgins and saints, many with strangely elongated necks. A shop owner observed my perplexed expression and explained that this particular style of art was the combination of a virgin or an archangel morphed with the delicate and pristine *vicuña*. She clarified that the vicuña was an animal similar to the llama but was officially part of the camelid family. *Camelid?* I wrote down the word in my journal, excited to find a way to incorporate it into my vernacular.

The friendly artist educated me on how the vicuñas produced small amounts of extremely fine wool, which was expensive since the animal could only be shorn every three years. When knitted together, the vicuña's fur was snuggly and warm, and during the Incan empire, it was against the law for anyone but royalty to wear vicuña garments. She let me pet one of the sweaters that was on sale for a whopping three hundred dollars, whose price, she assured me, could be dropped by 10 percent because it was my lucky day. No, gracias, but I did have high hopes that it was going to be my lucky day.

Arriving at the small San Blas plaza, I admired the church, which, according to my guidebook, was the oldest parish church of Cuzco, built in 1563, and whose spectacular pulpit was considered the greatest expression of baroque-style wood carving of that period.

I chose not to go in and instead continued on my mission, forging up a multiple of wide stone steps—up, up, up, up, and still more up. The higher I climbed, the more frequently I came across local Cuzqueños in their traditional dress, unaffected by tourism. The cliff-side village was only accessible on foot up long staircases terraced into the mountain. The neighborhood was unreachable by car, therefore a taxi couldn't retrieve me at night—or drop me off. This would mean I'd be trapped in the hostel unless I woman-ed up and braved the alleys after dark.

After the long sweaty march up, I dropped my heavy backpack overloaded with bulging plastic bags that I had tied to the external straps. I sprawled out on the steps, avoiding piles of llama poop pellets, feeling exhausted, dispirited, and thirsty. I took out a bottle of water and tore the top off a bag of roasted plantain chips, which were addictively mouthwatering. Slurping the last sip of water, I heard a faint "mew" to my right. Up the cobblestone alley strutted a friendly tabby kitty who requested that I follow her. Being a cat lover and having owned an orange kitty nearly my entire life, it was an irresistible invitation.

She catted about, eventually allowing me to stroke her neck that vibrated with contented purrs. I pursued her until she brought me to the front door of a quaint hostel featuring a cartoon alpaca on the placard.

If the cat brought me here, this has to be the place! After a few farewell scratchies for the gato, I rang the bell and was received by an apathetic, middle-aged man in the lobby. The space was lit up with brilliant sunlight and offered stunning views of Cuzco. I immediately noticed a large, domed adobe pizza oven in the middle of the room, along with a few long tables and chairs. I could already see myself savoring homemade pizza, reading and writing my evening away in a welcoming comfort zone.

Squeezing through the doorway of the bedroom I would be calling home, I was discouraged to discover it was more like a closet than a bedroom; the panoramic view mesmerized me and clouded my rational thinking. In my typical assessment of the bathroom, I felt relieved to splash my face with the fresh, cool water sprinkling out of the shower since I was extremely overheated from the uphill climb. Maybe if I could just get warm enough prior to showering, then it would be possible to cope with the cool water temperature. It would all be worth it just for the picturesque vistas!

I ended up paying in advance for one week at ten dollars a night. That evening, I delighted in choosing a pizza from the menu without prices but wasn't fazed since practically everything in Peru was dirt-cheap. Waiting patiently, I warmed my hands in the mouth of the oven as the crust bubbled. I hoped to engage the owner while he prepared my meal, but he was not to be bothered with conversation.

After dinner, I read a book and sipped tea until about 8:00 p.m. which was when he brought me the bill for seventy-five soles and asked me to move to my room, since the common-room time was over. *What? Already?*

Seventy-five soles was equivalent to twenty-five dollars, which was outrageous for a pizza in Peru, or anywhere, for that matter. *That can't be right!* I could stretch twenty-five dollars on food for almost a week in Cuzco. When I challenged the stony-faced man, he informed me that if *I* wanted to walk up the stairs with all the ingredients to make the pizza then perhaps it wouldn't be so expensive. He stood over me impatiently, waiting for my payment.

I paused, feeling agitation surge. This was highway robbery! Then it hit me. This man had a key to my room and I had yet to see another guest in the hostel. I was a female, all by myself far away from town, and not a soul knew where I was. Very possibly, at that moment my parents could have been looking at a map of South America, pointing at Cuzco and saying, "Hey, isn't Annie suppose to be there right now?" That was as much as anyone knew of my whereabouts.

I paid his price, rationalizing that I wouldn't hesitate to spend twenty-five dollars on a good meal back at home. A cup of tea cost three dollars more, came in a doll-sized teacup, and was not allowed to be taken from the dining area. As I took the tea down like a tequila shot, the man reminded me again that I needed to move out of the common room. I shuffled indignantly down the dark stairs away from the comfort of the heat-radiating stove as the chilly caress of night fingered my skin.

After turning the key and strongly yanking on the knob, the door flew open and a frosty *swooosh* of frigid air blew over me. The space was so small that the door hit the side of the bed. I side-stepped in and stood in the corner until the door closed just so I could enter the rest of the room.

A bald lightbulb glowed dully from the ceiling, revealing the water marks and peeling paint. There was no television and the view out the curtainless window was darkened by night. The daylight had really livened the place up, but now it felt like a dumpy, depressing chamber. Maybe I could sneak my new kitty amigo in to keep me company?

A shower was out of the question since I could see my own breath. I also realized I had poorly prepared since I'd finished the last drop of water after the salty plantains and now would not be able to brush my teeth. "Never, ever drink the water, not even to rinse your mouth out after brushing your teeth!" I remembered being warned numerous times.

My teeth were furry (like a camelid), but it was not worth the risk. My thirst, on the other hand, would be another story. Hoofing it to the nearest shop was now out of the question. Bundling up in every item of clothing, including gloves, a beanie, and a hooded jacket, I decided to read and listen to my iPod. Once my eyes got weary, I pulled the earphones off but became confused at what I heard.

From above, below, and all sides, the walls pulsated with penetrating noise. I faintly recalled Kylie telling me that the San Blas district was not only an artists' haunt but also a hipster barrio for clubbing. The trendy spots were cave-like bars and discos carved out from within the mountainside, which just so happened to be beneath the hostel.

I peeked my head out the window into the brisk chill of night and craned my neck to the left. Horrified, I saw a roof deck overflowing with partying patrons that butted up to my sidewall, which was the smoker's escape from the bar below. To top it off, the owner was above me with his television brazenly set at maximum volume, probably to drown out the throbbing beat from the discotecas that infiltrated the hostel.

I laid my head on the paper-thin pillow, mummified in all the clothing I owned and enveloped in three stinky alpaca blankets that smelled like sour body odor. Listening to audiobooks on my iPod kept me distracted until I finally fell into a restless semi slumber. Although beyond miserable, I was contented to know that at least I could sleep in since I was far, far away from the pre-dawn pyrotechnics by Marisol's house.

* * *

I awoke at 6:00 a.m. to what felt like a rocket being launched through my brain. Shooting straight up in bed with the iPod cord knotted in my hair, I roared with the recognition of what the noise was. My eyes were wickedly bloodshot, my mouth suffered from a deathly thirst, my teeth were caked with thick slimy-grime, and my veins pulsated with a diabolic intensity.

That's it! I was going to figure out what the hell that noise was and who the hell was making it! Since I was already wearing all my clothes, including a sports bra, I only had to put my boots on. I stomped down the cobblestone alley and took the stairs two at a time. Following the white streaks in the skyline, I was directed to the Plaza de San Blas. It was there I first laid eyes on *him*. Rocket Man.

He had a wooden launching station with fifteen three-foot rockets set up, ready to light. He tapped black gunpowder on the platform where the fuses touched. A barrage of bulbous firecrackers all twisted together covered the ground. I sat on a bench to observe and could hear ominous singing in the church at one end of the plaza. Positioned in front of the doorway on an immense wooden platform was a pudgy-faced saint depicted as a dark-haired, Caucasian female adorned in gaudy red and white lace.

Rocket Man took out his lighter and the mayhem commenced. The rockets practically split my eardrums as I dodged the sizzling pieces that tumbled back to earth after blowing up hundreds of feet in the air. He then detonated the highly explosive sausage firecrackers, which popped off like rapid gunfire, causing birds to take flight, dogs to run in circles, and all nearby car alarms to siren.

White smoke filled the air, and I couldn't see my hand in front of my face. I coughed and rubbed my stinging eyes. I stalked the Rocket Man as he cleaned up pieces of cement that had been blown to bits from the previous detonation. While he was arranging the next set of explosive projectiles, I crept up behind him.

I cleared my throat. "Perdón, señor."

He turned to me, his face blackened with soot and his bangs standing on end.

"Why are you lighting firecrackers so early in the morning?" I asked in Spanish with obvious disdain.

Unaware of my contempt, he cheerfully explained that each church in town had its own saint. He was honoring La Virgin del Carmen, who was not only the mother of God but also the mother of the Earth, along with being the patron saint of all the mestizo population.

OK, so she's justifiably big time. That's if you believe in a large doll that represents the divine goddess of the universe.

He pointed to her mounted statue with his hand over his heart. "Ay, mi Carmenita!" He described his duty with great pride since it was his sole responsibility to let everyone know when mass began, when it had reached its midpoint, and when it was finished. This happened all across Peru at the churches that honored Carmen as their patron saint. Other churches revered additional saints on other days. I mentally sent Marisol a quick apology for doubting her church rationalization for the fireworks.

Weren't the people who needed to know about mass already in the damn church? What ever happened to good old-fashioned bells? I cursed Carmen, and I cursed the damn cat for pretending to be a "sign" for me to follow. I wrapped up my conversation with Rocket Man. "So, how many more days of this madness, señor?"

"On and off for the next month," he replied. "If not Carmen, it's another saint we honor or other religious traditions. There are many, many celebrations in June, so you will be blessed to hear me a lot."

With my back slumped and my head hung low, I mumbled to myself like a crazy person. I stomped my foot at a gathering of pigeons, sending them into flight as I miserably made my way back to the death cave. As I came to the alley, I heard a familiar mew. Picking up a handful of rocks, I was ready to launch an assault on the innocent gatito. I hissed at her venomously, sending her scampering down the alley. It was then that I heard a familiar cacophony.

The Shit Birds were coming in for a landing.

A saint similar to Carmen being carried through the Plaza de Armas.

28

THE INCA MASSAGE

In an attempt to eliminate the nighttime ruckus, I jammed plugs deep into my ears. The consequence of this was that it prevented me from hearing the 5:45 a.m. alarm that would have warned me to wake up prior to Rocket Man's detonation. Even with my ears corked, the blasts shocked me into the reality of another day in my holding cell.

The morning dragged as I aimlessly wandered the streets, grunting with heavily hooded eyes and a crushing headache. Eventually it was late enough for a café to open, so I took a seat at a tiny wooden table more appropriately sized for a diminutive Peruvian. A thick, potent coffee and a dry Frisbee-shaped bread disc were placed before me as an eerie grumble echoed through the empty cavern of my stomach. It felt more ominous than hunger pains as paranoia settled in my weakened state of mind.

Maybe I had gotten the flu that was tearing through Cuzco like wildfire? Many volunteers had suffered through it, describing it as a death-like vomit-arrhea nightmare. Maybe I should have swallowed my pride and worn a face mask in the Lima airport, or even better, at the school!

A new strain of the AH1N1 virus had been attacking the general population with a vengeance. Public schools in Peru were closed for fifteen days to keep kids from passing it around. And, just my luck, Arco Iris School, which was where I was to teach that afternoon, was open for business.

The coffee did nothing to stir my unconscious state as I sat listlessly on a park bench watching street dogs inhale each other's rear ends. One scruffy pooch trotted over, rested his butt-sniffing nose on my thigh, and gazed up with persuasive eyes that pleaded, "Pet me, pet me, pleeeeease!"

A wave of dirty-dog scent wafted through my nostrils, which could very well have been my own stank since I had not showered in more than three days. Unconcerned with his filth, I rubbed the fly-bitten ears of the potentially diseased mutt. I just didn't care any more. It was exhausting to constantly avoid, prevent, and fear potential viruses. It was either going to get me or not, and I sensed that it finally had me in its grips.

My brain felt like it was in a vise, my throat was constricted, my skin was unusually sensitive, and my forehead was sweat-beaded. How could I possibly teach that afternoon? In order to do that, I would have to hoof it back up to my unwelcoming homestead, design a lesson plan, *and then* traverse the crowded streets to Arco Iris.

I had become a vital component to the smooth functioning of the school, or at least in my own mind I had. How were they going to do it without me? My motto in sobriety was to suit up and show up, even if I didn't feel like it. My old self would try to get out of anything that I didn't want to do. A righteous voice shouted from within, *You must rise above your own selfish desires!*

What did little homeless Paula do when she didn't feel like doing something? I bet *she* didn't feel like being abandoned. I'm certain *she* didn't feel like eating out of the trash. What if she felt sick? What if she didn't like her sleeping arrangement? Paula would probably give her left arm to spend the night in my bed, and here I was, complaining like a pathetic, self-centered ninny.

While lost deep in self-deprecation, my hand lay motionlessly in my lap, and my new canine companion nudged it with his nose to encourage more petting. Tears poured uncontrollably as sickness encroached and hopelessness descended. Wise, caramel eyes sympathetically stared up at me, blinking innocently. Wiping my nose spigot on my sleeve, I consulted with the furry face. "What should I do?"

I had hoped for a definitive bark that would somehow indicate my next step, but he just alternated arching his wispy brows. Giving up, I closed my eyes, took a few deep breaths, and surrendered myself to prayer and meditation. An indefinite period of time passed when out of the depths of my subconscious a gentle voice surfaced.

Take care of yourself, little Annie. To be of service to others you must first have your own affairs in order. You have permission to take this day to heal.

When I opened my eyes, the dog was sitting patiently at my feet, tongue out with what looked like a grin pulling his lips back. I couldn't help but crack a smile. "Was that you, lil' guy?"

A bark in the distance distracted my mongrel messenger and sent him dashing away.

A flash of relief soothed me now that my decision had been made, but I had no idea in that moment that I would never return to the Arco Iris School again.

* * *

My decayed brain chugged with repetition as I practiced over and over the impending phone call in Spanish to Javier about being absent. However, after all the rehearsing, he never even answered his phone. Wading through the thick sea of Cuzco chaos, I made my way across town to say my final good-bye to Kylie and bring her my lesson plan to relay to the unknowing victim who would be replacing me at school that afternoon.

I still felt responsible for pulling together an outline for the volunteer who would be teaching my wild bunch of kids. Hopefully, my cookie bribes weren't going make it even more difficult for the substitute who probably didn't come packing Nutter Butters like I did.

Kylie's extended hugs, kind words, and vegetable soup warmed my insides but also reminded me of how much I would miss her. I clenched my teeth to keep myself from desperately begging her not to go and instead strained a smile and wished her well.

"When will you be back?" I asked in a whimper.

"Not sure, really, maybe a few days, but most likely a week or so."

"Facebook me as soon as you're back."

"For sure, honey, now take care of yourself. You don't look so good," she said, wrapping her arm around me.

Now what was I going to do if I didn't teach? I was too weak to venture off at the high altitude with my whopping backpack to find another place to stay. Would I be condemned to sit in my cubicle and listen to audiobooks on my iPod? Or watch dogs sniff each other's privates? Or sit in another café and people-watch? None of the ideas sounded inviting in the least.

My throat was too raw to smoke a cigarette. There was no place to get a legitimate cheeseburger. No hot shower. No television to vegetate in front of. No recovery meeting to find consolation and support. No one to take care of me and no way to check out of my reality. Then a slithery word squirmed into my brain with determination. *Ayahuasca.*

I recalled with the utmost clarity the leathery-skinned shaman in an alley who had lured Kylie and me in with his spiel about ayahuasca and how he would be willing to facilitate our ceremony. Ayahuasca wasn't a specific plant but rather a psychedelic combination of plants varying in potency according to the skills of its maker. He'd asked with clear-eyed serenity, "Ladies, do you want to open the window into your souls?" *Yes, please!*

He'd counseled us that the ceremony was only for those who were truly looking for an authentic way to pursue their personal quest for expanded awareness and that through the sacred ritual, a hallucinogenic experience would bring profound self-exploration and personal integration with the Great Creator. His last claim was that it could cure any illness far beyond the frontiers of any conventional treatment.

Kylie was ready to sign up on the spot, whereas I was afraid that doing an ayahuasca ceremony would be considered using a drug and I would lose my hard-earned sobriety. *No one will ever know, and besides it's not really a drug,* my mind rationalized, *it's a natural medicine for the body and soul.*

Kylie told me that a few of her mates had done it and after drinking the green concoction, they'd vomited and actually shit a great deal during the ceremony. Ayahuasca is a purgative, and one of the ways it heals is by causing the body to expel all the nasty toxins that have accumulated over a long period.

"Besides the vomiting and shitting part, it sounds amazing!" I'd said to Kylie.

"Let's do it!" she'd proposed spiritedly.

I'd dug my nails into my palms. "I can't. *Fuck.* I just can't. I've worked so hard for my sobriety and if I do ayahuasca, I'd want to do it again and again. I know myself. Even if I didn't tell anyone and kept my sobriety date, that secret would eat me up alive."

"Hey, all good," Kylie had simply replied as we continued up the alley away from the shaman.

Ever since our interaction with the Ayahuasca Wizard, I had done research online to verify whether it was considered a drug or not. The spectrum was wide and each website held its belief to be true, which leaned more often toward ayahuasca being a medicine rather than a drug.

As I continued my sluggish journey back to my hostel from Kylie's, my mind chanted, *It's a medicine, it's a medicine, you need to be healed. Find the shaman.*

I stood at the crossroads. Turn right and go to my bed and rest? Or turn left and search out the weathered medicine man? My destiny was then diverted in only a moment.

A mixture of female voices caught my attention, "Hey, laaadeee...massage?"

The industrious women of the bustling Triunfo Street were busy hawking their finger talents, competing for my attention.

"Lady, I give you massage for cheap."

"Twenty dollars for hour!"

"Masaje, lady? You want masaje?"

"¡Masaje terapéutico!"

"OK, five dollars ¡Sólo cinco dólares!"

I usually waved them off with a definitive "No, gracias" or simply ignored their persistence, but on this day, one señorita caught my eye. Although incredibly tiny, she had an air of experience and her hands looked strong.

That's exactly what I need! I thought optimistically as my body immediately relaxed with the new possibility of relief. Her specialty was the fifteen-dollars-an-hour Inca Massage. Agreeing to the bargain price for her custom massage treatment, I followed her through the back passageways of an artisans' market and up two sets of makeshift stairs to a rusty metal shed on a shaky balcony.

A massage table was set up inside (minus the face hole) with a single, thin sheet, candles thoughtfully arranged, and Enigma playing on a small CD player in the corner, all of which helped me to feel a bit better after the unsettling route to get there.

I stripped and collapsed face down, pleased to find a solution to the despair that had nearly consumed me. It was awkwardly unsanitary being directly on the table with the thin sheet on top, but my body gratefully exhaled as I sunk into the sticky vinyl, eager for the soothing rejuvenation to begin.

As one who often gets massages, I expected that momentarily she would fold back the sheet and gently start on my upper back. I could almost feel the healing already. She introduced herself as Florisol and yanked the shed door closed. Lightly walking her fingers up my back, she abruptly launched into the Inca Massage by aggressively pulling my hair and karate-chopping my skull.

OK, actually that didn't feel very good, especially with my headache. But I bet it gets better from here, I thought hopefully.

Florisol then climbed on top of me like a mini-Amazonian spider monkey, squatted over my butt, and unexpectedly cracked my back so forcefully that bones I didn't even think I had popped. Scooting up my back, she flipped her position and straddled my head as if my skull were an egg she had just laid. Without a hole in the table to absorb the contours of my face, my nose painfully flattened to the table, making breathing nearly impossible.

I tried to vocalize my discomfort, but my voice was muffled into the tabletop as she squeezed my head with her thick legs, which were bent back on each side of my face. I whimpered as my illness encroached, dreading which technique was next. The Inca Massage continued with pinching my back skin and furious, rapid slapping. She then lay on my back and rested her head on my bare buttocks while pressing all her weight on my elbows.

What kind of massage school teaches that? The next stage was to lather me up with a thick, oily cream. "Oh, no, Florisol. No lo quiero!" I cried out. But it was too late. My body was already layered in filth since a shower had eluded me for days. Getting that oil off would require a strong stream of water, and all I had was a cold driblet.

"¿OK, amiga?" she asked.

In a pathetic whisper, I replied, "No, Florisol, please, no more oil."

I could say no more than that as I lay paralyzed, unable to speak up or remove myself from Florisol's torturous Inca Massage. Helpless and hopeless, I felt certain that life was paying me back for all the bad I had ever done.

But Florisol was not finished, as she pulled out scalding stones from a mysterious hot-rock location and lined them down my spine, sizzling my skin as I lay limp like a ragdoll. "No más," I squeaked out, barely audible.

But there was más. Actually, there was quite a bit más remaining in the Inca Massage program. Ignoring my previous request, Marisol squeezed squirts of oil in her palms, and before I could stop her, she rubbed it in my hair and scratched my scalp with cat nails, all the while knotting my strands in a million greasy dreads. Florisol wrapped up the session by aggressively finger-slapping my face, then thanked me for my business with a final swat to my butt cheeks and left.

What the hell just happened? I wanted to make a loud, desperate wail like baby animals do when they call their mothers to come rescue them. But my mommy was thousands of miles away. There was no one to come rescue me.

I slid open the metal door and stepped out into blinding daylight. Florisol sweetly approached me for payment.

You are the devil reincarnated as a Peruvian woman, my mind growled.

Once again out on Triunfo Street where I'd started just over an hour before, I made the mistake of checking my reflection in a restaurant window. A messy bird's nest of knots haloed my head, and the sun brilliantly shined off the layer of thick massage oil coating my pale face. *Pleeeease let there be hot water in my hostel!*

Trudging the endless stairs to the hostel, I hunched over like an elderly woman, shivering even though the sun shone strong. Women still bombarded me with offers for their personal massage program, which I responded to with an unrestrained "No!" and "Hell, no!"

My naked body trembled as I stood on tiptoes in the gritty bathroom with my hand under the sprinkling of arctic water. *Please, God, just a lil' hot water, pleeease!*

After waiting fifteen eternal minutes, my body began to quiver uncontrollably. I couldn't do it. With the dexterity weakening in my fingers, I pulled layers of clothing on my greasy body, tried unsuccessfully to tie a handkerchief around the matted tangle of what used to be my hair, and climbed under the heavy alpaca blankets. Moaning through shallow breaths, I resigned myself to the possibility of dying a lonely death in a cold coffin in the hills of Peru.

29

MURDER ON MY MIND

By the evening, I still lay lifeless and numb, rolled in the blankets like a burrito. After enduring the Inca Massage earlier that afternoon, I thought it could get no worse. Entangled in the convoluted depths of fevered sleep, I was abruptly and cruelly awakened at 8:00 p.m.

Unfurling myself from the fetal position, I crawled to the window to find a musical extravaganza in full effect in honor of the saintly Carmen. A rickety stage bowed under the weight of a sadly unorganized marching band wailing away at their instruments. I figured it'd be over by 10:00 p.m. since it was a Wednesday night, and, really, how long could a trumpet be played to honor a saint?

Once the marching band screeched out their last note, speakers were plugged in at the far end of the plaza facing my window. The penetrating voice of an overexcited man shouted out long-winded, incoherent speeches. Every few minutes the amplifier would scream with ear-piercing feedback, which no one seemed at all concerned with and therefore no one did anything about it.

Leaning my elbows on the windowsill in disbelief, I observed the commotion until the rumblings of deep fury reverberated the walls of my sanity. Guzzling down half a bottle of NyQuil would have been the perfect solution, if only I weren't sober. It was probably a good thing that I didn't have any nighty-night juice since it would have been hard to resist taking more than the allotted dosage, especially since the celebration outside was just getting started.

At 10:00 p.m., the classic Peruvian flute ensemble microphoned their instruments, each subsequent song sounding exactly like the previous. There were more enthusiastic speeches, and at 2:00 a.m. the snare drum battle commenced. An epic war of offbeat rhythms with interludes from the yelling man mixed with electrical high-pitch squeals. It felt like someone was beating each side of my head with a metal rod, with intervals of electric shock treatments.

The windows rattled and cement chips fell from the ceiling onto my sickly, cocooned body. I cried pathetically, begging for the imminent sweet silence that would kiss my ears as soon as the endless ode to Carmen concluded.

Sickened, delirious half-sleep hurled me into torturous dreams and realistic hallucinations. During one, I purchased a rifle from a toothless Incan man and from my windowsill massacred all the people in the plaza. The obnoxious man on the microphone was my first target, and then I knocked off all the drummers—one by one. I was calm, determined, and unremorseful.

The marching band was next, along with any celebrants participating in the pointless fiesta. With silent resolve, I crept upstairs to the room of the hostel owner, knocked down his door with one swift kick, and eliminated him too. Then, I returned to my bed with a serene smile and easily went to sleep.

* * *

In the morning, the Carmen rockets woke me bright and early, but this time I had no strength in my filthy, disease-ridden body to be disturbed. Stuffing my belongings in my backpack and plastic bags, I departed without informing the owner, unconcerned with the money I had paid for the rest of the week. Stopping every few steps, I leaned against crumbling adobe walls and put down the heavily loaded bags that cut the circulation off at my wrists.

I threw up a few times along the way until I eventually came across a hostel that offered a room with a TV (praise the Lord!) and an adjoining bathroom with hot water—sometimes. I paid, then immediately forced myself back outside to find a place to buy purified water, which was undeniably vital.

After returning, I asked the sisters who ran the hostel the question I had forgotten to inquire about upon my arrival.

"Is Saint Carmen celebrated in this part of town?"

"Sí, señorita, of course."

30

PERUVIAN HEALTH CARE

Not much could be worse than being crippled by illness in a third world country all alone, and that was exactly what was happening. Perhaps being unaided in finding a solution to my urgently ill condition was therapeutic misery, but although character building through suffering might be all right for religious folk, it did not appeal to me.

The sagging bed in my new homestead cushioned my feeble body as I proceeded to hibernate for the day. Hoping recovery would take place during the comatose state was a wasted expectation since, upon awakening, the sickness was far worse. Why hadn't I listened to my doctor and brought the intestinal virus medication?

My imaginary veil of protection from germs using Annie superpowers was obviously not working. I couldn't possibly go to work, and I had no strength to even get to a phone to let someone at the school know that I wasn't coming or, more truthfully, that I needed help.

Food had eluded me for days, so I forced myself to prepare noodles in the communal cooking area but only threw it all up again once I got back to my room. Evil slime from the lining of my stomach burned my throat, causing it to nearly swell shut. Swallowing felt like jagged glass being forced down my gullet.

If only I could have just called up my mommy to come take care of me, or at least give me advice about what to do. I had learned early on in my foolhardy international ventures that it was cruel and unusual punishment to call my mother when (a) I was lost, (b) I was injured, (c) I was in danger, or (d) I was sick beyond the remedies of a phone conversation. I couldn't imagine what life was like for my mom having to endure those calls. In my younger years, I never had the awareness to provide a follow-up call after a desperate phone call.

Nowadays, being a better daughter was important to me. Calling her in my condition would not be a loving thing to do. Besides, taking the few steps to the bathroom, I might collapse, never to recuperate. Actually dragging myself all the way to the city center to find a phone was really out of the realm of possibility.

Recently I had discovered the phone stores called locutorios that provided booths to call locally and internationally at a very decent rate, which was far better than the phone-on-a-rope option. Even still, any kind of telephone was far out of reach—and so was any assistance.

My motto prior to getting sober used to be "I don't need anyone's help." With very few relationships to manage, I thought I was *free*, but in hindsight, I was just *separate*. After many years, my attitude of complete self-reliance was not paying off. It became a juggernaut that aided my demise and left me to valiantly suffer through my difficulties alone.

Once I got sober, I was taught to rely less on my own will and to lean on a Higher Power, which was like God, the Universal Energy, or the Force—however I chose to believe in it. In the beginning, my fiercely guarded autonomy was a hard trait to let go of, until God decided it was time for my gut-wrenching submission.

* * *

It was September 2006 and I had just over one year of sobriety. Somehow, I was balancing a full-time teaching job, daily practices, working a recovery program, and traveling on the doubles pro beach volleyball tour. The first half of the beach season was brutal. I felt raw, vulnerable, and insecure, which were not the best traits for playing a highly competitive game in a tiny bikini beneath the eyes of thousands of fans. It felt as if I had lost my edge, and, even though it sounded crazy, I was certain that I had played better before I got sober. The urge to drink was fierce each time I lost or played poorly. The continual blows to my pride left me feeling devastated and darkly depressed.

Luckily, I had a strong recovery program with a lot of people who cared for me, even though I did not know how to return that kind of emotion yet. All my sobriety angels buoyed me through the harrowing first year of recovery and supported me unconditionally. Groups of sober men and women attended my games, standing as a cluster of non-beach-savvy people smoking cigarettes and cheering me on no matter how I played.

By holding onto my seat and riding out the unpredictable rollercoaster of new sobriety, everything started to shift by the middle of the volleyball season. I was weathering the highs and lows of playing a professional sport with a new sense of purpose and clarity. An elite training facility offered me sponsorship and a nutritionist to fine-tune my body inside and out. A brilliant sports psychologist graciously worked with me to build a solid toolkit of skills to bring my best self to the court. He also taught me how to walk off the court satisfied with the effort I gave—win or lose.

The best gift of all was that Saralyn, my original volleyball partner who had let me go when I had reached my bottom, asked if we could team up again. Gradually, I became a reliable member in our partnership. I was no longer playing for myself, but rather for *us*, and having a great time doing just that. Saralyn and I had an energetic spark to our partnership that was palpable. Our matching bathing suits, braids, fiery attitudes, and a few fantastic upsets of higher-ranked teams made us a crowd favorite.

By the end of that season, I had reached the pinnacle of my volleyball career. I also felt I had made progress in turning over my own will. I had accepted help from others and opened myself up to learning how to be a better player physically, emotionally, and mentally. Saralyn had been the first person in sobriety to whom I had been a stable and trustworthy friend. She had been patient and loving in the evolution of our friendship on and off the court.

Once I got sober, the recovery program was teaching me how to get out of my ego, but being a professional athlete was making that virtually impossible. Still identifying myself as a volleyball player, I didn't hesitate to share my glories and highlights with others. I still felt terminally unique and different than my fellow sobriety seekers. I had kicked drugs and alcohol and I was kicking butt at volleyball like never before!

I had heard many times in my recovery meetings that "edging God out" was the spiritual acronym for ego. Clearly, by being in ego, I was not allowing the Divine Spirit to flow through me and was still living in my will. Old-timers in meetings would often say, "God's will, not mine." This never really made sense to me, but I would nod and smile as if it did. I had also learned the "ism" in alcoholism could be referred to as the "I, self, and me" disease. And it was true, even with the alcohol and substances removed, the "ism" was still in full effect as if the world revolve exclusively around me.

That was until one sunny Saturday afternoon in September when the God who had been edged out decided to take back over.

My self-esteem had gotten a big boost when, for the first time since graduating more than ten years prior, I was invited back to Pepperdine University to play in a match slated for the alumni against the current team. My indignation had been intense during my time competing with the college team. From my distorted perspective, I had been unappreciated and had graduated feeling disgruntled with a "someday I'll show you!" attitude.

Now the opportunity was before me to show off and prove to my coach what a horrible mistake it had been to keep me on the bench most of my junior and senior years. I was just coming off my successful beach season, so I was in prime condition and springing high off the hard court after training on the soft sand. I could hardly contain my enthusiasm at my own performance as my heart raced and my veins zinged like I was getting high.

Moving toward a ball, I took one defensive step back when suddenly it felt as if someone had taken a baseball bat to the back of my foot. I heard a deafening crack that sounded like a thick tree branch snapping. My hearing went mute and my vision whitewashed as an atomic bomb of pain exploded in my leg. The agony was so tremendous that it almost ceased to be pain—as if the conscious mind got blocked off and sent to another dimension.

I turned to the referee standing on the back line and demanded to know, "Who did that to me?" It was puzzling to see that no one was near me, let alone someone holding a bat. Standing like a flamingo with one leg bent up and a ghostly pale face, I made the substitution signal with my hand. A player was sent onto the court to switch in for me, but I could only stand still like a statue and stare blankly. A medical trainer helped me hop off the court and I was put in a wheelchair. It was confirmed that my Achilles tendon had completely detached from my foot.

Game over. I never returned to the volleyball court again.

* * *

Lying in bed staring at the chipped ceiling of the Cuzqueño hostel brought back those memories of having my identity completely stripped from me, bringing me to my knees in humble submission. If I wasn't Ann the volleyball player, then who the hell was I? I remembered feeling so empty and hopeless without that socially glorified label.

I had had plenty of down time to think that one over as I lay crippled on my back for weeks. I had to move in with my parents to get full-time care and then have a sign-up list for people to help me daily once I moved back to my own place. The pain was nearly unbearable, but my medication had to be regulated so I didn't abuse it and lose my sobriety. Although I wasn't the pill-popping type, I did have insatiable cravings to completely check out and not have to feel every emotion that was coming up about how my volleyball career was over.

In hindsight, I see that besides getting sober, snapping my Achilles tendon was one of the greatest blessings life had given me. I had not been willing to let go of the sport and open up to what God really had in store for me. Finally, "God's will, not mine" was starting to make sense. So I started turning my will and my life over to the Divine Energy to see where it would take me.

Resentfully at that moment, I realized it had taken me to a dark and scary place in Peru with no one to help me. I really needed someone to come to my aid, but I had pushed away the only person that could help. I had no way of contacting her, but if Helen knew I was in trouble, she was the kind of girl who would go to any length to come and help me. But what had I done? Snarled at her, ignored her, spoken condescendingly to her, and shut the door on the opportunity for a relationship with her. Why? Because she dressed funny? Because she asked a lot of questions? Because she wanted me to help her learn Spanish?

Although I had come a long way with friendships and being nonjudgmental of others, it was quite clear at that moment that I'd burned an important bridge for no good reason. The only person whom I could truly count on was good ol' Kylie, but she was off meandering through the Andes, unaware of my frightening condition.

My semiconscious existence in the hostel room was clearly reaching a perilous crossroad and action was needed. The night was long and torturous as the fiery flames of hell flickered through the gates at me. By morning, the Saint Carmen fireworks didn't even provoke me but awakened me so I could immediately find help. Swallowing was agony and my stomach threatened another eruption of bile. There was no one in the lobby to direct me to the nearest hospital, so I staggered into the alley on a mission to find one.

Finally, I spied a narrow passage with a red cross symbol and arrow directing me toward a clinic. A small door creaked open to the one-room facility where a vacant-faced woman sat behind a desk. She didn't lift her gaze as she fiddled with a staticky Andean radio before addressing my presence. She simultaneously tried to write down my personal information with her right hand as she continued to fidget with the radio knob with her left. Since the static was so loud, she couldn't hear me as I excruciatingly repeated each of my answers.

My brain strained to speak Spanish, causing her to roll her eyes when I misspelled my last name for the third time. Giving up with a moan, I lay down sideways on the folding chairs, holding my stomach and praying that the situation would miraculously improve. She finished her initial questions, abruptly turned off the radio, then inexplicably stared out the window.

"Please, is someone going to help me?" I finally whimpered in Spanish. "Is there a doctor here?"

Looking annoyed and unsympathetic, the woman picked up a phone and spoke in Quechua to the person on the other end.

"The doctor is coming," she said blankly.

Curled up in a fetal position with tears streaming sideways down my face, I eventually drifted off to sleep. I awoke to find a gentle hand on my shoulder as a concerned face looked down at me. Doctor Torres introduced himself, touched my back, looked down my throat, and asked a few questions.

"You need to go to a hospital with me—immediately," he said.

Wrapping his arm around me, he led me out to the street where he hailed a cab. I lay curled up helpless in the backseat, pleading with God that this man was trustworthy. My frail mind somehow still had the strength to wonder if friendly Dr. Torres was going to harvest my organs or perhaps sell me into the sex trade.

Thankfully, as it turned out, he was a very respectable, caring individual who made it his mission to help sick foreigners who often rotted away at tiny clinics in dark alleys. We pulled to the curb in front of a small hospital where a welcoming staff greeted me. They sampled all my bodily fluids and handed me a miniature Styrofoam cup with a wooden tongue depressor in it.

"For feces," the nurse said.

Seriously? What's the stick for?

A comfortable private room was provided and an angelic nurse brought me tea and toast. She even wiped my tears when I started crying out of deep gratitude for someone taking care of me.

The results came back that I had an arbitrary strand of a swine virus, which could be combated with strong antibiotics and rest. I was told that it would take a few days for me to start feeling better and it would be advisable for someone to look after me. I didn't have enough cash to pay the seventy-five-dollar fee, which was pricey for any type of service in Cuzco but worth every penny to me.

Dr. Torres sent the matronly nurse in a taxi with me back to my hostel so I could get my ATM card. She took my arm and helped me to the bank and then to a market to pick up local food remedies. It took every ounce of pride I had not to beg her to come back to my hostel and take care of me. I was willing to offer her a ridiculous amount of money to stay. I stood whimpering on the corner as she hugged me good-bye and caught a taxi back to the clinic.

I popped my medication, settled for the clearest television channel I could find, pulled up the alpaca blanket to my chin, and slept. I was on the road to physical recovery, but emotionally and spiritually, I was ruined.

In the morning, I saw with great relief that Kylie had updated her Facebook status. "Machu Picchu was magical, but touristy—now headed back to Cuzco."

31

GOING ON AN ANNIE HUNT

Regrettably, e-mail was the only method of making contact with Kylie, and it might have been days before she checked it again. My appreciation intensified for not only a simple cell phone but for my iPhone, with which I could practically do anything. The familiar chime in my pocket that let me know I had an e-mail, text, or phone message was greatly missed.

During my sickness, the only mode of communication was the hostel's one sluggish computer that worked only 50 percent of the time and, most often, was occupied by other guests. Hopelessly, I sat on the edge of my bed, head hung low like a wilted flower, checking every five minutes to see if the computer was available. The feeling of powerlessness was overwhelming—Kylie was my only hope.

Once the computer freed up, I faced another obstacle. Locating the hostel after I left the hospital was challenging enough, but trying to describe its whereabouts through an e-mail was insurmountable. A GPS system would even find it challenging to pinpoint my location. Too bad there wasn't an app that could project a gigantic A into the sky for Kylie to follow.

The hostel was on a street with no name. It had no address. And the hostel was named Hostel. In my deliriously sickened state, the best directions I could write to Kylie in my Hail Mary e-mail were visual cues.

"Head toward the gigantic Inca by the twelve-sided rock, turn left where we saw that huge pile of llama poop, and then go right at the street with the hole in the sidewalk that could easily swallow a child. Look for an archway on the left-hand side that opens into a court-yard with half a dozen artisan stalls and a dirty dog tied on a rope. There you will find an incognito door between the alpaca ponchos and the cases of silver jewelry."

A prayer was sent out that Kylie would check her e-mail and decipher the treasure map to find my sickly self.

The only luck I did seem to have was finally receiving an e-mail from the Central Office of Alcohol and Drug Recovery for Peru. It had taken them four weeks to reply with the address of the few Spanish-speaking meetings in Cuzco.

Since getting sober, I've gone to meetings anywhere from one to five times a week, every week. My life is radically better when I attend them, and I am unbalanced and live selfishly when I don't. Once I'd finished the twelve steps, I'd made the lifelong commitment to my own growth through recovery. The process was essentially learning how to recover my authentic self, which drugs and alcohol and years of false beliefs had concealed.

When I work my program, the delight in my life continues to exceed my wildest dreams. I have tested the theory enough times to learn that I need to make sobriety my number one priority. Not going to a meeting for four weeks was risky business and enough time for the Shit Birds to start convincing me that once I got healthy, a celebration would be in order with an ayahuasca ceremony and a frothy pitcher of pisco sours.

Good thing I had the location of a meeting because it was certainly time to get to one before the demons started having their way.

* * *

Later that night I was lying in bed when there was a gentle knock on my door. An angel sent from heaven with a familiar Australian accent asked, "Ann, are you in there?" After over three hours of scouring hostels using her basic Spanish to ask for a sick American girl, she'd eventually found my location. The two women who ran the hostel but were rarely present just happened to be in the lobby at the very moment Kylie entered.

"Yes, I'm here," was my feeble reply. Captain Kylie to the rescue!

Kylie brought clean water, food, and her priceless friendship. Apart from being ill, I was torn up about what my next step would be. With my immune system so weak, I couldn't imagine going back to the school where germy mucus was exchanged through constant physical contact. At that juncture, perhaps the illness was a bit cathartic. It forced me to shut down, restart the engine, and choose a new direction.

"I'm not inspired to work at the school anymore. Depression drowns me every time I consider going back."

"I know," Kylie replied, "I felt like that too. So I left."

"But is this it? I had promised to stay until the end of July. I can't just give up."

"Nah, honey, you're not giving up. You've done so much already. You have touched their lives, and perhaps there are other kids out there you can help. It doesn't have to be at Arco Iris School."

"Yeah, good point," I paused as resentment surfaced. "But I'll never know what's going to happen with my donations."

"Didn't you already make peace with that?"

"You're right. I'll have to completely let that go."

"Besides," Kylie said, pointing at a bag in the corner, "you've got a shitload of those supplies you swiped back from Javier right there. I bet you can figure out how to help more kids around here."

I laughed for the first time in a long while.

"Listen, Ann, you don't have to move mountains to make a difference," Kylie said.

I paused to let her words sink in, and then it hit me. I had wanted to be extraordinary. To do something so grand that *I* would be somebody special. Clearly I didn't want to be a worker among workers at Arco Iris. I wanted to be in charge and make such a huge difference that I would become legendary. Perhaps they would have even added my image to one of the many murals around the school. I had even fantasized about someone suffering from sleep deprivation one hundred years in the future as the fireworks exploded in the early morning over a gigantic goddess with my likeness, honoring Santa Ana.

How quickly I had turned to my old self-centered behaviors, even though they wore the veil of philanthropy. But what if I could help other people to be extraordinary? It didn't have to be about what *I* could do, but rather what I could teach others to do for themselves. I had no idea where to begin, but a healthy Ann was critical in order to have a helpful Ann.

* * *

A new sense of purpose inspired me, but I could not say the same for the town of Cuzco. Being bombarded by locals hawking their wares had become infuriating—and also depressing. It broke my heart having to give a firm no to a five-year-old boy asking to shine my trekking boots or to a dirty-faced toddler handing me an ad for her parents' wool sweater business. Thick, black car exhaust was inescapable on narrow streets. Many times, I had nearly been smacked in the back of the head with side view mirrors from vans stuffed with people whose heads and limbs stuck out the windows.

The town center felt like a pulsating, machine-like state run off the greed of the locals that trumped general hospitality. There was no personal connection. I wanted to get to know the residents deeper and learn about their struggles and their victories. What was life like behind closed doors with their families? What were their traditions? How did they find joy and happiness in their daily routine?

Something tugged at me to stay and help the community, but I just didn't have it in me to continue there. So what was I to do?

32

CARMEN'S LAST LAUGH

The next morning, Kylie and I soaked up the rich sunlight while watching the mayhem of yet another parade circling the plaza. Finally, it seemed as if my immune system was rebooting, and I was able to keep down a light breakfast at our favorite perch on one of the balconies overlooking the city center.

It soon became evident after spending a month in Cuzco that every Sunday the main streets were blocked off for a celebration, parade, or protest. The locals certainly worked hard, but, apparently, they were eager to let loose and rejoice too. The range of festivities that Cuzco celebrates is expansive, from celebrating the Lord of Earthquakes to the Festival of the Cross to the Snow Star. There's Corpus Cristi, the Inti Raymi festival of the Sun, Independence Day, and, of course, my favorite, the Virgin Carmen. Besides parades, there were perpetual strikes and protests, along with gatherings of individuals zealous about their causes.

On this Sunday morning, it was the Day of the Student, honoring all children who attended school.

Lines of animated adolescents in their school uniforms arranged themselves from oldest to youngest. Frantic, last-minute hairstyling took place all across the plaza since brightly colored bows and braids seemed an important component of the female student attire. A band played on the steps of the church while fireworks popped and zinged wildly. Many of the attendees were indigenous Indians in their traditional dress who were visibly consumed with pride as they waved at their children or grandchildren. Many of the students participating were the first in their families to get an education.

Kylie pointed out an amusing breaking of rank as a young, eager boy attempted to march with the older boys, kicking his legs out stiffly in Peruvian military style. But my amusement was halted by a deafening screech below our balcony. A rocket shot through the wood below, pierced the side pocket of my purse, and hit a lighter that abruptly blew up and hurtled plastic lighter shrapnel in all directions. Charred stench filled the air as I touched my cheek where a hot piece of plastic had bounced off my face just below my eye.

"Un-fucking-believable!" I shouted.

"My hair is going to turn gray with all these Peruvian shenanigans!" Kylie growled.

After all my complaining about fireworks, rockets, and celebrations for Holy Virgins, in the end Saint Carmen got the last laugh.

33

LUPE

Back at the hostel lobby, I scanned the tattered paperbacks on the book exchange shelf, eager to finally read now that my eyes were fully functional. The adventure classic *The Lost City of the Incas* was the ultimate find. Since Machu Picchu was on my radar for the near future, I couldn't contain my excitement about reading one of the most famous chronicles of Hiram Bingham III and his discovery of that very site.

I positioned myself against a wall in the small courtyard where a few isolated handicraft booths conducted business. It felt like I was breathing in life again with the sun on my face, a soft breeze to keep me cool, and a renewed sense of gratitude for my health. The semi seclusion of the courtyard kept the street vendors at bay while providing me the luxury of being outdoors.

The book pulled me into the story of Bingham, a Yale University lecturer who was passing through Cuzco in 1909 when he heard of a four-hundred-year-old unsolved mystery. So the story goes, when the Spanish conquistadors invaded in the sixteenth century, a group of Incas escaped to a mysterious fortress in the clouds where they took many treasures of the Incan Empire. During the time Bingham was first in Cuzco, the hidden city of gold was considered just a legend, but he was unwaveringly ambitious and methodical in his approach to unearth the ruins.

Taking a break from the absorbing read, I gave my eyes a rest and examined the courtyard. I noticed a girl, about eight years old, with precisely braided hair sitting on a stool in front of an artisan's stall. Just then, a woman, who appeared to be her mother, entered the courtyard with a jewelry display board, which I presumed she carried around through the city to sell to tourists—like me.

I couldn't count how many traveling vendors I had snubbed with the palm of my hand and a definitive no. Clearly, her store was in an undesirable area with little to no foot traffic, so she had to bring the business to the customer. I guessed that the little girl was instructed to watch the store and do business if necessary while the mother was out trying to make a living for her family.

"Did you sell any jewelry today?" I asked the woman in Spanish.

"No, ma'am, not today. Not yesterday, either. It has been many days."

"Maybe tomorrow," I replied hopefully, but felt uncomfortable that I had inquired at all.

Eager to know more about Bingham's quest, I returned to the book, but concentrating was difficult. The young girl swept the front walk and then rearranged the knickknacks in the glass display case, all the while keeping an eye on me.

I smiled and asked," ¿Cómo te llamas?"

"I am Lupe," she replied softly in Spanish.

I continued in her language. "Lupe, do you like to read?"

She paused. "I like…stories, yes."

"Have you learned to read at school yet?"

Her eyes dropped. "I only go to school sometimes, when my mama doesn't need me to work."

"Oh," I responded awkwardly. "Would you like me to read you a story?"

Her face lit up as she twirled her braids nervously. "Sí."

"Just a minute, Lupe, I'll be right back."

In my room, I selected from my supply bag the children's classic *Green Eggs and Ham* by Dr.Seuss that had been translated into Spanish. Back outside, Lupe positioned her stool in front of me as I sat on the step holding the book up so she could see the illustrations.

"Huevos verdes con jamón," I began.

She giggled with delightful anticipation.

"¿Te gustan los huevos verdes con jamón? No, no me gustan nada, Juan Ramón. ¡No me gustan nada los huevos verdes con jamón!"

By the end of the story, she was chiming in with each stanza as her mother stifled laughs while watching us from her shop. Handing Lupe the book, I told her it was now her very own. With her mouth parted in awe, she carefully cradled it, brushing her delicate hand across the hard cover, tracing the cartoon images with her finger. She skipped over to her mother, who scooped Lupe up in her arms and embraced her with the book sandwiched between them.

"Your very first book, mi hija!"

I waved goodbye with a visceral tingle and told Lupe and her mother Teresa that I'd be back the next day to read more. For the first time in over a week, I was starting to feel remarkably better.

* * *

Cross-legged on my bed with the Bingham book cradled in my lap, I got lost in reverie. When I was eight years old, like Lupe, my mom was a special education teacher in Torrance, California. At the beginning of every summer, she would take me to one of my favorite places—the book depot. It was a multi-leveled utopia for teachers to check out their required reading for the school year. The rows upon rows of metal shelves housed endless possibilities of escaping into new realms.

Pushing a shopping cart, I'd meticulously go up and down every aisle collecting as many books as the cart could hold. Once I was home, I laid out my treasures in a long line around my room, abandoning myself to creating an order with which I planned to read them. I'd lose myself in the words and took on characters as my very own.

It was troubling for me to think that Lupe didn't know how to read or that prior to my giving her *Green Eggs and Ham* she had never possessed her own book. Books were the portals to my imagination, opening up the doorway to infinite new worlds. When I was a child, stories and novels allowed me to vicariously try out new experiences and test new ideas, with no negative consequences in my real life. I often met characters in books whom I returned to for comfort when I needed a friend.

Seared into my memory was the image of Lupe clasping her first book with an expression of joy in its purest form. A penetrating wave of inspiration washed over me, but then it abruptly withdrew into the abyss of my subconscious before I could fully grasp the message.

34

THE THREE AMIGOS

The slip of paper with the address for the recovery meeting was making a handy bookmark for the *Lost City of the Incas* book. Every time I opened the novel, the meeting location stared at me, as if to remind me of the sobriety support that was waiting. While traveling internationally, showing up at an unfamiliar meeting can be nerve-racking and wildly unpredictable. Although the format is theoretically universal in its presentation, more often than not the members customize the structure to make it their own.

While in Spain a few years prior, I was often the only woman in a room full of chain-smoking men who gawked me shamelessly. On one such occasion, two men in their fifties got in a verbal altercation that turned into a fistfight resulting in the two fellows falling on a table and breaking it in half. All of this mayhem was instigated over who would keep track of the phone list.

That kind of behavior, along with the man-to-woman ratio, often turned me off to seeking out meetings while in foreign countries. However, there have been some occasions when I stumbled across meetings that were like little treasures tucked away, just waiting to be discovered. Many sober folks have crossed my international path and lit up my life, appearing like angels out of nowhere.

These people have given me stellar suggestions when I was traveling alone and have invited me to coffee or to their home for a meal as if we were old friends. Even after only knowing me for minutes, I've been invited to birthday parties, social events, and local excursions with other sober people. It was as if I had an instant network in every city all over the world if I was patient and willing to search out meetings. It opened doors to unforgettable relationships and new experiences, but also presented the risk that I could find myself worse off than when I walked in. It was *always* an adventure, and I was certain that in Peru it would be no different.

My body was still in the healing process, so navigating the complicated Cuzqueño streets was not at all appealing. With the address in hand, in the plaza I hailed a cab that proceeded to speed away before I had even closed the door. The driver immediately hit a tourist in the crosswalk who sprawled out on his hood, staring through the windshield, traumatized. Shaking a fist at his new hood ornament, the cabbie dropped the taxi in reverse, violently removing the poor pedestrian off the vehicle, then swerved around his crumpled body. He raced off, cussing at the miniature saint swinging from his rearview mirror.

I held on for dear life as the cab traversed the city NASCAR-style until eventually we turned up a familiar street. He pulled to a screeching halt directly in front of the door to my previous residence at Marisol's.

Still shaken by the drive and confused as to why I was there, I remained in the backseat studying the slip of paper. *Did I give him Marisol's address by accident?* He bellowed at me to get out since we were holding up traffic in the narrow alley. After I paid, he accelerated up the street, expelling a large black puff of exhaust in my face.

Coughing, I stood in front of Marisol's door, completely dumbfounded. I double-checked my address number again—02. Marisol's was 01. Shifting my view and walking five steps, I came to a small door with the familiar triangle and circle symbol etched in the wood. Out of this vast city, the meeting had been *here* all along? All those nights sitting on a broken chair in the garden and petting the cross-eyed dog and there was a meeting across the damned street?

No one answered my first knock. Awkwardly, I stood pressed against the wall so the traffic squeezing down the cobblestones wouldn't run me over. Ready to give up and go back to the "comfort" of my hostel, I gave one last knock. The door cracked open, and a small, elderly man sporting a derby cap looked me up and down.

"¿Usted es amigo de Bill?" he asked cautiously in Spanish. Are you a friend of Bill's?

If I hadn't been in the recovery program, I would have had no idea what he meant. But I was part of the universal club of sobriety. The question he had asked was like a secret code to know if someone was sober and working the program. With an anxious smile, I introduced myself.

"Welcome, sister," he said, "I am Octavio. We have been waiting for you."

He led me to a tiny, windowless, chilly room with a wooden table, four chairs, a coffee pot, and the wall décor typical of sobriety clubhouses. Sitting at the table were two other men wearing hats similar to Octavio's and who all looked identical in stature and age. I was introduced to Miguel, who had wildly bushy eyebrows, and Francisco, who sported a finely groomed mustache. They were visibly pleased to see a new face and immediately offered me a cup of coca tea. It was a relief to see that they too were sipping the tea, and therefore I was assured it was nonnarcotic.

As with most people working a recovery program, culture, age, and gender gap melted away in mere minutes as we exchanged our stories. Octavio, Miguel, and Francisco all had double-digit years of sobriety, and the three of them had been meeting in that room every week for decades. They each gave me a rare insight into the lives of alcoholic men in Peru.

"You see, Ana," started Miguel, "the men in our society often turn to the drink because it is easily accessible, even for the very poor. This becomes the outlet for many who live a life of poverty, stress, and hardship. Alcohol becomes their solution. They often put the burden on their women and detach themselves from their responsibilities as fathers, husbands, and upstanding men of society. I think Octavio and Francisco can agree that we used to be these kind of men, but through this recovery program we have found a better way to live."

Francisco added his thoughts. "Historically, the Inca Empire had excessive drinking habits, which could have been caused by the trauma of the Spanish conquest or all the continued wars, but the result was that the culture took on behaviors that became self-destructive but acceptable. If the government or society as a whole cannot see it as a problem, but rather a custom or tradition, it is hard to fix, prevent, or to provide support."

I immediately became grateful for the strength and availability of recovery programs in my own country. It seemed that in the US, alcoholism is widely understood to be a disease requiring treatment. Most people know someone who is either working a twelve-step program or someone who should be. Television programs like *Intervention* have helped demonstrate to a wide audience the signs of addiction and how an alcoholic or drug addict can be helped. It was hard to imagine living in a country where destructive, alcoholic behavior was accepted as the norm.

Rarely did these men get the gift of a new attendee, and their gratitude at my spontaneous attendance was evident. Octavio read from the approved literature, and we each shared our experience in relationship to the text. Many times, I had to ask them to repeat themselves or slow down since their dialect and manner of speaking was challenging for me to interpret. It was comforting to hear the familiar words spoken by individuals who were sober, especially coming from men as wise as these three fellows. Their unconditional love, kindness, and honesty helped me to eventually feel at home in their company.

My emotions started bubbling up when I shared how tortured I felt about the fact that I was considering leaving the school I had come to volunteer at. They alternated giving me their handkerchiefs to soak up uncontrollable tears that seemed to be melting away from a long-forming iceberg in my heart. Octavio kept his worn hand on top of mine, giving periodic squeezes of reassurance. They understood the journey of an alcoholic like me who used to live only for herself.

"Why am I here?" I kept repeating. "What's the purpose? To abandon my original goal for the school and then nearly die in a bed all alone?" I went on to describe how difficult my recent sickness had been and how scary it was to go through it by myself.

"Ana! Why didn't you come here sooner?" asked Miguel, raising his thick eyebrows. "You could have stayed at my home, and my wife would have taken care of you!"

"Believe me, Miguel, if I had known you wonderful men were here, I would have come long ago! But for some reason, I think it was supposed to happen this way." I paused, lost in my own musing. "But now what do I do? Part of me wants to stick it out at the school. Although it wasn't easy, I really started to care deeply for those kids. How am I supposed to just walk away? I want so badly for my heart to be into it, but it's not."

The three men just nodded patiently.

"I have such a strong yearning to fly free and explore," I went on. "I want to breathe fresh mountain air and connect to the magnificent energy of the land. But isn't that selfish? What about helping people and taking contrary action to how I used to be? One of my old ways of dealing with difficulties was to run away, lose myself in nature—and escape all my troubles."

Octavio looked me directly in the eyes. "Ana, I think you cannot see what is clear to us. From what you have shared, we can see your heart is in the right place with your service work, but something even greater is trying to get your attention. Do you follow what I'm saying?"

My brain was working overtime to focus on translating his message. It was still as if I were one step away from what he was trying to express. "No, Octavio, I don't understand."

"It is the importance of nature in your life and your connection to it. You used to desperately seek it out, not necessarily because it was an escape but because it was calling you."

Francisco was next to chime in. "We appreciate what you are trying to do for our people, Ana, and your intentions are good, but perhaps Pachamama has another plan for you here in Peru. Something bigger."

"Something bigger? How can there be something bigger? I've hardly done anything. And Pachamama? Isn't that the goddess from the Inti Raymi festival? What does she have to do with me?" I asked.

All three men nodded with knowing smiles. Octavio even removed his glasses and wiped the moisture from his eyes. Francisco smoothed his mustache with his thumb and forefinger and answered.

"Pachamama is Quechua for Mother Earth. In our culture, she holds much power, and many people worship her as the deity that controls our planet. She is perceived as a living consciousness and is vital to our spiritual lives. The Spanish brought Catholic religion to Peru, but many of us still believe in the gods of our lands."

Miguel began to laugh. "Ana, do you know how they say, 'Let go, let God' in our program?"

"Yes, of course," I replied.

"Well, think of it like 'Let go and let Pachamama guide you.' Your soul is congested, but the energy of our lands will clear you out and create space for the glorious inspiration that is coming your way. Be patient, Ana, and listen to your intuition. You just need to find your way to the heart of Pachamama."

"The heart of Pachamama? I'm not sure what you mean."

"There's more to be revealed, Ana, but you need to explore and go discover it for yourself. She will show you the way."

Sitting in contemplation, I suddenly felt a warm sensation burning in the middle of my back. My eyes lit up with recognition. Laughter bubbled up. Pulling my jacket off, I turned my back to the men and then pulled down the collar of my shirt, exposing my world tattoo.

"It's Pachamama! Years ago I marked myself with Mother Earth, and I had always wondered why I did it. I figured I was just out of my mind back then."

I wasn't sure what the elderly men actually thought of this new revelation, but their eyes widened and they shook their heads in disbelief.

"Oh, Ana," chuckled Octavio, "you are such a curious girl."

The three men embraced me in a womb of courage, wisdom, and faith. Miguel put his hand on my shoulder and squeezed. "Just trust, Ana. Trust the power of Pachamama."

"Please join us for coffee tomorrow," said Francisco as he turned off the light in the small room.

"Yes, yes," added Miguel, "we meet every morning at nine. Please come."

I agreed as we stepped out into the brisk night air.

"Octavio and I will walk you back," said Miguel, "and we can show you where to meet us tomorrow."

Towering over my two escorts, I hooked each of their arms, and for the first time I was able to relax and enjoy a night stroll without feeling unsafe in the dark streets. Hugging them each tightly, I promised that I'd join them in the morning.

That night I lay back in my bed and sighed long and deep. I could feel the influence of Pachamama reinvigorating my soul and pulling me toward my destiny. "To the heart of Pachamama," I said to myself. "Just trust."

35

ADIÓS, CUZCO

Crossing the plaza, I stopped to toss a coin in the fountain and sent out a prayer to Pachamama. Next stop—the three amigos at their local coffee shop.

It was a simple place filled entirely with old-timers who all looked like cookie-cutter versions of my new buddies. The clanking of coffee cups and small talk ceased the moment I stepped through the door.

Immediately, Octavio stood up and greeted me with a big grin and extended arms, saying, "Ana!" All three men hugged me and kissed my cheek; each looked at me proudly as if I were his long lost daughter. The shuffling of tables and chairs commenced as the sober trifecta rearranged their acquaintances so I could sit at their table. Miguel stood and declared proudly to the men, "This is our friend Ana from California."

"Say something, Ana!" Miguel said, turning to his coffee shop comrades. "You should hear her speak Spanish, it is very good."

Standing awkwardly in front of the men, I smiled and greeted them. The others nodded their heads in approval, a few stood to greet me personally. Francisco pulled out my chair and called to the waiter to bring me tea.

"So, Ana, what's your plan?" asked Octavio.

"Well, I thought about it a lot last night, and I decided it's time to bid Cuzco farewell."

"Where to?"

"Tomorrow I'm taking a bus to Arequipa."

"Ah, yes, it is a very beautiful town. You will find a lot of Pachamama there!"

"Then after that, I think I'll go to Puno and visit Lake Titicaca."

Miguel's eyes lit up. "If you go to Puno, my friend Rodolfo lives there and is sober. He can help you find a meeting."

"Great, thanks, Miguel," I replied.

"According to the mythology of our people," he continued, "Lake Titicaca is the place where the world was created, when the god Viracocha came out of the lake and created the sun, the stars, and the first people."

A renewed sense of optimism and anticipation surged with the intrigue of an unknown adventure resting on the horizon. I promised the men I would be back to Cuzco in a month and would seek them out for another meeting and fellowship. Filled with confidence and a transformed sense of hope, I headed back to my hostel to pack.

Lupe was sweeping the walk when I returned. She lit up and scurried to me, giggling and repeating lines from *Green Eggs and Ham*.

"My brother read it to me last night five times, and my father too. I am going to memorize the whole book!"

"Good for you, Lupe!" I said. "Want to read some more?"

"¡Sí! ¡Sí! Mamá, can I?"

"Sí, mi amor," her mom responded from behind the jewelry counter.

I returned with *Where the Wild Things Are* and a little bag filled with a coloring book, crayons, kid scissors, glue, and a small pad of construction paper. Lupe's focus was undivided as I read.

We soon gained the attention of other children who mysteriously appeared, their eyes gleaming with excitement as they sat in front of me. Once the last page was read, the group chanted, "Más, más, más!" I asked Lupe to get her *Green Eggs* book, which then entertained the kids for the next hour as they learned how to repeat the lines at the end of each stanza and would shout out, "No me gustan, Don Ramón!" I don't like them, Sam I am!

I said my good-byes to Lupe and gave Teresa the bag of supplies.

"Where are you going now, señorita Ana?" she asked, clutching the bag gratefully.

"Arequipa, then Puno."

She smiled, nodding her head. "Yes, Ana, you are very lucky. I hope one day to visit some of those places." She paused, as if second-guessing her next question. "And what does your husband think about your travels?"

"Oh, no, there's no husband," I replied. "Someday I hope to find a good man, but until then I travel alone."

The look on her face was a combination of amazement and sorrow. "Don't you want to have children?"

By her cultural standards, I was probably long past due to be married and have children.

"Yes, but it's different in my country."

She shrugged her shoulders. "One moment please, I have something to give you."

She brought back a tiny cloth sack cinched together at the top with a red string.

"I want to thank you for what you have done for Lupe. She will never forget you. Please take this, it will keep you safe on your travels."

Inside was a dark green, three-stepped symmetric cross with a hole in the center, a charm that I had seen in most of the tourist shops and carried by all the jewelry-board-toting women in the city center.

"It is the chakana, the Incan cross," Teresa explained.

The curtains parted from the back of the tiny storefront and an ancient-looking woman joined Teresa. "This is my grandmother, Saywa."

"La cruz Andean," said the older woman, taking the charm from me and turning it over in her weathered hand. "Do you see the hole in the heart of the cross? It represents our city of Cuzco, which we consider the navel of the Incan world."

She pointed to one of the steps on the bottom side of the cross. "Surrounding this circle are four sides of the cross. Each one is meant to represent one of the three worlds of the Inca belief system. The underworld, or Ugh Pacha, is represented by the snake; the middle world, that of the humans, is called Kay Pacha and is represented by the puma. Finally," she said, pointing at the top edge of the symbol, "the upper world of the gods, Hanan Pacha, is represented by the condor."

Teresa then added, "These three animals, along with the chakana, are in a lot of our architecture and artwork. Have you seen them around the city?"

I realized that I hadn't seen any. Had I been so occupied with my frustration with the school that I hadn't noticed? Or was I walking with my head down so no one would have eye contact with me and try to sell me something? It seemed I was blind to some of the intriguing details about the culture.

"Did you know that Cuzco was built in the shape of a puma?" Lupe chimed in. "The head is the fortress Sacsaywaman, the heart is the main plaza, and the two rivers…"

Lupe paused, digging in her brain for the names.

"Huatanay and Tullumayo represent the tail," Teresa said, filling in.

"No, I didn't know that, Lupe, how fascinating!" I said.

Saywa held the cross in the palm of her hand, looked at me through her cataract-clouded eyes, and continued with her captivating Andean mythology lesson. "There are many philosophies about this symbol, but in our family we believe that the top of the cross represents the god of creation, Viracocha.

I interrupted, remembering what Miguel had told me that morning. "Viracocha was the god who rose from Lake Titicaca, right?"

"Yes," she affirmed and continued, "and the Mother Earth or Pachamama anchors the bottom of the cross."

I couldn't help but smile at the mention of Pachamama.

Teresa placed the powerful chakana in my hand and folded my fingers around it. "Wear this on your travels to keep you safe." She shook out the small stitched bag as five brilliant red seeds with a black marking fell into my hand.

"These are huayruro seeds and have been a part of our culture for centuries. They bring good luck and ward off negative energy. Maybe they will even bring you love," Teresa said with a wink.

* * *

Kylie and I met up that evening for one last trek up to the White Christ. It was a pleasant escape from the random fireworks, the exhaust, and the touristy hustle-bustle. We thought we'd be out of reach from the vendors but were asked four times if we wanted to rent horses. She chuckled when I showed her the repaired hole in my purse from the firework debauchery the previous morning. I had taken the beautifully stitched purse to the sewing machine aisle at the locals' market. There, an indigenous woman using an archaic Singer repaired it on the spot while I read a book to her daughter.

"This time I avoided the fruit smoothie aisle," I said laughing. It very well could have caused my horrific illness. In any case, I wasn't willing to take the risk, no matter how irresistible.

Sitting beneath the grand statue, I pointed out to Kylie the puma outline of the city and how we were in the belly button of the sacred animal when we stood in the plaza. We reminisced on our experiences in Cuzco, both knowing we were at a crossroad that would send us in separate directions. Kylie was off to Bolivia, and I had purchased a ticket for an eleven-hour bus ride south to the "white city" of Arequipa.

Adiós, Cuzco. Pachamama lead the way!

36

THE BUS RIDE FROM HELL

L etting out a deep sigh, I bent over to touch my toes and alternated bending my knees. The ritual of stretching prior to long flights or road trips was habit. While bystanders typically stared curiously, I would pretzel myself into creative positions using railings, stairwells, and walls for support. The morning of the departure to Arequipa was no different as I stretched my Achilles on a high curb, arched my arms up, and exhaled deeply.

The bus terminal was bustling with a curious mix of travelers. Backpackers were splayed on the ground, leaning on their packs and munching on snacks. These vacationers were most likely gallivanting around the country on adventurous holidays, unlike the locals who would probably never have the chance to visit some of their own country's most famed locations. I wondered if traveling for pleasure even factored into Peruvian dreams as it did for so many Americans.

The previous day, I had ventured to the bus station to search for a reasonable ticket price from one of the numerous bus companies competing for business. After haggling with multiple vendors, I proudly walked away with a ticket for ten dollars. Little did I know at the time that buying the cheapest ticket to traverse the rough countryside would be the worst choice I could have made.

It was only later that I became utterly disgusted with myself for quibbling for a better price on items that were already far below what I would normally be willing to pay. Why this obsession with getting a bargain? Why not support the local economy instead of wanting everything cheaper, cheaper, and cheaper still? It was as if my American competitive nature wanted to assume the advantage over the perceived opponent so as to walk away confident that *I* got the better end of the exchange.

After watching clusters of indigenous women stuff their oversized loads into the lower storage area, I realized it was one of *those* kinds of buses. As I finished my last cycle of stretches, I caught the glimmer of eyes watching me from the other side of the bus's grubby windshield. The driver saluted and hopped out of the cab. Realizing he was heading directly for me, I removed my earphones.

"*I* am the bus driver," he declared assuredly, as if it were a profession that deserved the greatest of reverence. The green stains on his teeth made it clear he habitually grazed on coca leaves.

"Are you married?" he asked directly after our brief introduction.

"No," I said, certain that I should have lied. "How about you, are *you* married?"

"Así, así," he said with a wink.

Kind of? I had a hard time holding back my revulsion, but realized I should have known better than to return the question.

Since it was going to be an eleven-hour ride, I snuck into an empty row as far as possible from the stench of urine that radiated from my original seat in 12B. My hope was that the breathtaking countryside would somehow make up for the odor. I was a bit hesitant about such a long drive since I had read about the country's many traffic fatalities, but the bus company had guaranteed me that the drivers changed shifts every four hours for safety purposes. Remembering these words of reassurance, I relaxed and settled in.

I turned to survey the other guests waiting to board and quickly realized that there would be no landscape-viewing through the windows caked with grime. I have a bit of an obsession with clean glass and take every opportunity to make sure my own car windows are crystal-clear. I even keep a squeegee in my classroom to keep those windows sparkling.

For a moment, I considered dashing outside with a wet tissue to clean a porthole to gaze out from. My discouragement with the viewing situation was substantial and coupled with disgust at the seats, which were covered in crumbs, stains, and moisture. At least there was a television screen connected to the paneled wall at the front of the bus, which would provide much-needed en route entertainment.

My stomach rumbled with the ever-present discomfort that had remained since my illness. Craning my neck backward, I felt greatly relieved to see that there was a bus potty, which would probably save me if my grumbling tummy worsened.

The bus filled quickly with many of the men wearing hand-woven ponchos and women in colorfully stitched peasant dresses and bowler hats. Most had blankets slung over a shoulder hauling mysterious contents. The only other out-of-place travelers on the bus were two college students sitting in the first row, both sporting matching red University of London sweatshirts.

Only a few minutes into the journey, the real en route entertainment began. A traveling salesman had boarded and strutted the aisle shouting warnings to the native people about carrying their goods over one shoulder. He displayed large photos of indigenous folks with humped backs and grotesquely enlarged shoulders.

"Do you want to look like this?" he bellowed. "Don't worry, my friends. I have the solution! Super vitamins!" He diligently passed each seat and shook a pill bottle, pointed at particular travelers, and clucked his tongue with disappointment.

"Oh, no!" he said to one finely weathered fellow. "You, sir, are well on your way to having a deformed back." The man stared at him without a trace of concern. The salesman gave one last shake of the plastic vitamin container then exited at the next stop without making a sale.

A laxative vendor followed and then another man selling petroleum jelly for cracked feet. The foot salve seemed most necessary since the majority of Peruvians living in the countryside wore year-round sandals made from recycled tires. I had observed some feet that had ceased to even look like feet, so blackened and cracked that they appeared to have actually become tire tread.

As true countryside charlatans, each peddler shouted long-winded monologues. The first few minutes of each pitch were fascinating but then quickly became highly irritating. The next to board was a teenage boy who scraped the ridged edge of two shells together in the most unbearably grating tempo. He shouted a song, spouting spittle, and every so often added a few off-tuned blows on a flute hanging from his neck.

Appalled at how horrible his singing was, I sat up on my knees and looked around, wondering if any of the other passengers were as deeply bothered as I was about being held hostage to his music. One of the university students from the front row turned back to watch the boy and rolled his eyes comically at me, shaking his head in astonishment.

"Hey, I'm Dexter!" he shouted over the musical ruckus in a thick British accent.

"That little fucker really sucks!" he said, bellowing over the heads of the dozen non-English-speaking passengers between us.

Laughing out loud, I sunk back in the stinky, crumb-covered seat. I couldn't help but think about how Dexter stood out in Peru with his dark chocolate skin and immaculate smile, bright red sweatshirt, expensive jeans, and perfect white sneakers. At least I wasn't the only one who was disturbed by the entertainment. Then I remembered my recent discovery that most Peruvians seemed to have a remarkably high tolerance for boredom and irritation, unlike myself, and obviously unlike Dexter too.

A man with coal-black hair meticulously greased to one side opened the partition from the front of the bus. I guessed he was the second-shift driver who would soon be taking over for the sort-of married man currently at the wheel. He began checking the tickets of each passenger and by the time he reached me, I already had an excuse ready. I fluttered my eyelashes, then begged and pleaded, but he firmly directed me back to seat 12B.

My nostrils filled with the stink emanating from that row as I threw my bag over the seat, nearly flattening a boy sitting silently in the aisle seat. I introduced myself and dug in my bag for treats. Carlitos was about ten and gladly accepted a Spider-Man sticker and a piece of gum, which he cradled in his lap as if not sure what to do with them. The urine scent was sourly abundant, but I became momentarily distracted by the sound of a movie crackling through the speakers.

Good timing, I thought.

Staring at the black screen, I waited eagerly. Would it be a classic Peruvian film? Or perhaps a good English movie with Spanish subtitles? There were a lot of fantastic films Spain had produced that would be great for a bus ride.

I recalled the torturously never-ending bus ride I'd taken to Madrid after walking five hundred miles on the Camino de Santiago. The movie medley was back-to-back Steven Segal flicks, complete with voice-overs.

It was my first glimpse of television after full nature immersion for a month, and it was the worst possible return to society I could have imagined. But, contrarily on the Peruvian bus, all I wanted was to be amused for the next few hours, no matter how awful the movie was.

I stared expectantly at the blank black square mounted on the front partition. The volume was full blast, but there was no picture. I soon figured out the movie was something like *Saving Private Ryan*, with machine guns, bombs, painful screams, and total mayhem. It echoed through the bus as if an invisible war were actually taking place inside the confines of the vehicle.

By this point, I wasn't surprised that the other docile passengers were undisturbed, but I knew who would be. I peered over the seats to see Dexter's reaction. Much to my amusement, he was already knocking on the wall partition that solidly separated the passengers from the drivers. This blockade not only separated us from them, it also prevented forward viewing, which was incredibly unsettling.

Nice, Dex, I thought.

A small panel slid open and the non-Spanish-speaking Dexter mimed to the person on the other side. I gave Dexter double thumbs-up and settled back in my seat, ready for the action. Five minutes went by, then ten. Nothing.

We stopped at a town where I could see vendors on the sidewalk with packaged snacks and drinks. I turned to my seatmate. "Hey, Carlitos, I'm going to get a snack, you want something? I hope they have plantain chips, they're my favorite!"

"No, señorita," he said with surprising firmness, "you cannot get off the bus."

"¿Por qué, Carlitos?"

"You will not get back on."

Minding Carlitos's warning, I stayed on the bus, pulled out my meager supply of munchies, and shared them with him, wondering what his mom had brought to keep him busy for the long ride. Soon enough it was evident that he had nothing but a hangnail to play with. My iPod shielded me from the war movie as the soundtrack continued to blast. Carlitos, seemingly unperturbed by the intense audio, stared contentedly at his Spider-Man sticker.

The bus filled up fast and soon adults sat on each other's laps. The driver didn't come to a full stop for indigenous people, so women ran breathlessly alongside the bus, their children clasped to their hips, their black braids airborne. The bus door slammed open and they leapt onto the step and hung on for dear life.

Every hour or so, the second driver abruptly slid open the partition and shouted at the passengers, as if he were exerting some illustrious power over those beneath him on the social totem pole. It was hard to pinpoint exactly what he was so furious about, but it seemed to have undertones of disdain for those indigenous passengers who were culturally inferior. It was just my observation, but no matter the reason, I was not thrilled to have such an aggressive and irate person responsible for our safe delivery to Arequipa.

After six non-stop hours, only pausing for gas once, the driver had yet to be replaced. My stomach condition was quickly deteriorating thanks to the building stress of the journey, and I feared I might have to test out the restroom.

* * *

Being an official member of the frequent pee-pee club, I am destined to spend time with some of the most undesirable toilets known to man. Because of this, I carry a handy GoGirl, a female urination device, which actually allows a girl to pee while standing up. Just hold up the bright pink rubber contraption and pee comfortably like a man! The catchy advertisement says, "It's neat. It's discreet!" What they neglect to mention is that peeing down your pants is probable if you don't suction it tightly, which I sadly discovered on a camping trip during which I had only brought one pair of trousers.

With a cramping stomach and tissues in hand, I maneuvered around the obstacles in the aisle. The moment I touched the metal doorknob, blistering heat sizzled my fingertips. Yanking my hand back with a little squeal, I looked around, stunned. An ancient Indian lady caught my eye and slightly shook her head, smiling sympathetically.

Padding the doorknob, I successfully opened the door, only to be met with a wave of the authentic fragrance—eau de toilette. My stomach churned, and I crossed my arm across my face to protect my mouth and nose. Peeing through a tennis-ball-sized hole that opened directly onto the highway was going to be impossible. Clearly, others had attempted it and also missed.

I cautiously straddled the hole, watching the highway race by below, but the driver took a curve at high speed. I flew to one side, slamming against the wall.

I bellowed out an inhuman howl upon feeling the scorching heat from the nearby engine. I burned both palms and my forearm and peed all over my shoes. To top it off, in order to not touch the walls the next time the bus accelerated, I crouched to my knees—and landed right in the muckity-muck. Upon exiting the torture latrine, the tiny, old woman winked at me as if she knew some piddle secret I was not privy to yet.

Defeated and soiled, I returned to my seat. I was determined to recall my mother's words of wisdom about Kegel exercises for those with a weakened pelvic floor. Mom had the same problem of incontinence and once declared, "Ann, you have a naughty bladder!" as if it were a disobedient child. "It has learned how to control you. You must take back the reins."

She'd then described a few exercises for contracting and relaxing the pelvic muscles that would strengthen the region. She completed the lesson by showing me awkward drawings in a Kegel book. At the time, I rolled my eyes, convinced it wouldn't work.

Sitting next to little Carlitos, I strained to remember her advice as I Kegeled with the utmost determination. I couldn't seem to get my face to stop tensing with each cycle of contracting, which made me wonder what Carlitos thought I was doing.

Jerking to a sudden halt, the bus stopped in the middle of the highway. Without the option to see out the front windshield, passengers never knew what was coming. Pulling down the dirt-caked window, I craned my head to look forward. Rocks, glass, and cement chunks covered the road. Transportation-strike extremists, who had wanted the strike to last forty-eight hours instead of the predetermined twenty-four hours, were now punishing all those who were driving during that time. All the buses and trucks were at a standstill and various drivers stood in small huddles.

Our green-toothed driver stomped up and down the highway, furiously kicking rocks. Piling off our bus, every single male passenger began peeing on the highway. There was no discretionary stepping behind a bush or nonchalantly next to a rock. It was an all-out peeing free-for-all. The old fellow from seat 10A peed right on the bus tire.

I searched out Dexter and his travel companion Silvia, and we amusedly observed the indigenous women lift up their layered skirts and squat like they were laying eggs on the highway. None seemed too concerned with toilet paper since they could simply wipe with the hem of their skirt.

"I bet they don't wear underwear," said Dexter.

"Oh my God, do you think they pee directly on the seats too?" asked Silvia.

My stomach turned and I understood perhaps why the bus reeked so badly of urine. Unable to face the bus's death latrine again, I too found a spot on the highway to lay my own egg.

After an hour, the roadblocks were moved and we were on our way. A barren expanse of open landscape filled the next few hours, when on the horizon appeared a primitive village with perhaps a few hundred inhabitants. Food vendors ran up to the windows and stood on buckets to sell random food items. Corn on the cob, dry bread discs, and bright red corn juice in dirty plastic bags were offered. There was no way I was going to drink what looked like blood in a baggie, plus I was restricting my liquid consumption. A disheveled woman stared at me eagerly through the dirty window, trying to sell me a grisly skewer of unidentifiable meat.

Suddenly, I caught a glimpse of the distinctive red sweatshirt and swanky white shoes strolling behind her on the dirt path. The locals gawked, moving to the side to let Dexter pass through. He approached a man who could have been anywhere from thirty to one hundred years old. The vendor had a wood crate on wheels with identifiable snacks. Dexter pointed to a pack of Oreos. I held my breath nervously for the risk he had naively taken by getting off, but secretly hoped he would buy a few packs to share.

Without warning, the driver gassed it, pulling away from the stop. Dexter was oblivious, still contemplating the cookie assortment. As if in slow motion, he turned and his contented expression abruptly transformed. His lips formed a long, drawn out *Noooooooooo!* The whites of his wide eyes were visible through the dust kicking up behind the bus. Silvia was immediately up and pounding on the partition.

"Stop the bus! Stop the bus!" she shrieked hysterically in English.

I made my way up to the front while keeping an eye on Dexter, who was now chasing after us, Oreos in hand.

"¡Señor, señor, por favor pare el bus!" I pleaded through the closed partition.

He slid the panel over, revealing his wild eyes and thick, green goo oozing from his lips. He waved his fist and shouted in Spanish, "Idiot shouldn't have gotten off!" and kept on driving.

Dexter pumped his arms, racing to catch up. Soon he was alongside the windows with a crazed, desperate expression. I appealed to the driver with a sweet smile and a calm voice.

"Ay, mi corazón, how about you just slow down a bit, mi amor, let him jump on." I could see a momentary flicker of possibility in the driver's eyes of what this favor might get him. "Be a sweetheart and open the door, please."

The glass doors folded open and, with the bus still in motion, Dexter jumped in, gasping for breath and covered in a fine layer of dirt. I wondered what he would have done if he were left in the middle of nowhere, unable to speak a lick of Spanish, with only enough money for cookies.

"Dude, what were you thinking?" I asked.

Ignoring my question, he wiped the dust off his spiffy shoes and declared, "I'm gonna give that driver an ear-bashing when we get to Arequipa!"

We soon arrived at another village that was a bit bigger than the last, and it seemed the driver received news that there was another strike down the highway. He decided to take his own route. The driver had not changed after nine hours, and it was clear that the green-toothed monster was on a dangerous mission to get to

Arequipa. Did he get paid more if he arrived quicker? Had he tied up the other driver so he'd get paid the full price for the journey? Did he have a date? Was he in a crazed coca-leaf frenzy?

There was no GPS to guide him, so he flung the doors open and shouted at local villagers who were probably more accustomed to directing sheep than a huge bus. The detour began as the bus forced its way through the tiny streets, scraping the adobe walls. Skeletal dogs barked and children pointed at the over-sized vehicle attempting to maneuver down streets designed for carts and stock animals. We worked our way through the labyrinth of narrow alleys, which was visually entertaining from an upper bus-window view. My amusement was curbed the moment we got to the edge of town and I saw the bleak, roadless wasteland that lay ahead.

It was then that the off-roading adventure began. The bus driver acted as if he were by himself in a Chevy 4x4. This went on for the next two hours, during which he not only drove on a rocky dirt path populated by bushes, ditches, and ravines, but also drove at remarkable speeds. Everyone in the bus was thrown in every direction.

Passengers shouted in protest, others threw up, and some hunkered down below the seats and moaned. Since the driver was not responding to the desperate pleas to slow the bus, one man boldly hung out the window to get the driver's attention in the side view mirror. Abruptly, the driver stopped the bus, whipped the partition back and barked, "If anyone has a better fucking idea how to drive this bus, then come on up and try!"

By this point, I was ready to volunteer since it felt like death was on the horizon for all.

Once we passed the strike, the bus jumped back on the paved highway just as night encroached. The driver proceeded to race like a bat out of hell, passing cars and other buses on curvy mountainous roads. I sunk down in my seat to keep from obsessively watching out the side window. Riddled with sickening anxiety, I was sure we'd soon meet our demise as our bus rocketed toward the bright lights of oncoming trucks.

After thirteen hours of mayhem, the driver abruptly pulled the bus off to the side of a sheer cliff and turned off the engine. The passengers sat restlessly in the pitch black as traffic dangerously whizzed by on the dark, winding road. I moved up to sit with Dexter and Silvia. The driver finally confessed that he'd run out of gas and the battery was dead. He would not let us off the bus as we sat on a precarious precipice in the dark, without hazard lights.

Dreadfully famished and shrouded in fear, I felt imprisoned in an epic nightmare. I glared out the window at the driver who stomped the ground and shouted into his cell phone. Fed up, a heavy-set man with a cowboy hat stormed down the aisle, kicked the door out, and started swinging his meaty fists at the driver. All the passengers excitedly pulled the windows open and watched them go at it.

"Kick his ass, cowboy!" Dexter shouted.

Thinking he was going to join the fight, we watched the old man in seat 10A get off the bus, pull down his pants, and take a shit right next to the brawling men. Without wiping, he pulled his pants right back up and returned to the bus. With his first step back through the door, he brought with him a rancid smell powerful enough to stop a grizzly bear.

Dexter cringed. "What the fuck, Grandpop?"

Delirious laughter consumed me after his remark and catching my breath became impossible since each inhale brought with it excrement fumes.

Three hours later, another bus came to transport us the rest of the way to Arequipa. Dexter never did give the driver an ear-bashing, but I was sure we all felt he could have used one. As we exited the bus, I asked Dexter what he would have done if he had been left in that isolated village.

"Don't know, sweets, and I am glad I didn't have to find out," he said with an unconcerned wave of his hand. "And, hey, I think at least I owe you some Oreos for saving my ass."

My stomach rumbled in anticipation as I gratefully tucked the prize in my coat pocket, heaved on my backpack, and pulled out a map to locate the town center. After the eighteen-hour odyssey and it being now close to midnight, I was about to navigate the town to find a place to sleep.

As I started to walk away, I heard a slithery voice call after me. There, in the dim glow of the bus station, was the green-toothed, kinda-married bus driver waiting for me. Was I the date he was in such a hurry for? He started to walk in my direction.

Desperate, I waved down one of the dozens of tin-can taxicabs and flung my pack in, shouting, "¡Al centro, señor, y rápido!" To the town center, and quickly!

Indigenous women load the bus with their goods.

37

CHICHANI THE GREAT

Arequipa is known as La Cuidad Blanca, the White City, since the buildings are constructed out of white volcanic rock called *sillar*. Arequipa also has accessibility to a multitude of distinctive adventures, such as the Colca Canyon tour, white-water rafting, mountain biking, the Misti volcano excursion, or a chance to scale up Chichani volcano—supposedly one of the easiest 19,700-foot mountains in the world to climb.

Taking into account that I was still recovering from being deathly ill, I decided on the Misti volcano overnight excursion, which would be a bit challenging but provided unparalleled views of some of the most rugged landscape in Peru. I settled on a price, which was first eighty dollars, then sixty—not including equipment—and finally sixty-five for everything, but it was to be kept a "secret price." That night there was a knock on my hostel room door from a representative of the outfitter company.

"Sorry, we are not doing the Misti trip tomorrow, so you will do the Chichani expedition instead. Same price. No problem."

"Isn't that trip much more difficult?"

"Oh no, señorita, it's easy. No problem. It's like a stroll."

"Well, OK," I said hesitantly.

"You'll be fine, señorita. It'll be fun."

Later that night, I looked up Chichani in my guidebook and read that it was close to 20,000 feet, which at the time meant absolutely nothing to me. I had never hiked at that altitude before, and I had no frame of reference for what that number actually translated to in terms of physical suffering.

* * *

At eight in the morning a 4x4 Land Cruiser picked me up in front of my hostel and then sped off to the next stop to collect a trio of hikers in their early twenties hailing from Quebec: Pierre, who looked like an Abercrombie and Fitch model, Veronica, his girl-friend, and Quentin, their gangly, redheaded pal. We departed the well-kept central tourist area around the Plaza de Armas and headed out through the uproar of unregulated traffic, black exhaust puffs, and unre-strained horn-honking.

The SUV stopped at a street corner where a woman stood with a massive nylon bag of extra gear. We piled out and tried on trekking boots made for extreme expeditions. Clearly, they had been worn by countless other trekkers, and I was none too thrilled about wearing a stiff boot that didn't fit quite right. My repaired Achilles was permanently distended, causing shoes not sized correctly to agonizingly rub on the tendon.

So I demanded to use my own comfy hiking boots, but the woman was vehement. I was no longer sure that this wasn't going to be a high-risk expedition. Why did I specifically need alpine mountaineer boots?

"Yours are not waterproof. You will wear these," the woman said definitively.

We were each given pants, a fleece jacket, and a hat. Mine ended up being an orange clown cap with dingleberry balls hanging off the tips, which I put over my own beanie. I told the woman I had my own and didn't need one, but she responded with, "You'll be sorry." The pants she gave me were two sizes too small and bright turquoise. The waist only reached the V of my womanhood and was impossible to zip up, completely inhibiting movement. "No importa," she said, brushing off my concern.

I stuffed all these essential items in my pack along with the five liters of water we were each required to carry. The water alone weighed over ten pounds. Crazy Kite made my backpack a tight fit. She was already poking her head out the top. I had envisioned myself skipping along the volcano top overlooking the 360-degree view of the sweeping terrain, the bright Peruvian sun on my face, and my rainbow kite dancing in the wind. My reverie was broken as the lady thrust an ice axe in my hand and a pair of archaic crampons.

On the way out of the town, the driver of the Land Cruiser told us that batteries were not included in the price for equipment, so we had to buy them separately for the headlamp. Entering the small, run-down market, I couldn't help but roll my eyes when he high-fived his buddy behind the counter.

Quentin confided that he had just flown into Cuzco the previous day and had directly caught a flight to Arequipa. His friends, Pierre and Veronica, had already been in Peru for over a month and he was joining them for the last leg of the trip.

"You didn't even have a chance to adapt to Cuzco, and that's over eleven thousand feet," I said with concern. "Most people take a few days just to acclimatize there. Seriously, what are you doing, Quentin? You're gonna get brain damage or something."

He shrugged his shoulders. "Don't worry about me, I'll be just fine."

The views from the Land Cruiser windows were amazing once we got above the dingy brown air hovering over the city. The driver pointed to the distance at the slightly lower of the two peaks and said it was Misti volcano, which was where I was supposed to be. Romel, our actual guide, added nothing to the conversations since he was busy pecking away at his cell phone.

The two-and-a-half-hour off-road journey began with a stomach-turning, head-jarring, seat-beltless, rollercoaster ride up to the base of the volcano. Quentin looked oddly pink—one of the many colors he would rainbow into over the next thirty-six hours. I had taken the altitude sickness pills the night before and one in the morning to prepare for the ascent. I could already feel side effects, including frequent urination and tingling body sensations. It felt as if I were covered in ants, especially my lips and fingertips. My stomach churned, and my body prickled as my nervous excitement grew with my ever-expanding bladder.

The only wildlife we saw on the drive up was a small herd of guanaco that were feeding along the road. The driver told us they were cousins of the llama. They had long necks and short fur; their backs and sides were a warm shade of cinnamon and their undersides were cream-colored. Two dozen big brown eyes fixed on us. Even those that faced away curved their long necks back to see what we'd do next. I was hoping they would watch us turn the truck around and go back to Arequipa.

We continued to drive into the folds of the mountain until we reached our drop-off point. The road instantly narrowed into a trail, and it was clear that from here, we walked. My neck cricked as I regarded the looming monstrous mountain capped with snow and whistling wind.

Romel disappeared behind a large boulder and returned dragging a gigantic canvas sack from a secretly stashed location. "Here's the rest of the gear and supplies. We must carry it up to base camp." He instructed me to translate for the others.

With a blank stare and mouth ajar, I growled at my fully loaded backpack, already stuffed with gear and heavy with water. Nevertheless, I had to reorganize and add in food, dishes, and a rolled-up mat that strapped to the back. The down sleeping bag and large dented metal pot wouldn't fit, so I had to carry them in my hands.

Romel told me I would be sharing a tent with Quentin and, thankfully, he offered to carry it up.

The sky was blue and clear and the sun beat down, but it didn't provide much warmth. My legs quivered as I yanked on my pack. Sighing deeply with a titanic, sickening knot in my stomach, I looked up to the incline of dirt, sand, and rock divided by zigzagging switchbacks.

"Hey, guys, it's only a mile to base camp," Romel said, nudging us to get started.

"Yeah, but it's over a thousand-foot gain to get there," added Quentin.

"And that looks like deep sand," said Veronica.

The dread weighed heavier in my gut than the backpack did on my shoulders. This was not what I had signed up for.

Pierre was far from complaining as he eyed the mountain with anticipation and began marching up. I, on the other hand, nearly puked after fifteen minutes, taking big gulps of air, gasping desperately for oxygen. I kept hunching over with all the weight tabled on my back while setting down the cumbersome items in my hands. At one point, the pot began sliding and skipping down the hill; luckily, Quentin was further behind and was able to snatch it up. I felt the same as the pot and wanted to slide my butt back down the hill—never to return to the mountain of doom.

To get through it, I switched to machine mode, as I had learned to do on the long walk across Spain. My Achilles was already stiffening up, which reduced the ability of the left foot to push off. Digging deep, I braved my way to base camp where the icy gale whipped over the ledge and stirred up suffocating volcanic dust that forced its way into every facial orifice.

Quentin and I struggled to set up the tent, weathering the extreme wind, dust, and his intermittent vomiting. I wasn't too thrilled to be stuffed into a tiny tent with someone so vomitous, but at least it might be warmer together since the temperature had dropped dramatically. Inside the cooking tent, Romel prepared soup and quinoa mush with coca tea and dirt seasoning.

We sat huddled together, attempting to keep warm. Although the adventure company had claimed the guides were bilingual, I had a feeling that Romel much preferred to speak his mother tongue and rely on me to translate all conversations. Romel insisted we practice putting on our antiquated crampons for the ice and snow the next day. I recalled a documentary on the English mountaineer George Mallory, who died on his ascent to Everest in the 1920s. He had worn boots with nails sticking out of the bottom. Even though he died, his shoes actually seemed safer than the strappy, rusted contraptions in my hand. Then Romel dropped the bomb.

"I'll wake you all up at 1:30 a.m. to start the ascent. We'll have a hearty breakfast, then trek up for about seven hours. You'll have to take your crampons on and off about eight times. So prepare now because it will be very cold and you will need to take off your gloves to do it. Then it will just be three hours to come down."

The others looked at me to translate, but I couldn't swallow the dry bread in my mouth. *Did I hear him right?*

No one had said anything about trekking at night, nor did anyone say it would be for ten hours! I felt deceived, horrified, and consumed with fear. After I translated, Quentin turned a distinctive green and threw up before he could get two steps away from us.

"You'd better go to bed now," Romel said, looking at his watch.

"It's only six!" I rebuked.

"Yes, Ana, but we'll get up early. Plus, you probably won't be able to sleep well because of the altitude."

"Well, yeah, and because it's only six o'clock!" I said, sounding like a bratty five-year-old.

Pierre dug in his coat pocket and pulled out a flask.

"Here, take a swig of this, it'll keep you warm and help you sleep."

He took a long drag, smacked his lips, exhaled, and then handed it to Veronica. It went to Romel and then Quentin, who passed it up. Warming up from the inside out seemed like the perfect solution. No one would know. But I would, and so would the Shit Birds, who certainly knew how to fly at high altitudes. When it got to me, I wanted to grab the bottle, run out of the tent, and hurl it off the edge of the cliff. This was one of the moments when I really despised being alcoholic. Instead, I smiled politely and passed it back to Pierre.

* * *

It became crucial that I gather my wits and find some sort of master bravery to face the task ahead. Sitting cross-legged on a colossal boulder at the edge of a cliff, I meditated on the view that spanned over the terraced Inca lands. Platform clouds listlessly floated at eye level.

Ego and common sense were in the throes of a furious battle. Deep down, I knew I was not capable physically or mentally to reach the volcano lip, but I had come this far. So I might as well force myself to suffer through the great challenge. Then I could bask in the intensely sweet sensation of overcoming an impossible feat while literally standing on the mountaintop.

As I visualized the glory, icy winds snuck in through every crevice, making me shiver all the way to the core. I thought of Sir Edmund Hillary, the man confirmed as one of the first climbers to successfully reach Everest's summit—and stay alive. He was quoted as saying, "It is not the mountain we conquer, it is ourselves. If you can overcome your fear, you are frequently able to extend yourself far beyond what you normally regard as your ability." Suddenly, with a wave of optimism, I convinced myself. *C'mon. Let's climb this bitch!*

Having to relieve myself yet again, I reluctantly pulled down my pants, hopefully for the last time that evening, and mooned the moon. Inside the flimsy tent, I layered up in my long johns, trekking pants, petite turquoise pants, two smart wool socks, tank top, T-shirt, long-sleeved shirt, North Face fleece, Peruvian fleece, North Face down coat, gloves, beanie, and the goofy clown cap they gave me. Still, I shivered uncontrollably.

The wind viciously whipped the broken tent door flap, bringing in gusts of dust and arctic chill.

Quentin lay on his side moaning and told me to leave it as I repeatedly attempted to rezip it with frosty fingers. Finally, I was able to channel my clever inner MacGyver and tied it shut with my hair bands. Since it was impossible to sleep, I listened to books on my iPod for a few hours, then reviewed the strapping tie system for the crampons over and over in my head. Interrupting my thoughts were the jerky movements of poor Quentin throwing up in the plastic bag positioned by his head.

I painfully realized that I had to go to the bathroom *again*. I nearly brought down the tent trying to get out of the jerry-rigged door. As I stumbled between the boulders to take care of business, I gazed up to the sky and nearly fell back into the dirt. The Milky Way was a spattering of twinkles, with bright planetary buttons and shooting stars pulling through the sky like diamond zippers. We were on the north side of the mountain, and, looking down the slope, the Big Dipper was upside down and stretched across most of the visible horizon. Hyperventilating from the lack of oxygen and the shock of the incomprehensible magnificence of the universe, I was unable to truly catch my breath again.

At 1:30 a.m., Romel threw stones at our tent as the wake-up call. We silently ate a "hearty" breakfast of coca tea and rock-hard biscuits. Quentin threw up after one sip of tea and didn't eat a thing more. We put on lighter packs—including crampons, axes, snacks, and water—and headed out under the star-studded sky. After what seemed like a long hour of a brutal incline, I requested a short break since I could not catch my breath.

"Ana! It has only been *ten* minutes. We'll never make it if we stop now!"

"Seriously? Only ten minutes?"

I knew I was in trouble. Abercrombie model Pierre trekked ahead like a champ, while Veronica, Quentin, and I struggled behind. My brain whirled, taunting me incessantly. *What if my other Achilles snaps? What if this makes me sick again? What ever happened to volunteering? Has my addiction cunningly manifested itself into the endorphin rush that comes through dangerous pursuits?*

I felt defeated, but my egoist, athletic warrior and the craving for adrenaline-through-risk pushed me to continue. Trudging on with my back bowed, I shined the headlamp on my next careful step. Grimacing in agony, I could feel a portion of my Achilles scar being rubbed raw by the tight boots.

When we reached the snow, I pulled out the crampons quickly, replaying in my mind the strapping system. Unfortunately, I proceeded to put them on upside down, with the spikes going into my shoes instead of the snow. So much for mental preparation! My brain had no functional clarity at that altitude. The gloveless exposure to the cold left me with finger pops.

I noticed Veronica quietly crying, as she was also unsuccessful in putting on her ice-cleats. Romel instructed us to step hard in order to pierce the packed snow, especially when we forged the cliff on the ice wall. *The what?* When we got there, I made the mistake of shining my funnel of forehead-light below, only to see a vertical sheet of ice.

I started a mantra. *Breathe in. Left (icy crunch). Right (icy crunch). Axe (snowy squeak). Exhale.* It worked for a while, but soon fear seeped through my body. I was feeling nervous and clumsy when suddenly my right spiked shoe got caught on a loopy knot, causing me to trip and fall forward. Instinctively, I heaved the ice axe into the solid snow, which barely held me onto the edge. Quentin pulled me back to the narrow trail as a long moan wailed from the depths of my being.

Frozen tear crystals stuck to my face. What if I had fallen all the way down into that bottomless crevice? I could have been left for dead, only to be found millennia later like the famous Juanita mummy. She'd been discovered after the Peruvian volcanic eruption melted the ice tomb where the little twelve-year-old girl was frozen. I could imagine the year 3000 when Chichani would spew lava again, uncovering the thirty-three-year-old American girl frozen in time. *Come see the Anita exhibit, ice maiden found intact from the year 2009!*

"This is so fucking dangerous!" I shouted hysterically. "We have no business doing this!"

Attempting to provide myself a mini-dose of comfort, I pulled out my ration of Oreos, but after one bite realized they had transformed into glacially petrified rocks. It was too late, I already had a chunk in my mouth, but the worse was yet to come. While attempting to take a sip of water to wash it down, I discovered the liquid was frozen solid. Desperately thirsty and my mouth encrusted with dry cookie, I had reached the edge of my capacity to persevere. Staring out at the expansive universe, I sent out a desperate prayer for Pachamama to guide me.

Then I remembered the Andean cross the wise grandmother, Saywa, had given me back in Cuzco. It hung around my neck somewhere beneath the multitude of layered clothing. Untying it from my neck, I pushed the thick stone cross inside my glove to rest directly in my palm. I repeated my new mantra—*Pa-cha-ma-ma, Pa-cha-ma-ma*—while gasping for breath through a thundering headache.

Transforming into a zombie, I carefully stomped my feet with every step, as if clawing the ice on the narrow trail. Bizarre contemplations wiggled through my mind like tadpoles caught in the mud. *I wonder if I'm close to the heart of Pachamama*, I thought curiously. *Nah*, responded another voice in my head, *more like climbing her boob.*

Peculiar mental dialogue continued as we pushed on for two more frightful hours, at times having to free-climb slick ice rocks on the edge of an abyss.

"Just four more hours up to reach over nineteen thousand feet," encouraged Romel, "but at this pace it's going to take longer than that. ¡Vámanos, chicos!"

Squeezing the chakana in my hand, I suddenly had a miraculous revelation. It was actually weakness for me to continue, and it would take a great quantity of courage and strength to speak up and request *to go back*. This type of suggestion would go against all my self-will and pride. Historically, *I* would never be the one to give up, but maybe I needed to now.

I quickly analyzed the scenario. Veronica was certainly on board with going back. She cried, shivered, and was upset at disappointing her boyfriend. Quentin was a barfy mess and had also fallen and twisted his knee. Pierre, a robust twenty-year-old buck, was the only one powering through like a true mountaineer. No one was willing to be the one to say it, but they were all feeling the same—I was sure of it. So I swallowed my pride and expressed myself with a purity that radiated out of me.

"I have to be honest with all of you," I said. "This is not what I signed up for, and I feel very unsafe and scared. I would hope you can all speak your truth about where you are with this journey. I vote to turn around."

Pierre immediately snapped, "Romel has a sleeping bag. We can tuck you in the cliff until we get back."

Veronica started sobbing that she wanted to go back too, and Quentin nodded in agreement. Pierre sighed in defeat, and we turned around. Going down, I was elated with a renewed burst of energy. I promised Crazy Kite that she'd get to spread her wings on a different site since there was not going to be any volcano flying on this day. However, at one of our rest stops my euphoria quickly drained upon realizing that my camera had frozen solid. It was only later that I discovered that the mountain not only stole my sanity but also nearly all the pictures taken over the previous few weeks. *Damn you, Chichani!*

The feeling of euphoria from actually taking care of myself in a very precarious situation was more of a deeply satisfying sensation than summiting a mountaintop. I had reached the pinnacle of self-preservation on that day and learned that it was not necessary to reach the apex of physical suffering to attain illustrious triumph.

The sun had just risen as we reached base camp. I climbed onto the rock where I had sat the previous evening and let the dazzling rays of sunlight shoot through me like fire-tipped arrows. I outstretched my arms, offering my humble thanks to Pachamama for keeping me alive and providing me the courage to summit my own mountaintop.

An unforgettable moment captured by Quentin upon our return to base camp.

38

THE COLCA CANYON

R emaining in the charming, white-walled town of Arequipa was an easy choice. The sun was plentiful and the cost of living and adventuring was dirt cheap. Five dollars a day could get me a private hostel room, and a meal was about the same. I had no intention of leaving until I had taken advantage of every unique experience the town had to offer. Helen Keller once said, "Life is either a daring adventure or nothing." At the counter of the expedition company, I stared hungrily at the menu of extreme activities that covered the wall, floor to ceiling. I channeled my inner Helen and declared, "I choose daring adventure!"

It was almost like drinking; once I had one sip, I wanted more. Also like the hazards of excess alcohol consumption, I quickly forgot the consequences of my previous experience. It was like the mind tucked away any negative memories and cleaned the slate to blindly make the same mistake again.

Less than twenty-four hours after recovering from the Chichani volcano semi-ascent, I was standing in the early morning mist waiting to be picked up for the four-day Colca Canyon trek. The canyon was promoted as being the deepest in the world, even said to be over twice as deep as the Grand Canyon. It was also home to the Andean condor, which I was told could be seen soaring gracefully, riding thermals near the canyon walls.

The twelve-passenger minibus pulled to the curb, and I eagerly jumped in with my bulging backpack slung over one shoulder. I noticed that most passengers were overweight, mature adults who carried day bags. They were clearly not planning on trekking down the deepest canyon in the world for four days.

Certain that I was on the wrong bus, I waved my hands, trying to get the tour guide's attention. Brushing me off with a flip of his hand, he positioned himself in the swivel chair facing the passengers.

"I am Juan, your tour guide for this trip," he announced through a microphone pressed to his chin. "Arequipa is a region blessed with spectacular nature as it is crossed by the Andes mountain range dividing an extensive coastline and an area full of Andean valleys, canyons, volcanoes, and snowy mountains."

"Perdón, Juan," I interrupted, standing up from the last row of seats, "is this bus going to the Colca Canyon?"

Taking a deep breath in through his nose, he exhaled noisily through the microphone. "Please sit down, ma'am."

Like a scolded child, I sat back down, figuring he would answer my question. Instead, he just continued on with his lecture in strongly accented English.

"To preserve its varied ecosystems and unique biodiversity, there have been many nature reserves created in Arequipa, some of which contain species that are in a state of extinction."

I turned to the older gentleman to my left wearing all khaki and a camera slung around his neck. "Excuse me, sir, do you know where this bus is going?"

"As far as I know, it's going to Chivay."

"Chivay? Not the Colca Canyon?"

"Not sure, my dear, maybe ask our guide."

"Yeah, I tried that already."

Digging my fingernails into the palms of my hands, I glared at Juan as he described in detail the Salinas National Preserve.

"Among the most representative of the reserve are the viscacha, fox, condor, and the Andean flamingo. Scientists have determined the existence of 169 animal species, of which three are mammals, including two domestic forms of South American camelids, 138 species of birds, three reptiles, four amphibians, and three species of fish."

I could feel the bubbling of rage heating up in my belly and I wanted to shout out, "Was that *camelid,* you said? Wow. Juan, that's *really* fascinating. But I need to know if I'm on the right bus!"

My vicious head was getting the best of me. With a scowl, I headed toward the front of the bus. Standing directly in front of him, I obstructed his view from the hostages of his Peruvian factoid sermon.

"Juan," I said in the fiercest Spanish I could muster up, "I need to know *right now* if this bus is going to Colca Canyon—or not."

He put his palm a few inches from my chest. "Don't worry," he said sarcastically, "it's all worked out."

"What's that mean?" I said through clenched teeth.

"Go sit down, ma'am."

Hot, angry tears streaked my face as I stormed back to my seat. It felt like bile had surfaced from my stomach and surely a few blood vessels had popped in my eyes. After feeling deceived by the trekking company with Chichani, and now with this situation, I had little patience for any further carelessness with my personal safety. Feeling completely powerless, I stared out the window as a rainy snow began to fall. Juan droned on over the loudspeaker.

Finally, the bus pulled through a large archway with Chivay written in stone across the top. The rains had done serious damage to the town, leaving the streets flooded. We came to a stop in front of a series of rustic cottages.

Hey, all right, this looks nice, I thought as my spirits dared to lift.

Juan began calling out the names of passengers who would be staying at the enchanting guesthouses. With my pack balanced on my lap, I sat on the edge of my seat, waiting to hear my name. Everyone filed off the bus, even Juan. He had called everyone's name, except mine. With a patronizing grin, Juan waved at me through the rain-streaked window. Exhaling like a bull, I screamed out my preferred Spanish expletive, "Cabrón!"

The bus driver turned back to me.";Habla usted español, no?"

"Sí."

"I will take you to *your* hotel now," he continued in Spanish.

"What's going on, señor? Why am I not with the others at that nice hotel? And why is Juan such an hijo de puta!?"

"No sé, señorita," he said, laughing. "The touring company that organized your trip has booked a different hotel for you," he said as he pulled up to a small door with the hotel sign hanging sideways off half the hinges.

Soaked by the rain, I stood in the doorway of the bus wanting desperately to plead with the driver not to leave me there.

"Don't worry, señorita," he said gently, "tomorrow you will go to Colca Canyon."

* * *

An expressionless woman with a large mole on her cheek showed me to my dark and dingy room. Inside the room seemed colder than outside, and a large, grizzly bloodstain covered the top half of the bedspread. *Are you kidding me?* Trying to make light of it, I asked the woman at the front desk if someone had been murdered in my room. She just glared. I demanded a new bedspread and any type of heating device. She charged me five dollars for the heater, which was probably the same price as the room.

With my back concaved into the bowing mattress, I took a moment to consider Juan and his treatment of me. These days I rarely caused such a reaction from people. I kept my side of the street clean and, for the most part, was honest, well-mannered, and kind. What could I have done to cause him to treat me so poorly? My stomach was in knots and my brain refused to stop analyzing every conversation I'd had with him. I fantasized about putting him in a headlock and whacking his head with his precious microphone.

Wearing every scrap of clothing I'd brought, I curled up in a fetal ball near the weak ray of warmth emanating from the heater and pleaded for sleep to take me. After a restless night, I was horrified to awaken to the pillowcase on the floor and my face directly on the filth-stained pillow.

Reboarding the bus, I attempted to confront Juan again about my trekking tour. I'd like to think I approached him calmly and appropriately, but I guess he didn't agree since he commanded, "Cálmese," relax yourself, as if I were a hysterical woman—which I most certainly was not.

"You know what, Juan? You are *the* most rude and unhelpful guide. As soon as I return to Arequipa, I will be reporting your conduct to your company. You'd better tell me right now what the plan is, or I will do everything in my power to have you fired!"

I sounded like a stereotypical disgruntled American, but it seemed to work since he went on to explain that I was going to meet with the trekkers that afternoon at the Condor Cross where I would switch buses and continue the journey. *Why couldn't you have just told me that in the first place, asshole?* I then made the mistake of asking if he knew the weather report for the next few days, since it seemed quite dangerous to descend the canyon in the current weather.

"It's the dry season," he said with indifference.

"Yeah, okay, Juanito," I said, pointing outside. "Does that look dry to you?"

He repeated his answer verbatim. I eyed the microphone and considered acting out my fantasy but instead grumbled back to my seat.

Now with at least a thread of understanding of what was to come, I began to look forward to the famous Condor Cross, hopeful see the nine-foot wing-spanned prehistoric bird. Unfortunately, once we arrived there weren't any to be seen, even though a woman shouted, "Condor!" when she saw the fluttering of an incoming Andean swallow, causing everyone to run around hysterically with their cameras. I asked the khaki-outfitted gentleman to take a few pictures of me pretending to be a condor as I stood on a rocky outpost with my arms out, but at this point I considered jumping.

Suddenly, Juan shouted at me to grab my backpack and then shoved me in a rushed frenzy toward a public bus. "Your bus is not coming because of the snow, so you need to go to Cabanaconde Village and look for Miriam."

"What? Who?"

Then he added condescendingly, "The bus fare is already taken care of, so you won't have to worry about it."

"Yeah, well, it better be!"

As I boarded, I took one last glance at him.

"Bitch," he called out cowardly from a distance; it sounded more like *beach*.

The bus twisted down the precipice, forging pebbled shallow rivers and barely scraping the edges of cliffs. My capacity for dealing with the unknown was gone. Normally, I am not one to express uncontrolled anger or get into inane verbal scuffles with people. So the tug-of-war with Juan left me miserable.

When the bus arrived, I dragged my large backpack down the aisle as the bus driver gruffly asked for my ticket. I tried to explain that it was already taken care of. My hands shook in fury as he shouted at me to pay up, to which I replied in English, "Make me!"

Fuming past him, I got my backpack awkwardly wedged in the doorway. Finally, after a furious yank, it popped through like a cork, and I stormed away without looking back. I now faced a tiny village plaza scattered with local people in their traditional garb sitting on curbs and random dogs sniffing for scraps. Turning around in a slow circle, I scanned the plaza looking for…Miriam? Lacking the strength to go on, I plopped down, unable to think, speak, or move.

Eventually, a woman in typical Cabanaconde attire, which included a distinctively stitched hat and layered skirts, with long braids approached and motioned for me to follow. *Is this Miriam?* She gave me tea in a chipped cup and told me to wait on a curb in front of a small restaurant for the trekking group.

After two hours of waiting, I took to exploring the nearby streets. Finding a tiny shop with food, snacks, and other sundries, my eyes fell on the rack of cigarettes. The demon in my head encouraged me to buy a pack since my recent trauma certainly qualified me for a stress-releasing smoke session. With the pack in one hand, I hesitated for a moment and reached up to the Andean cross hanging from my neck. A slight vibration tingled through the hand that held the chakana.

Paralyzed for a moment, I eventually handed the cigarettes back to the woman behind the counter and grabbed a cold Fanta. A bit surprised by my own actions, a surge of pleasure greeted me. I had resisted the temptation in the face of a situation where I would have normally felt justified to smoke. Perhaps it was time to make consistently healthy choices for myself. Very likely I would be able to hear my intuition better without voluntarily introducing toxic chemicals into my system.

Returning to the meeting point for my trekking group, I was instantly charmed by a puppy who had wriggled under a gate. Climbing on my leg, he stared at me expectantly. I couldn't have asked for a better companion at that moment as he chirped happily. The little fur ball curled up in the cradle of my lap while I gave a local boy my old crackers and a Spider-Man sticker—and waited. And waited. And waited. For six hours, I waited. I considered taking a bus back to Arequipa but didn't have the strength to do anything except sit and pet my new amigo.

A group of eight with their guide, Leo, finally arrived from Arequipa telling of their nightmare journey in the rainy snowstorm and the scary van driver who nearly killed them multiple times. We all compared stories and realized that trekking companies did a number on tourists. They combined tours to save money, which caused solo travelers to get the short end of the stick as they were tossed around to fill group quotas.

When I told the others of my awful experience with Juan, one seasoned trekker told me how many of the guides have a mission to take tourists from point A to point B and were paid accordingly. He also warned that trekking companies frequently tell foreigners exactly what the travelers want to hear so they will put down their money. Trips that would otherwise be deemed extremely unsafe by first world country standards, with dangerous road conditions, would be described as perfectly safe by an insistent salesperson. A girl with jet-black hair and a nose ring, who was also traveling alone, explained that she had had a similar experience with a male tour guide who withheld information about her trip. She felt it was the cultural *machismo* trait of some Peruvian men who acted out their self-righteous superiority over woman. Although disturbing, this information put my experience a bit more into perspective.

Despite the rain, Leo assured us the weather would be beautiful down in the canyon and went on to educate us on its history. The name Colca referred to small holes in the cliffs of the valley and canyon. These holes were used in Incan and pre-Incan times to store food, such as potatoes and other Andean crops. They were also used as tombs for important people.

After a group lunch, we began the five-mile descent over three thousand feet into the canyon. The trail was steep and mostly made of gravel. So, despite being downhill, it was a challenging hike. We passed colorfully dressed local people who still maintained ancestral traditions and continued to cultivate the pre-Inca stepped terraces.

The first night was spent in the village of San Juan, and once everyone was asleep, I climbed out to the grassy terrace and was welcomed by a pleasant balmy temperature. Surrounded by bushes heavy with fragrant flowers and an expansive ceiling of stars, I put earphones in to let the gentle melodic music move my body. I stretched, danced, meditated, and breathed deeply with relief at finally finding a peaceful pocket.

In the early morning, a jolly rooster took his job seriously and cock-a-doodle-dooed without rest. When I exited our hut, I nearly stepped on a young rust-colored dog curled at the doorstep. I named him Colquita and scratched his ears. He diligently followed our group as we traversed the canyon over bouncing, cactus-woven bridges and inhaled the lush flowers that were becoming more and more abundant.

We soon descended to the magnificent Colca Oasis, which sat ten thousand feet deep at the base of the canyon. It was a sanctuary of magical enchantment: palm trees, giant blooms of flowers, natural pools, and brilliant sunshine. Colquita stayed by my side and barked when I dove from the rock into the sparkling turquoise water. Laying comfortably on a smoothed, scooped-out rock, the sun quickly dried me off as a gentle perfumed breeze danced across my skin.

The last amber rays lit up the narrow valley, igniting the colors of the canyon walls and dancing on the translucent pools. After pushing my body to the limit for so many simultaneous days, it was necessary to put in a thorough stretching routine to recover. Soon trekkers asked to be guided through stretches. The next thing I knew, more than a dozen hikers were spread out, following my lead. Colquita even impressed us by rolling on her back while we did yoga poses. Later that night, I shared my grilled alpaca dinner with her and, in turn, she never left my side.

When the stars appeared, most of the trekkers headed to their bamboo huts to rest for the long hike out the next morning. By the light of the moon, I climbed onto a rocky perch overlooking the deepest layer of the canyon and lay back with Colquita snuggled against my side. Shooting stars rocketed across the sky as blissful satisfaction washed over me, soothing my fears and filling me with an indescribable sensation of being loved.

Maybe this sweet, private paradise was the heart of Pachamama? Would I find my answer here? Staring up at the sky from the depths of the deepest canyon in the world, I smiled with the realization that this sweet and private crevice was probably *not* her heart.

Starting at 3:00 a.m., we dug in deep and climbed out of the canyon in four hours. Colquita was underfoot the entire way, racing ahead and looking back with a curiously cocked head, as if she were saying, "Come on, slowpoke!"

Leaving Colquita was devastating, but I knew she'd find a new friend soon enough. She ran alongside the bus while I waved and knocked on the window as if I was leaving my best friend. On the drive back, the bus stopped at the Cruz de Condor and this time the massive birds were soaring off the lip of the cliff, regally shadowing the land below.

"Look!" pointed a man with binoculars and an Ohio sweatshirt. "There's a dead mule down there! The locals probably threw it over to keep the birds here and that keeps us tourists coming."

Gazing down, I spotted the rotting carcass. "Hey, thanks for pointing that out," I said sarcastically.

Mr. Ohio was happy to fill me in on all his knowledge of the Andean condor. He explained how the bird's dull red-colored neck and head were nearly featherless and actually changed color in response to the creature's emotional state. He described the interesting mating ritual of the large vultures, during which the birds flew close together in unison, as if they heard a whimsical harmony just for them. And without a wing beat, they elegantly glided like they were dancing on the wind. Condors choose a mate for life, and if one dies, the other won't take another mate.

I watched in awe as a pair of condors, who perhaps were courting, flew in majestic circles with remarkable grace. Taking a few deep breaths, I channeled into my heart the eternal love they pledged to one another. Then a bit of envy crept in when I realized that big, old ugly vultures had an easier time finding love than I did.

My loyal friend, Colquita.

39

THREE BLIND MICE

The day after returning from the Colca Canyon, I marched right back to the touring company store to file a complaint about Juan. The supervisor acted sympathetic to my complaint and graciously offered me a discount on another trip.

The whole afternoon was open, so I took to wandering the systematic streets of Arequipa to find something to drink. Tea was the most commonly served hot beverage in Peru, and by this point of the trip, it was clear the locals hadn't a clue how to prepare a proper cup of coffee. Peruvian beans are exported all over the world, but it seems the Peruvians neglected to keep some for themselves.

Every time coffee was a menu option, I would fall under the illusion that *maybe this time* I would get a real cup o' joe. Instead, I often got a two-liter thermos of hot water, a tiny tube of instant coffee, a cup with thick, hot milk, and a separate cup for mixing it all together. I practically did a cartwheel upon discovering a genuine coffeehouse, with WiFi, fantastically clean windows, and funky music. Perching on a stool with a steaming cup of *real* coffee, laptop before me, and sunshine beaming through the windows, I smiled contentedly, knowing I could joyously spend the entire day in that exact spot.

With the windows facing a busy street, the people-watching was abundant and colorfully diverse. A local newspaper left by a coffeehouse patron caught my attention. The front-page image made my heart stop. A touring bus traveling from Cuzco to Arequipa had been in a fatal collision, killing over a dozen passengers and disfiguring many when they were launched through the windows. My mood changed dramatically and I had a hard time getting back to the previous carefree pleasure of being highly caffeinated.

Meandering the streets, I suddenly felt emotionally overwhelmed. What the hell happened to volunteering? I was clearly exhibiting the old behavior of recklessly indulging in adventures when my first attempt at being of service hadn't worked out as planned. In what direction did I want to take my life? What did I want to stand for? Who did I want to be? Did I truly want to make a difference in other people's lives, or did I want to make my mark in the world by being a bloodstain on a highway? At the rate I was going, it would be the latter.

I needed to have a heart-to-heart with my Divine Spirit, and the convent Santa Catalina was just the place. Checking my map, I figured out the route and headed directly to the divine sanctuary where perhaps I would find some answers.

After taking one step inside the monastery, it felt like the walls were impregnated with centuries of true devotion. A brochure explained that Maria de Guzman, a rich Spanish widow, founded the monastery for nuns in 1580. Traditionally, the second-born daughter from upper-class families entered the nunnery to devote her life to God and live in poverty, giving up material possessions. It gave me a new perspective imagining the women who had surrendered their lives to service. Here I was struggling to help others for one summer when these women cloistered in this nunnery had dedicated their entire lives to a cause not necessarily of their choosing.

Santa Catalina was a magnificent example of colonial architecture, covering over 200,000 square feet and making it like a city within a city. Relief washed over me with each step inside the maze of narrow cobblestone streets with vividly painted walls, ornate fountains, and tiny plazas laden with flowers. A bench lit with sunlight lured me into a hallway painted bright indigo blue with red geraniums overflowing from hanging pots. It actually didn't seem like a bad place to spend a lifetime.

Folding my hands in my lap, I closed my eyes and prayed for Pachamama to show me the way. After a period of quiet meditation, the wise words of a woman I knew back at home swirled through my mind. She had once illustrated for me a clever metaphor to help me through a difficult time. "Ann, do you remember going to Disneyland when you were a kid?" she'd asked. "There was a ride called Autotopia, where you could drive a little car around on a track. When you were young, you thought you had the power to direct the car. You turned the wheel, jerking the vehicle from side to side, but it always hit the center rail and kept you going in the direction it intended.

"This is comparable to the road of your destiny. You might grip the wheel tightly, forcing it to go where you want, thinking you have control, but, really, it's already in motion, headed in the direction of your divine destiny—where you can do the greatest good. The more your own self-will tries to alter the course, the longer and more difficult the ride. Get quiet inside and listen to your intuition. Let go of the wheel, Ann, and let God do the driving."

The gentle trickle of the fountain nearby brought me back. I realized that even if I didn't have the answer yet, all I needed to do was find that quiet space within and listen for each next indicated step.

* * *

When I entered my hostel that afternoon, I was a few seconds too late to stop a guy with gauze eye bandages from walking into a wall. Another man with one eye patch entered the hall and guided the poor fellow to a chair. Then, another, wearing oversized dark glasses and using a cane, hobbled through the common area to join the other two. I could tell by their accent they were Argentinean, and I couldn't help but notice that they looked like the three blind mice.

"Hey, are you guys okay?" I asked in Spanish.

"No, not really," one of them replied wearily.

"Were you in that bus accident?"

"No," said the guy with the pirate patch. Then the three said in unison the three-syllable word that brought chills down my spine. "Chi-cha-ni!"

Their story was even more tragic and scarring than my own. The trekking company hadn't advised them to wear sunglasses to protect against the intense exposure to UV light at altitude, so they figured they wouldn't need any, especially since it was a cloudy day. This made me even more grateful that our group didn't make it to the top, since I 'd not been counseled to bring shades either.

The sun's glare at the top of Chichani and, worse, its reflection off the snow and ice had caused them to go temporarily blind. They actually hadn't started to lose their vision until they were back at base camp, when suddenly all three of them noticed their eyes were watering excessively, had become red, and were quickly swelling shut. It had already been four days, and only recently had the two gotten partial eyesight back, but the third was still completely blind and feared he would never be able to see again.

Although feeling deeply sympathetic to their story, a deep sense of gratitude washed over me that, one, I wasn't blind, and, two, I had followed my instinct and spoken up on Chichani. I sent out a prayer of thanks and promised my Divine Spirit that I would slow down and check in with the Universe daily. It was about time I slipped on over to the passenger seat and let God take the wheel.

* * *

After a ten-minute meditation at a recently discovered secret spot on the hostel rooftop, I felt the intuitive awareness for my next step. If I wasn't going to volunteer and extreme adventuring was eliminated, then how about educating myself on the history and culture of the people of Peru?

Lake Titicaca was just the place. Ethnic heritage was richly abundant in that part of the country, as I recalled from the words of the three amigos back in Cuzco and the wise old Sawya. All of them had pointed their fingers in that direction for me. Only now was I ready to hear their message. I even remembered Helen telling me about how the Incas considered Lake Titicaca to be the birthplace of their civilization. If I really wanted to educate myself on Peru, that was clearly the place to begin.

The Sir Edmund Hillary quote that I had repeated in attempt to motivate myself to the top of Chichani now echoed through my head again: "If you can overcome your fear, you are frequently able to extend yourself far beyond what you normally regard as your ability." So, really, what was I so afraid of?

My mind was a tangle of opinions, but I could feel one clear intuitive thought beginning to surface. What I feared was stepping into the ring of possibility for what the Universe had in store for my highest-level potential. How could I be of the greatest good?

I had spent so many years sabotaging my potential, the idea of embracing it and allowing it to carry me to the next stage of my life was intimidating. In order to do so, I would need to forgive myself for the actions of my past. To absolve myself for not only how I'd treated others, but also how I'd treated myself. It was finally time to give myself the love I had spent most of my life seeking from outside sources. It would be important to fill my tank with confidence and compassion so that I could give freely without worrying that I was losing a piece of me.

What would it feel like if fear was replaced with love? If I could overcome my fear of not having enough or being good enough or of not ever finding love, if I just relaxed into being whole and complete right here and now? What might that do to my life?

I took ten deep breaths and let the whirlwind of thought blow through my body as I settled into meditation. For a moment, the story of my life was wiped clean from my mind and replaced with a vision of the future. My mind led me to look through the eyehole of a kaleidoscope to experience the beautiful and infinite mosaic of possibilities of what my life could look like if it came from a place of love.

40

LAKE BOOBYPOOP

Lounging on the roof of the boat, I relaxed in the dazzling, high-altitude sunlight with the crisp, fresh air and surrounding sparkling water. The boat dipped and swayed, gently skimming over the waters of Lake Titicaca—or, as I preferred to call it, Lake Boobypoop.

According to the Andean mythology, Manco Capac and Mama Ocllo, children of the Sun God and founders of the Inca Empire had emerged from its waters. It was also known for being the world's highest navigable lake at over twelve thousand feet, covering over three thousand three hundred miles. The surrounding mountains towered above like proud guardians of the "lake of origin," as the native people called it. The afternoon sun was tinted gold, and the cotton clouds nestled snugly in the peaks. Like a peacock showing off, the geometrically arranged terraces stepped up from the waters in every shade of green.

When I'd first arrived in Puno, the jump-off city for Lake Titicaca, I'd signed up at my backpacker-friendly hostel for a tour of a few islands on the lake.

I'd declined the recommendation of the typical single night stay, certain that I wanted an extended experience with an indigenous family. Alfredo, the jolly Uruguayan hostel owner, laughed heartily and teased me that I wouldn't last three full days.

But I was determined to adopt my new commitment to embrace the culture. He booked me to stay with a local family and suggested that I bring edible offerings since certain foods were not cultivatable on the islands. Spurred on by Alfredo's challenge, I high-fived him and marched out of the hostel with my pack stuffed full with fruits, vegetables, three liters of potable water, my warmest clothes, and, of course, Crazy Kite.

* * *

My first glimpse of the islands of Uros was a vision beyond extraordinary, yet also depressing. The guide on the boat explained that Uros was an ancient lake colony of natives who were murdered by the Spanish to near extinction and probably fled to these tiny islets to escape forced labor in the silver mines. It was also thought that they might have come earlier to isolate themselves from the aggressive Collas or Inca tribes.

It was mesmerizing to witness how their lives completely revolved around the *tótora*, or reed, which was cut and piled to form floating islands anchored to the shallow lake bottom. The houses were made of the same material, so were boats, furniture and hats. Tótora was eaten at most every meal. I couldn't fathom eating reeds as part of every meal for my entire life.

I pondered what it would have been like to take one of these families to a Costco. The Uros certainly kept life simple and seemed to be incredibly content. Guess they didn't need super-sized excess. By observing these people's lifestyle, it didn't seem as if *want* was even a factor in the native philosophy. Tourism introduced additional income, but I wondered who initiated the concept of consumerism. Certainly not the people of Uros. So it must not be an innate trait of all humankind.

Perhaps my culture had created in me the toxic pollutant of believing I didn't have enough. The constant nag that I was lacking something in my life was ever-present. The drive of consumerism and relentless marketing continually suggests that I don't have what I need to be happy. It was as if layer upon layer of false belief had been built on top of my initial state of total completeness. Maybe I actually lacked nothing and I already had everything I needed. I just needed to learn how to access that and step outside the thick walls of my own society's belief system.

The boat docked at the floating property of one of the tourist-friendly islands where barefoot women with brilliantly fluorescent skirts welcomed us. They clapped and sang, swinging their hefty bodies from side to side, as everyone on the boat snapped pictures as if we were at a theme park.

I too found it hard to resist capturing their images since it was like nothing I had seen before, but it felt intrusive and almost disrespectful. We were invading their tiny, natural sanctuary and tromping on the rotting, waterlogged foundation of their homestead.

The welcoming family had many elderly members who stayed half-naked despite the sharp chill in the air. Tourists flashed money for handmade reed items, took pictures, then piled back on the boat, giddy for the next fascinating stop.

The Uros people fish, hunt birds, and move about the lake in huge tótora rafts that look almost like Viking ships with massive animal heads on the bow. I wondered if the young people cruised up and down the waterways between floating neighborhoods showing off their fancy rides. The family we visited had a double-decker dragon boat made entirely of reeds, whereas the family across the canal had just a canoe with a mediocre snake head.

After thumbing through my guidebook for a moment and confirming some facts with the tour guide, I asked another tourist to help film my first educational video. I greeted the camera as if I was speaking to my students and proceeded to do a spontaneous lesson on the history and culture of the Uros people. Reboarding the boat, I stopped taking pictures and just honored the simplicity of their lifestyle and their absolute and total dependence on nature.

Legends say the Uros people were protected from the extreme cold in that region by their thick, black blood. It seemed like the children of the area could have used more than legend to keep them warm. I had read in the paper that over the span of two weeks during the recent cold spell, more than seventy children in that region had died of pneumonia. With each stop of the bus from the warmer Arequipa to the chilly region of Puno, I had noticed the children looking dramatically unhealthier. Most were barefoot and unbearably filthy, with severely running noses and dead, scaly skin peeling off their faces like old paint. Even with their thick layer of grime, I still felt a deep yearning to scoop them up and wrap them in my soft North Face jacket to keep them warm in a hug.

* * *

After exploring various flotilla homes in Uros, the boat made its final stop for the day on the island of Amantani. It was home to the pre-Incan Aymara people, who opened up their homes to curiously adventurous tourists so the foreigners could experience the traditional way of life. The guide explained how the Amantani island was a barren place with many well-preserved terraces and home to about eight hundred families of farmers, fishermen, and weavers living in a few small villages without running water or electricity. My heart skipped when he said there were excellent hiking opportunities to the island's two peaks of Pachatata and…Pachamama!

Half a dozen local women dressed in colorful traditional attire waited patiently for their new guests. There was not one taller than five feet, and most of their faces were deeply creviced with decades of the elements. I was matched with Bonne, a proud Dutchman, and Maria, a lovely Swedish girl who was studying archeology in Peru. Our homestay mother smiled politely and then scurried up a rocky path at a pace impossible for us to follow with our large packs.

Communication with our Aymara-speaking host was impossible, so we were often left confused, not knowing what to do. Our room was more appropriately constructed for the diminutive; the three of us remained uncomfortably hunched while waiting for the señora to indicate our next move. Finally, she knocked and motioned for us to follow her, then pointed to a trail leading to a nearby summit. Guessing it was the well-known mountaintop the guide had talked about, we set out, breathlessly heaving ourselves up the trail toward the highest part of the island, the Pachamama peak!

All along the hike, I saw boys with homemade kites constructed from string and plastic bags. They aggressively yanked on the strings while running full speed, pulling their airborne trash creations. With giddy excitement I waved and shouted in Spanish, "Want to see the mother of all kites? Follow me!"

A gaggle of dirty-faced boys scampered on all sides of me like sprightly mountain goats as I huffed and puffed to the hilltop. Huddled around me in awe, they chattered in their native language while I put together the wings of my large, long-tailed rainbow kite. The sun was just setting, bathing the land in golden light that reflected off the expansive waters of Lake Titicaca, which was visible from all sides.

The boys popped up and down with anticipation. Before I could finish putting her together, Crazy Kite launched herself out of my hands and into the fresh air of freedom. Responding to the cheers, she dipped and danced across the horizon, showing off for her spellbound audience. One shy boy a bit older than the rest stood to the side, mesmerized with hopeful wonder.

Using Spanish instead of his native language, he introduced himself as Cesar. I told him my name and presented him to Crazy Kite as if she were a real person, which he didn't find at all strange. I proudly demonstrated how she could dive-bomb and hit just about any target on the ground. His eyes laughed, somehow understanding the personality of this inanimate object. The other boys ran around as targets, hoping to be hit by the diving, multicolored demon.

Moving on to more mature topics, he asked me if I knew about the spot where we stood. I told him of my fascination with Pachamama and he smiled, nodding with an expression of wisdom beyond his years. He explained how the ceremonial site was built to worship Mother Earth, and in the Incan mythology, she was the goddess who controlled planting and harvesting. Every January during the Fiesta de Tierra, the population of the entire island split. Half went to the Temple of Pachamama and the other half to the other peak of the Temple of Pachatata, Father Earth. The two peaks symbolized the islanders' ancient dualistic belief system.

"You're very smart, Cesar. Do you go to school here?" I asked.

"No, I study in Puno. Because of the money our family makes from tourists staying in our home, my parents can send me to a real school. I stay with friends of my father during the week and come back here on the weekends to help with the potato crops. This peak is one of my favorite places because I feel good when I am here."

Without hesitation, I gave Cesar the handle of string attached to Crazy Kite. "I want you to have her."

"Oh, no, señorita, I can't take your kite," he replied.

"Yes, Cesar, just like you, she feels good here. I can tell when she's flying. She needs to stay with you. I insist."

A smile exploded across his face and I knelt to give him a hug. Just then, an enormous full moon peeked from the horizon.

"Don't forget, señorita, you must circle Pachamama temple three times for a wish."

"Oh, I will, gracias amigo," I told him. Then I asked, "Hey, Cesar, are we in *the heart* of Pachamama?"

He looked at me strangely and said, "Señorita, I do not know what you mean."

"Never mind," I said feeling foolish. "Take good care of Crazy Kite!"

His answer was inaudible but obvious as I watched him dart away with a tribe of envious boys in tow, Crazy Kite sailing high above us all.

There was a vibrantly magical quality to the place that was palpable. I felt grounded and safe. The small circular temple was made of stone, standing about nine feet tall. It had a simple wooden door that was locked, which I presumed kept the sacred center closed to the public. Above the door was an arch made of stone with rays or teeth that served as a crown. I was beginning to sense that the two temples represented male and female—like the sun and moon. In Spanish, *el sol* is designated as a masculine word and *la luna* represents the feminine. I was starting to see how each functioned as separate entities but existed in marriage with one another.

Vibrating with delight, I began looping the temple, pulling my jacket tight to keep out the frigid night air while the perfectly round moon gazed with wide-eyed curiosity. As I sauntered around the stone building, I could feel the anticipatory energy stirring within, paired with a humble calm.

Suddenly, something reflecting the strong beam of moonlight caught my eye. There before me, atop a pile of stone, rested an old, rusty key. Perhaps to open the temple door? Slipping it in my pocket, I peered stealthily from side to side then headed toward the entrance. After a few tourists passed, I held my breath and stuck the key in the lock, my head whispering, *I am the gatekeeper!*

The key fit but would not turn. Discouraged but intrigued, I found a pile of rocks on which to sit facing the bold-faced moon. Inhaling and exhaling slowly, I closed my eyes and rested my open palms on my crossed legs, feeling the strong pull of the two energies present on the island. I could definitely relate more with the masculine energy; in control, grossly competitive, and simplistically efficient. My mode of operation always seemed to be seek and conquer, which I could see was a very masculine state of mind.

Maybe the key was a gift for me from Pachamama? Was she helping me open the door to my femininity? Perhaps gentleness, compassion, and nurturing needed encouraging. This was very likely one of the reasons why I hadn't been able to find a good male counterpart. If I was acting the part of the masculine energy in a relationship, there was no room for a man. I was sure men didn't mind a strong woman, but I bet they liked one who knew how to be feminine too. It felt like a sign, saying, "This is the key to your future. Right now, initiate the inner feminine energy within. Let it spread through you like the rays of the sun. Active Divine Love within your heart."

* * *

Little did the three of us guests know what we were in for after the meager dinner of watery soup, purple potatoes that looked like alien fetuses, and a small square of cheese that squeaked when chewed. The señora then brought piles of traditional clothing and mimed that we had to wear them to a party. Family heritage and marital status were publicized in the color and stitching of the outfit. In order to attend the celebration, we needed to be dressed appropriately in accordance with our homestay family's heritage.

Maria and I pulled stinky embroidered blouses over our heads and the señora wrapped us each in a wide, colorfully sewn belt that cinched like a Victorian corset. We both howled in pain, pleading for her to loosen it as she pulled it tighter and tighter still. Next was the brightly colored skirt that I sneakily pulled my long johns under since it already felt like a refrigerator in the room. Finally, she draped a long black cloth over my head. It smelled like the bottom of a lost and found hamper in a men's locker room. Bonne was dressed for a Clint Eastwood western. Instantly our camaraderie was built because of the bizarre situation we serendipitously found ourselves in.

We followed the señora by the light of the moon, heading toward the unknown. The second we stepped through the stone arch to the town hall, we were pulled into a crazy dancing frenzy. A conga line of sorts was snaking around the celebration, with a panpipe folk ensemble blowing their flutes with tenacious intensity. I spied other tourists from our boat, also decked out in traditional garb, trying to keep up with the fast-paced flute tempo. Many locals hovered around the exterior and watched us silly tourists dancing as if we were costumed monkeys in a circus. It felt like the tables had turned and we were the subjects of their amusement.

Preferring to observe the animated, rotating mass of stink rather than be engulfed in it, I tried to take a break along the stone wall, but the señora would not permit it. She kept pulling Maria and me out to dance in an endless dizzying circle.

After more than an hour of nonstop dancing, I was definitely over the celebration—and the suffocating corset squeezing the life out of me—but I had no way of asking when we would be leaving. Just when I thought the fiesta might be coming to a close, I clapped my hands up high in a "Hey, thanks for having us" gesture. But the small band of flutes restarted, picking it up a notch, continuing to play what seemed like the same song yet again, but now more quickly and fiercely than the last time. The señora approached me with arms out and a big, friendly smile and took my hand to continue the spinning flute-jig. There was no escape.

As we prepared to depart early the next morning after a sparse breakfast of hard bread and peppermint tea, I presented the señora with my parting gifts. She seemed most excited about the small package of sugar. Noticing one of her sons hiding behind her skirt, I pulled out the always-popular Spider-Man stickers.

I stuck one on his shoulder, and suddenly another boy's head popped out a window above, then another head out of the garden door, and another from behind a wall. They all stood proudly in a row with stickers on their chests as I taught them how to make Spider-Man web-launching movements with the palms of their hands. Then in through the gate came her last son, perhaps returning from early morning work in the fields. It was Cesar! My heart warmed knowing that the money I had spent to stay in Amantani went to his family and directly affected his future.

* * *

From the roof of the boat, I got an excellent view of the approaching island of Taquile, famed for its high-quality textile industry. Its steep terraced hills seemed to jut aggressively out of the water, stretching up to tiered platforms that dominated the landscape. The Taquile residents were occupied with pulling frayed wool from a spindle through their fingers into a streamlined thread and then into a pouch at their waists. Even young boys and elderly men carried a spool and spun unconsciously as they went about their daily business. Our tour was led to a semimodern structure that posed as the official artisan market. The goods were of extremely high quality with prices to match.

The original plan was to stay a night there, but I just didn't have it in me to go through another non-communicative night of the unknown in the freezing cold, without running water or electricity, and this time without my compadres to share in the experience. When I arrived back at the hostel, the corpulent Alfredo laughed like Santa Claus, then hugged me and said, "Ana! I knew you'd be back!"

Cesar and *his* Crazy Kite.

41

A BIRTHDAY GIFT

The rickshaw seemed to be a mistake during the first block of head-bobbling. With a full day to explore the city prior to my return to Cuzco, I thought a two-wheeled passenger cart pulled by a bike rider would provide a swift and efficient way to tour the city. Railroad tracks zippered across town, which the driver hurtled over at high velocity, causing my rear end to slap the splintery seat and my teeth to clatter. The locals watched in mild amusement as I held on for dear life, letting out squeals of discomfort.

Even though the city sat on the shoreline of the immense Lake Boobypoop, its existence didn't seem to revolve around it. Perhaps this came from my own perspective of the fun activities people *should* participate in if they were near water. Most residents of the California beach cities take full advantage of every possible water sport. Peruvians didn't appear to be occupied with the need for playtime. The main city of Puno was five blocks off the water, but not a soul was sailing, swimming, or fishing along its shores.

I hollered at the driver to stop when I spotted a paddleboat with a triceratops head. It sat abandoned in the mossy, stagnant shoreline. Not knowing the word for triceratops in Spanish, I asked him how I could rent the *dinosaurio*.

"No, no, señorita, no puede." No, you can't.

Momentarily discouraged, I gazed fondly at the big, green plastic head with its tri-horned face. I loved triceratops. To me, they represented safety, strength, and protection. My affinity for the dinosaur had begun when I was a little girl. Even in kindergarten on the "bring your teddy bear to school day," I brought Topsy, my beloved triceratops. Every night he stoically protected me from the evil clutches of E.T. (the Extra-Terrestrial). Consumed with fear, I was certain that the little alien would creep his crooked, glowing red finger up the side of the bed and touch me.

In 1982, when *E.T.* premiered, I was seven. Mom took me to the theater thinking I would love the movie, as most children did at the time. After the first scene with the unnatural creature running through the forest bleating like a goat being slaughtered, I lost it. I cried hysterically and choked on my sobs.

Over the course of the next year, my *E.T.* trauma became progressively worse. At night, I was certain he was in my bedroom watching me sleep. My dino-protector stood vigilantly on the exposed side of the bed and kept me safe from harm. Getting neurotically clever, I set up a series of chairs that I could hop across to get to the bathroom during the night so I wouldn't touch the floor (which was surely where E.T was lying in wait).

My dear mother had had just about enough of my nightly tragic performance and decided to have some fun with me. On Christmas morning, I eagerly raced to my stocking, only to find an E.T. doll stuffed inside. Clearly, Santa and E.T were in cahoots. The Christmas incident was traumatic, but absolutely nothing could compare to what was to come for me at Universal Studios.

Mom and I did the typical mini-train tour around the studio lots. Jaws launched from the lake, followed by a simulated flash flood that almost overtook the tram. The final stop was the movie production set, which highlighted popular films and included special demonstrations. With my favorite hoodie sweatshirt pulled over my head, I sat on the edge of my seat, excited for the next part of the show. A woman approached me and crouched to my level.

"Hey, honey, would you like to be in our next scene?" she asked.

With a big grin, I squealed at the opportunity. I told my mom, "This is gonna be better than kissing Shamu at SeaWorld!"

Stifling a smile, my mom patted my back. "How fun!"

The woman led me backstage as I pulled off my hood. She patted me on the head. "Oh, sweetie, keep your hood on, it'll be perfect."

Unsure of what she meant, I followed her instruction. She directed me to hop up on a bike seat and hold on tight. Suddenly the seat jerked as a mechanical arm elevated me up and out toward the stage. A bit confused, I looked out at the applauding audience. Turning to my right, I could see what was so entertaining. A ceiling-to-floor widescreen made it look as if I were flying over a city on a bicycle—with a bundle in the front basket. Then the first few beats of the theme song to *E.T.* began.

With the shocking realization of what was happening, I desperately searched for my mom in the audience and spotted her doubled over with laughter. She dabbed her eyes with a tissue and waved at me. Practically unable to swallow, I clutched the handlebars and clenched my teeth. When I thought it could get no worse, the bundle suddenly jolted to life. I held my breath as the blankets parted and a wrinkled, brown head popped up. It lifted its arm to point its red, glowing finger to the sky. I nearly passed out, but clung onto the bike until the demonstration finally concluded.

* * *

Watching the triceratops float lifelessly in the Lake Boobypoop waters, I couldn't help but laugh at my silly childhood fears. Continuing down the bumpy, half-paved road, I considered asking the driver to take me to an address written in my journal. Prior to the trip to Puno, I had reached out to Rodolfo, who was friends with Miguel, one of the three amigos in Cuzco. Rodolfo told me there was a meeting at 5:00 p.m. on Tuesday and that he would meet me there. Even though getting to a meeting was definitely good for me, I still didn't want to go.

Unfortunately, I had already told Rodolfo that I'd be celebrating four years of sobriety on the actual day of the meeting. Birthdays in sobriety were usually a pretty big deal, almost as if it were the date of a rebirth, a reemergence into one's true self. Sometimes in meetings, a cake was given to the birthday recipient with the designated quantity of candles to indicate the years sober. The same cake might be used over and over and the birthday song sung numerous times depending on the number of birthdays.

Unsure if birthdays were celebrated in Peru, I was not too motivated to share mine with unfamiliar faces. Then the wise voices of my recovery program echoed in my head, reminding me that the purpose of acknowledging a milestone was not just for the person celebrating it. It was even more important for other members to witness a transformed life and to provide hope for those with less time sober. Looking up to the towering, majestic mountains surrounding the city, I took a deep breath, exhaled slowly, and told the driver the address of the meeting.

A half dozen men in their forties were sitting on metal folding chairs lining the walls. None of them were talking. It was quiet and awkward in the barren room— that was until the jubilant Rodolfo burst through the door. Two apprehensive young ladies followed him in. He could have easily been the fourth amigo with the Cuzco crew.

Light danced in his eyes as he introduced me to the girls, Joviana and Mayu. Since there were few women in recovery in their region, they didn't have many female examples to follow. Even though the meeting was considered "mixed," Rodolfo explained that it had been a long time since they'd actually had a woman in attendance.

Gratefully, I thought of recovery at home and the hundreds of sober women who had shown me the way. I couldn't imagine walking the rough road of sobriety in a place where there were hardly any other women doing it too. Once Rodolfo had heard from the three amigos that I was coming to Puno, he'd rounded up all the women he could find to come meet me, as if I were some rare creature. *A sober woman? Really? In these parts? Nah, it can't be true.*

The two women looked just like the newly sober ones I worked with back at home, the same empty eyes and fear betraying their every word. Mayu hugged me tightly with desperation.

Rodolfo went to the podium and got the meeting started. His Spanish was quick and clipped, making it challenging for me to understand. "Welcome everyone. Tonight we have a special guest, Ana from California!" There was light applause as the men eyed me suspiciously. "Today she celebrates four years of sobriety." More clapping followed, with some raised eyebrows and head nods. "We are lucky to have her with us because tonight she is going to tell us her story."

What? I swallowed hard. Did I hear him correctly? Maybe a little five-minute share on the topic. But the main speaker? And in Spanish? Nodding my head nervously, I smiled and remained glued to my seat.

"¡Venga, Ana!" Rodolfo said warmly as the two girls encouraged me by taking my hands and guiding me to the podium. The others were no longer studying their shoelaces or staring out the window. Joviana and Mayu returned to their seats and looked up at me with hope.

Taking a deep breath, I asked the others to do the same. Then I invited them to close their eyes for a few minutes of silent meditation, which I did just to calm myself. From there, what took place was nothing short of a miracle. I can't even recall the words said or what it might have sounded like in Spanish, but it seemed that those in attendance heard what they needed to hear. It was as if I finally just sat back and enjoyed the ride.

At the conclusion of the meeting, Rodolfo presented me with a pastry typically served in Puno with four candles and small shot glasses for everyone with a sugary, bright green liquid—non-alcoholic of course. The group put me in the middle of the circle, wrapped their arms over each other's shoulders, and swayed from side to side singing "Happy Birthday" in Spanish—feliz cumpleaños.

The energy in the room had completely transformed. Each person hugged me affectionately and had kind words, thoughts, or questions about what I had said. Arm in arm with my two new sobriety sisters, we walked the streets for the next hour. They led me to a quiet plaza where we sat amid the surrounding darkness of night, only one lonely lamppost shedding a funnel of light.

What I have learned in sobriety is that gender, race, culture, financial status, or age don't matter. Those who believe they are alcoholics feel the same on the *inside*. I had felt the pain they were feeling. The circumstances might have been different, but how we felt about it was fundamentally the same.

"Please, Ana, tell us more," asked Mayu.

"Imagine a rotted, old tree," I told them. "The roots are dead, the branches are bare. If you were to cut a hole in it, you might find insects eating it away on the inside. This is how I felt before I got sober. On the outside, I might have still looked like a tree, but on the interior, I was hollow and decaying. Roosted on the branches were large, evil birds that continuously cawed. These were the voices in my head that never gave me a moment's rest."

"I feel just like that. Dead inside," Joviana agreed, shaking her head solemnly.

"Yes! The voices. I thought I was the only one with those," said Mayu.

"Oh no, I think we've all got the birds cawing away," I said. "It's just that some of us have learned how to ignore them and, more importantly, how not to believe what they say. Funny thing is when you don't listen, they go away. And a voice will emerge that you can trust."

The girls sat transfixed on what that kind of change might look like for them.

"No one talks like that here," said Mayu with a genuine smile.

"It's so hard, though," cried Joviana.

"Believe me, I know," I said, putting my hand over my heart. "First, you've got to have faith in a power greater than yourself. It can be a god of your own under-standing. There are a lot of gods in Peru, right? There's the Catholic God that the Spanish introduced. And Viracocha. Isn't he the god that created the sun and moon from Lake Titicaca right here in Puno?"

"Yes, Ana. There's also Mama-Quilla, the Moon God who's married to the Sun," said Joviana, "and many more."

"OK, good, so you do have an understanding of a force or energy greater than yourself. Now is the time to rely on that."

"Pachamama. She's the one I trust," Mayu said, putting her hand over her heart.

Overcome with emotion I started to tear up.

"Pachamama?" asked Mayu. "Do you know whom I'm talking about, Ana?"

"Yes, I am starting to get to know Pachamama very well," I said.

Wrapping my arms around them both in an emo-tional embrace, I sensed this was what it was like to truly open up and love freely.

Topsy's Peruvian cousin.

42

HELEN

The next morning began the ten-hour bus ride back to Cuzco. The exorbitant price of thirty dollars for a "first class" ticket on a bus line catering to tourists seemed well worth it. The bus would travel at a safe speed, drivers would change places every two hours, and we'd make multiple cultural stops as we took various breaks for food and shopping. This was what the bus company pledged to do, but whether it was the truth or just a line fed to vacationers was yet to be determined.

Upon boarding, I found all the passengers were foreigners, the bathroom actually had a toilet and paper, the seats were clean, *and* the windows were recently washed! Overcome with pure joy, I sunk into my chair and released a deep sigh of relief. Each spontaneous stop delighted me since it allowed me to stretch, get a snack, and observe cultural facets of the Peruvian culture that were off the beaten path.

We visited a traditional Andean church, a wool market, and a plaza filled with decorated llamas and dancing children. Lastly, we pulled into a cuy farm that raised guinea pigs. Instantly, I became enamored with an irresistible cuy whom I named Clyde after I was certain that he had winked at me. Sadly, I realized he was probably going to be dinner that night.

The matronly guinea pig ranch owner (and chef) was happy to converse with me about her animals. I explained to her that guinea pigs were considered pets where I came from. Her eyes got wide when I told her that most dogs were also pets in my country and were often treated as if they were human. I went on to describe how some owners dressed their dogs in clothing and others even put little shoes on the dogs' paws.

After my portrayal of some dog outfits I had witnessed, I suddenly felt ashamed for telling her. It felt incredibly inconsiderate to laugh and joke about dog fashion when there were people in her country who hardly had warm clothes. With Clyde still nuzzled close, I wanted to beg the woman to spare him, but knew in my heart that she needed Clyde to survive, not to be her pet.

A few hours later, the driver announced we would be making a lunch stop in a town that was completely isolated and survived solely off the meal revenue from tourists. When we pulled up, a few other buses were also unloading passengers. The travelers began filing through an archway into an area where a traditionally dressed band played Peruvian flute melodies.

A snaking line of hungry foreigners slowly made its way up to the buffet tables. Ravenously, I eyed the rice and stew and then joyously yelped, spotting salty plantains. Consumed by hungry anticipation, I didn't realize that someone was shouting, "Annnnnn!" in a high-pitched voice.

And there she was. Helen. The Russian from Marisol's house, wearing her trademark fanny pack at her waist.

"I never thought I'd see you again," she gasped.

Yeah, me too, I thought.

"Wait a minute," she said, shaking her finger at me. "What are you doing here? I thought you left to go back to the States!"

"No. I just left Cuzco," I replied.

"You mean you left the school? Did you tell Javier? I thought you told everyone you were sick," she challenged.

"I was sick."

"Well, I am headed to Lake Titicaca! I just finished my two months of volunteering and now I get to have fun!"

"You've been at the school this whole time?" I said incredulously.

"No, actually, I've been at the juvenile detention center."

"Seriously?" I was dumbfounded. No one wanted to teach there. It was supposed to be the most challenging job, since the kids had been arrested and were being housed in a group cell in town. Javier had set up a system where the most brave volunteers could go in daily and help them learn to read or teach them a skill. I couldn't imagine what the conduct of those kids was like compared to the so-called disciplined ones at Arco Iris. I'd never even considered for a moment taking on that level of commitment.

She went on to explain her experience. "I really wanted to help the most unfortunate kids and thought that would be a good place to do it. But the kids were very cruel to me. They made fun of my Spanish and refused to do any activity I created for them. But I wasn't willing to give up on them."

A sharp pang of guilt stabbed me, remembering how vehemently opposed I had been to helping her learn Spanish. *Why wouldn't I teach her Spanish? Geez, what an asshole!*

Helen told me how she had diligently gone back to the detention center every day with new approaches. She'd translated the directions ahead of time for her craft ideas, like making beaded bracelets and painting small landscape scenes. She was determined to reach the kids and had not backed down when they'd insulted her. One juvenile had even physically pushed her to the floor and told her not to come back. She said she could tell they were hurting inside and wanted for someone to care about them. Eventually, after Helen returned with renewed resolve day after day and week after week, she finally broke them. They could see how much she truly cared for them.

I was speechless. I had made such a swift judgment because she hadn't fit *my* definition of a strong, resilient woman. I was wrong.

"Helen, you're truly amazing," I said, taking her hand in mine. "I'm so sorry. I can't believe how I acted in Cuzco. That's not the kind of person I want to be. You were so helpful to show me around town and teach me what you knew about Peru. You're so lighthearted and joyful." I shook my head with a new clarity. "Honestly, I'm inspired, Helen. Thanks for being a good example for me to follow. I can't imagine what you went through at the detention center. I wouldn't have lasted more than a day."

Helen's cheeks colored as she squeezed my hand. "Even though it was hard, I knew they just needed a little love, and I've got plenty of it to give. Ann, remember, you'll always be taken care of when you come from the infinite fountain of love that's in your heart."

I stood in admiration, shaking my head in disbelief, unable to find words to respond.

"So apology accepted, amiga!" she said with a smile. "Now let's eat!"

Over lunch we chatted like old friends and shared stories of what we had experienced since we had seen each other last.

"Don't worry, Ann," Helen said, giving me a hug by the entrance to my bus. "Arco Iris might not have been a good fit for you, but I know something remarkable will happen for you here in Peru."

43

LOOK, POP, NO HANDS!

All my worries about not being granted entrance into the magnificent Machu Picchu were completely unnecessary. It was common knowledge on the tourist grapevine that there was a bountiful supply of permits in Cuzco. It was just the online companies with a limited supply.

Perhaps it was my visualization technique that had caused the ticket to materialize. Whatever the case, I was bursting with excitement that finally I was going to realize my dream of experiencing the palace of the Incas. After visiting various trekking companies, I'd settled on one that spoke of the fair treatment of their indigenous staff as well as a commitment to help restore the Inca trail and the communities along the route. Whether they were telling the truth or feeding me a beautifully orchestrated sales line, I had to give them credit for their inspiring pitch.

Upon stepping onto the bus with six other *aventureros* for the four-day Machu Picchu trek, I was instantly struck with unadulterated delight. I knew that

this was a magical fusion of dynamic and joyful characters. After being on a myriad of multi-day tours, I had
come to the conclusion that each individual was a crucial ingredient in the group recipe. Lucky for me, the
bus to Machu Picchu was filled with outspoken, funny-
bone-poking jokesters with jovial personalities:

Isaac and Tara. The dark-haired couple from
Gibraltar were professional contemporary dancers traveling for one year through South America. They were
free-spirited, energetic, and clearly smitten with one
another.

Hendrick and Greita. The six-foot-nine-inch,
rail-thin Dutch acupuncturist amused every Peruvian
child with his height and fun-loving personality. He
was traveling with his girlfriend, who was infinitely
curious, with an insatiable appetite for Peruvian cultural
knowledge. Most of what I learned about Machu Picchu and the region came through her unique inquiries
to our guide.

Aiden. The Australian Jim Carrey look-alike was
a cowboy-hat-wearing, scraggly redhead who worked
with aboriginal children in the Outback. He was enamored with butterflies and chased them playfully right off
the trail. We frequently lost sight of him for stretches,
only to see him later appear out of the bushes with a
wild grin, hollering that he'd found a new species.

Magnus. The bald Swedish scuba-diving vid-
eographer who worked in Thailand became my closest
amigo. For some reason, he chose to look after me and
could predict what I needed before I did. A granola bar,
a jacket, a hat, a kind thought, creative conversation, or

a good laugh in a challenging moment—he provided it all with genuine pleasure. It was a comfort to know someone had my back.

Magnus even insisted on carrying a few of the heavy items from my backpack. I had thoughtlessly brought three books, which I was inevitably too exhausted to read. After my frigid experience on Chichani, I didn't want to take any chances, so I toted full winter gear just in case it was cold—it wasn't. My pack was unnecessarily overloaded and there was no ignoring the fact that I was struggling because of it. Magnus also graciously insisted on carrying enough water for the both of us. He was my angel.

Vancho. Our friendly, knowledgeable, and barefoot guide was clearly passionate about his job, his people, the country's history, and the Inca road to Machu Picchu. He always had a smile and a childlike glint in his eye. At one point in the journey, he refused to let me carry my pack and insisted I switch mine for his. Humbled and ashamed at my inability to carry my own weight, I finally conceded after much resistance. His daypack only contained paperwork and a few pieces of fruit that he handed out to children along the way.

The first day of our journey was thirty miles of downhill biking, starting at the Malaga Pass at 13,900 feet. Twenty-five miles were on a newly paved, black, snakingly steep highway. After the first twist in the road, I was hurtling down the mountain and away from the tour group. It felt as if I were riding on the unfurled tongue of the yawning mountain dragon that exhaled its chilly, misty breath. I raced past the chocolate chunk mountains whose peaks vanished in the clouds. It took every ounce of restraint not to put my arms out like wings.

It was a dangerous habit that I had learned to do expertly as a young girl on the extensive bicycle trips with my father. On one such expedition, we rode three hundred miles through Canada while carrying gear to camp along the way. I was fifteen and wasn't as inspired about the trip as was my father.

To keep myself busy, I kept a diligently rationed supply of candy in my pocket. I would only eat a piece if I had to ride past roadkill. Raccoons, flattened snakes, deer, small rodents, and dog carcasses were plentiful along the highway. The continual witnessing of dead animals was agonizing, as was the physical and emotional suffering of such an arduous trip. The sweets and my Walkman helped to ease the discomfort.

To release the fury at being roped into that trip, I rode without my hands on the handlebars while going downhill, screaming wildly with outstretched arms. This, of course, infuriated my father, but there was no stopping me. All the reprimands and consequences did nothing to deter me and my reckless binges of no-hands riding.

While racing down the twisting Peruvian highway, I sat up in the ready position to release my hands. My dad's voice echoed in my head. *Annnnnn! Don't you do it!* This highway was the worst possible place to ride hands-free since the road ahead was entirely a mystery.

Landslides were abundant, leaving enormous boulders and rubble scattered. I had already passed over a dozen rivers and waterfalls that flowed directly over the road, yelping as the cold liquid rooster-tailed up my back. The greatest hazard was the buses and trucks that suddenly overtook me on a bend. Worse still were the vehicles coming up the road that would pass each other. With all the dramatic curves, it was hard to predict when I would be coming face to face with an intervillage bus accelerating in my lane. Instinctively I knew that taking my hands off the bars would result in my becoming Peruvian road kill.

I took one hand off. *Annnnnnn!* Then the other. *Don't do it!* I laid them on my thighs and exhaled, finding my equilibrium. Once I found my groove, I unfolded my wings—outstretching my arms and closing my eyes as time stood still. Wind whistled through my ears and life raced by with the smear of a colorful landscape. The bike took over as the tires made the distinctive sound of tread gripping wet asphalt.

Digging for my camera while still moving at high speed, I finally pulled it out and took a video for my father. At that moment, he was most likely sitting on the sofa with his dog Dylan, watching sports, completely oblivious to what his daughter was doing. I squealed and hollered into the camera and then wrapped it up with my father's least favorite words to hear out of my mouth, "Look, Pop, no hands!"

I could hear Magnus before I actually saw him. His holler must have been a Swedish version of *Yaaaahoooo*! It was a universal sound of irrepressible enthusiasm. I could hear it echo across the canyon just as he rounded the bend with a glorious grin and took the flooded road at full speed, spraying water in a wild arc that soaked me.

"Holy shit!" he shouted in his strongly accented English. "What a ride!"

After a fifteen-minute break, no one had yet to appear from our group, so we continued on together. The scenery dramatically changed from what looked like rugged hunks of fudge to lush foliage twisted into olive-colored dread-locks. Massive palms arched over the road intertwined with dew-covered ferns outstretching spindly fingers. A sword-beaked hummingbird zipped alongside us, chirping gaily.

Nostril-busting freshness and the brisk prickle of biting air slapped my senses. The sun broke through the dense rooftop of clouds, radically changing the temperature. Finally, my fingertips and tingly earlobes could thaw. We whizzed past forests of deep plum bou-gainvillea and blood-red poinsettias interwoven with the emerald vegetation framing waterfalls that dropped from a hundred feet above. Concentrating on biking was virtually impossible with all the mesmerizing com-binations of dazzling colors.

We reached the end of the smoothly paved high-way and wheeled onto a flat, single-lane dirt road that linked villages. Pedaling over the ditches and rocks was challenging and took a lot of physical effort and focus. Trucks and buses still passed, leaving a dense, suffocat-ing cloud of dust in their wake. Feeling uninspired by this portion of the ride, I slowed down to look back at Magnus, ready to complain.

"Go fast, Ann! Go! *Now!*" Magnus shouted urgently.

Before I could question him, I saw why it was that I needed to go now—and fast. Charging toward me were three mangy dogs with their teeth bared. I shrieked and my heart leapt. Pedaling as if it were the final stretch of the Tour de France, I desperately tried to change the unfamiliar gears to gain more speed.

Dropping into primal gear, I lifted my back-side off the seat and pumped the pedals with all my strength. I could hear the dogs snarling, their paws tearing the earth directly behind my back tire. Now the reason there was an absence of bike riders in South America became crystal-clear. Looking back over my shoulder, I saw one mutt lunging, trying to bite the tire.

I yelled hysterically, "*No, perros, no!*" as I tried to defend myself by kicking awkwardly at their heads. With its lips curled back and fangs out, running on full throttle, one dog nearly clamped its jaw on my ankle, but got my shoe instead. I shook him loose, but the exchange caused me to lose balance. I swerved, nearly taking a fatal tumble.

In the forest ahead, I could make out a figure standing just along the tree line. As I got closer, I saw a short, dark indigenous man with a handful of rocks. Pumping the pedals with both feet, I streaked past him, only to hear a thump directly followed by a high-pitched yelp and a howl.

Afraid to look back and lose ground, I kept my frenzied pace. I rode and rode and rode until my lungs burned and my legs felt like helpless slabs of flesh. Eventually, I reach a thatched-roof village where I threw down my bike and bent over at the waist. I dry-heaved as tears streaked my sweaty, dirt-covered face.

Chickens pecked the ground at my feet and a skinny cat hopped on a fence nearby to welcome me. A young, barefooted girl in a homemade dress appeared from a doorway and handed me a bottle of warm Fanta. She sat down next to me and, without a word, put her hand on my leg, as if to tell me that everything was going to be okay.

44

THE ROAD TO
MACHU PICCHU

The tracking van collected us after the bike ride and dropped off our group in the tiny village of Santa Maria. Magnus, Aiden, and I shared a room and spent the late afternoon laughing about the high risk of stage one of our Machu Picchu journey.

Feeling the dried sweat and layers of mud caking my body, I decided to brave the frozen waters of the shower in the tiny outdoor bathroom facility. This was also where the toilet was located, which provided the unique opportunity to simultaneously sit on the toilet *and* shower.

For dinner, we were served quinoa soup and a basket of popcorn to sprinkle on top. Disappointed with the light meal, I was determined to find myself something more substantial that included meat.

With carne on my mind, I explored all five of the desolate streets that made up the town. Lost in a fantasy of seeing an arrow pointing me toward an In-N-Out

Burger, I suddenly came face-to-beak with an unnaturally large, blue-headed turkey. Whipping out my camera, I took a series of pictures of the colorfully plump bird. He wasn't too keen on the photo shoot and started scraping his feathery wings on the ground like a bull pawing the earth before a charge.

Ignorant of the language of turkey, I had no clue he was actually warning me of his imminent attack. I crouched to get a good shot of the crotchety old fowl when he burst forward in a flurry of feathers, making a disturbing screech from his red, swinging gobbler. Still jittery from the dog chase earlier, I turned in a panic and sprinted down the dirt road.

After turning the corner, I pressed myself against the wall. Peeking back around the edge of the adobe building, I was shocked to see the monster turkey just a few feet away, wings out, beady yellow eyes staring me down. I ran the entire way back to our lodging and burst into the room, where Magnus and Aiden were playing cards.

"Help! There's a turkey!" I said, panting. Bending over, I put my hands on my knees. "Seriously, there's a crazy turkey trying to get me!"

"Ann!" Aiden said, amused. "Will you just sit down and chill? You get yourself in a lotta trouble, ay?"

"No kidding," added Magnus. "Dogs *and* wild turkeys? What's next?"

"Don't even say that, Magnus!" I said with a laugh. "There won't be a next."

"Hey, ya know, Ann, it's hard for Magnus and I to come to ya rescue if you keep goin off by ya-self," said

Aiden. "Stick with me, I'll protect ya from all the wild animals!"

"Like butterflies?" I retorted.

"Hang on, ya don't know I once fought off a crazy packa dingoes with a stick!" He nodded with sincerity. "Seriously, they started to attack me dog Charlie. I went crazy and jumped in. Knocked the shit outta them bastards and saved 'em. Tore me up good, though. See the scars?" he said, pointing at two jagged white lines on his forearm. "Bloody dingoes!" Aiden took off his leather hat and put it over his heart. "Poor Charlie called it quits right before this trip. Man, I miss that dog, he was a real goer, ya know."

"Don't worry, Aiden," I said. "We'll find a good Peruvian pup you can take home. You can call him Carlitos—it's Charlie in Spanish!"

The next morning commenced the trekking portion of the trip, which was an ascent to the village of Santa Teresa. We started climbing out of the river valley and up the mountainside above the Urubamba River, partly following the old Inca trail leading to Machu Picchu. We were welcomed by the heady scents of coffee, tea, and cacao growing in the terraced fields along the way. Vancho explained that life in the Andes hadn't changed much since the Spanish conquest almost five hundred years before. The locals still plowed their fields by hand with sticks, and many still observed practices that honored Pachamama.

Surprisingly, many natives still kept time by observing the shadow cast across a local peak. The people of the highlands called the summits *apus*, which referred to the spirit of the sacred mountain. The apus were like wise and loving ancestors that looked over and protected the minerals, crops, animals, and the people. Special agreements could be made with a particular apu with the help of a village shaman who knew how to broker deals with the mountain deities.

Vancho's constant flow of facts and history helped to distract me from the difficult hike, especially with the heat, my weighty pack, and the altitude. He handed me a pinch of coca leaves and told me to put it in my cheek.

"Are you sure, Vancho? Isn't it kind of like a drug?" I asked with concern. Perhaps drinking it as tea was okay, but to put a bushel of it in my mouth might be another story.

"No Ana, don't worry. It will give you a little boost and help you with the *soroche*, the altitude. Coca helps the body adapt to the lower levels of oxygen in the thin Andean air."

Hesitant, I was willing to try it since he promised it would reduce my crushing altitude headache. Thinking it might taste like tobacco, it instead had the flavor of bay leaf and green tea.

Vancho pointed out numerous curiosities of the plant kingdom, like the world's smallest orchid and a poisonous fungus. He snapped off a handful of large, furry seeds from the achotie plant and cracked them open in his hand. Inside was a deep red liquid, which he used to draw stripes on our faces and give us the authentic jungle warrior look for forging the Inca trail.

"Vancho?" Greita began. "Do the natives use the achotie seed juice to dye their clothing?"

I hadn't thought of that, but I certainly had been curious as to how they got so many brilliant colors in their outfits.

"Good question, Greita. They do use the achotie seed, because red is a very important color to the Andean people. Since ancient times, red has been the brightest and most highly saturated color that could be produced with natural dyes. But actually, the cochineal insect is the most commonly used ingredient for red dye. It's a scaly bug related to an aphid, and it's found on the prickly pear cactus that is common to the Sacred Valley.

"The insect is ground using stones to release the deep red pigment, which is then added to water and boiled as the basis of the dying process. Other substances are added to alter the core color and create new hues. They can use, for example, lemon salt to shift a red to a carrot-orange. The spun yarns are boiled for varying periods, then after they are dried, they're respun and made into balls of yarn ready for weaving."

I rubbed the material of my purple North Face shirt between my fingers. Never had I considered how colors were created for clothing.

"How do they make purple?" I asked, thinking it might be fascinating to naturally produce one of my favorite colors.

Vancho smiled. "Do you really want to know, Ana?"

"Yes. Maybe I can learn how to make an organic purple."

"Well, you'll need the cochineal insect, lemon salt, and…urine."

"Urine? Ewwww." I said, wrinkling my nose in disgust.

Vancho laughed. "Cold urine sets the color."

"How about brown?" asked Tara, the petite dancer from Gibraltar.

"Actually, they use the wool from the alpaca or llama since they have naturally brown fleece."

"Man, them llamas are like a one-stop shop," added Aiden.

"Yes, and they easily negotiate the vertical Andean terrain," continued Vancho. "Their dung is also burned as fuel. And it is estimated that ninety-five percent of the meat consumed here is llama or alpaca."

I wanted to go through all the colors of the rainbow and have Vancho explain how they were made, but I was out of breath and struggling to keep up with the group. This was when Vancho took my pack, insisting that I would enjoy the trek much more if I wasn't so weighed down.

"Vancho, you are the best tour guide in all of Peru!" I proclaimed in Spanish, wrapping my arms around him. "Thank you. I am so grateful that you are leading us! And by the way, your English is top-notch!"

For our breaks, Vancho selected particular homesteads hidden amongst the leafy, tropical trees often filled with chirping parakeets. We bought overpriced water, Gatorade, handicrafts, and fruits and resisted the temptation to give things to the local children. Vancho had specifically instructed us not to since the kids were becoming reliant on the Machu Picchu trekker traffic and weren't going to school or helping with the crops.

They begged tourists and chased after tour groups for gifts or money. He let us know that he used a portion of his pay to help particular families in need.

There was an endless parade of puppies and kittens and even a hungry monkey that tried to eat my bamboo bracelet. In one village, I had a stare-down with a huge buck-toothed animal that looked like a combination pig-possum-skunk-beaver. It sat on a huge stump with a baby bottle in its claws. A sign read Do Not Touch, but still I stood nearby, captivated. Aiden approached me from behind and grabbed my shoulders.

"Ann! Don't even think about it!"

Walking with Hendrick, the six-foot-nine Dutchman, was entertaining to no end. With five foot five being the average height for men in Peru, Hendrick was of mythical proportions and caused a comical commotion each time the locals caught sight of him. Our group had a deep appreciation for the unique environment, and we'd often come around a corner and stand in a row, breathlessly observing some unbelievable treasure of nature. We felt blessed to witness a vast, mystical rainbow arching out of an intense waterfall spray. At one point, the rays of the sun broke through the architectural cloud pattern, shining ethereal cones of light as an eagle soared royally, owning the skyscape.

After eight hours of spectacular views and painstaking inclines, we gratefully reached the much-anticipated conclusion to day two—the thermal baths. We slipped in the steaming hot mineral waters, soaking ourselves until we were thoroughly pruned.

"Hey, Vancho," Greita said, getting his attention from across the steamy sulfur pool. "Where did you attend school? You know so much, and your English is superb."

"I owe it all to my mother, actually," he replied. "She was determined to have all her children educated so we could make better lives for ourselves. Even though our father left us, she did not give up. She worked three jobs and saved her money carefully. She would never let us miss school for any reason, and we learned the value of education.

"I was able to get a scholarship and went to school in Lima for a degree in tourism. I learned English there too. Actually, there was a British woman who befriended my mother and has helped our family a lot too. She writes me letters and that helps to improve my English."

"Wow, your mom sounds like quite a woman, Vancho," I said.

"She is. If only all the women here in my country could have the strength that she has. Not that our women aren't strong. They are. But she has a different kind of determination. You see, we have very traditional roles here. If only the women were able to unleash their true potential, it could turn this country around. It is the most misused economic resource in Peru. I think female empowerment is the solution to poverty in third world countries."

The baths were on the outskirts of the village of Santa Teresa and were where we stayed that night. After an inedible dinner of chewy, gristly alpaca, we all danced at the only disco in town. The dance floor cleared to allow Tara and Isaac the space to let loose. It was a treat to watch them flow together in a synchronized expression of beauty and grace.

Although I was thoroughly exhausted, it was difficult to fall asleep that night hearing the brutal hysteria of spousal abuse nearby. Magnus and Aiden were fast asleep, but I was unable to lie back and do nothing. Returning to my thoughts was the disastrous day at Arco Iris that had stemmed from me taking charge for Javier while he attended a forum on spousal abuse. A new dose of gratitude came over me for his work. He was going to extraordinary lengths to give a voice to the women and children of his country.

I climbed up to the roof to try to locate the violence. All I could see through the darkness was a labyrinth of patios and crumbling, half-built houses. It was gut-wrenching each time I heard a thump and a female crying. Feeling helpless to do anything, I crossed my legs, stretched my hands up to the nearby apu mountain peak, and asked that love be sent their way.

The following day, most of our walk was beneath the forest canopy on railroad tracks leading to Aguas Calientes, the base city of Machu Picchu. It was six miles of vigilantly careful steps on railway ties that paralleled the Urubamba River. Vancho pointed out the thickets of bananas and avocado trees rising from the mountain at steep angles.

We were all easy targets for mosquitoes and got eaten alive, but luckily I didn't get zapped as much as some of the others. By midday I only had a constellation of twenty-four welts on my right calf—and nowhere else. Other trekkers looked like they had the measles. My bottle of toxic 98-percent DEET kept the bugs at a distance but eventually caused my skin to decompose. I wasn't sure which was the worse of two evils. I just prayed that no mosquitoes were carrying malaria.

Eventually, we reached the town of Aguas Calientes, where the lodging manager promised us the ever-elusive hot shower. This, of course, should be the case in a town called Hot Waters. But, as usual, we were told what we wanted to hear at the moment.

During the icy shower, I cried out in frigid agony while attempting to rid myself of the poisonous DEET. I even shampooed my hair, which, after four days and sulfur baths, was a must, no matter how cold. Aiden and Magnus, playing cards in our room, laughed out loud, seemingly unconcerned with their own filth.

45

A CHEESEBURGER
IN PARADISE

The next morning, we were up at 3:30 a.m. to start the last leg up to the gateway of Machu Picchu. There was a lot of huffing and puffing and misstepping in the dark climb on the huge block steps up the mountain. It was hard to imagine the shorter-legged Peruvians making the lunge up each step.

"Why the hell didn't they make smaller steps?" Isaac cried out. He and his girlfriend were both five foot six and having a hard time with the ascent. Finally, at about 5:15 a.m., we reached the entrance gate and sat down to eat the bagged breakfast Vancho had given each of us prior to departure. The chill of the morning set in and we guarded our spot as all the other early morning trekkers arrived. A friendly puppy kept me warm by sitting on my lap. He was content to eat the "donkey stomp" from my breakfast sack, the flat, dry, and tasteless Peruvian bread.

"Hey, Aiden. I want you to meet Carlitos!" I said, handing him the puppy. The dog barked and licked his face. Aiden lit up.

It was still dark, but the plaza in front of the entrance gate was jammed with backpackers. It felt as if I was part of a mob waiting to get into a concert. The first thing visible once dawn broke was the mist-covered peak of Huayna Picchu. I was told that the looming mountain famously displayed in most of the images of Machu Picchu was actually this peak. It looked like a green rhino horn and only four hundred people a day were allowed to climb it. Everyone waiting seemed to be buzzing about getting one of the special tickets to reach the summit.

Much could be said about Peruvian inefficiency, but their system for this World Heritage site had to be one of the worst. Once I handed the guard my ticket, I was shoved by a mass of people who sprinted past as if chased by an axe murderer, or a wild turkey. Their purpose was to get to the other side of the mysterious, ancient Lost City of the Incas and line up at another gate to get a Huayna Picchu ticket.

The otherworldly architecture was swathed in ghostly mist as focused trekkers raced in a fury, passing vast grassy terraces where llamas quietly nibbled. One fellow dashed down the cobblestone path with his arm up to the side, wildly snapping photos without even knowing what he was taking pictures of. Feeling an odd pressure to run too, I fell victim to my own competitive nature and blindly followed suit. I laughed out loud when I saw Aiden running on the far side of a grassy terrace with Carlitos flopping under his arm.

Finally, everyone from our group was together as the unorganized line of people took on a personality of its own. There were arguments as those in line tried to sneak in their friends who were slower to reach the queue. It nearly got physical, cultures clashing when those from countries not accustomed to the unspoken rules of lining up tried to push to the front. Since there was a limited number of tickets, some were willing to fight to the death for their once-in-a-lifetime opportunity. Vancho handed me a waiver to sign that would relieve the INC of any liability in case I should fall off the narrow and dangerous trail up Huayna Picchu.

"Oh, hell, no!" I told Aiden and Magnus. "I'm not going up. Seriously. I am done climbing mountains for now."

"Ay, Ann! Come this far, you gotta go up!" encouraged Aiden.

"Oh, no I don't. I have learned that going to the top of a peak is not the destination. It's all about the journey. So I am just going to journey myself around this magical place while you guys go up there."

"OK, then. Enjoy yourself," Magnus said, putting his hand on my shoulder. "Stay out of trouble, OK, little Anita?"

"Yes, Magnus, don't worry about me."

"I worry, Ann. I worry," Magnus said with a wave as the group started up the trail.

I gave my ticket to a woeful traveler who thought she had lost the rare opportunity. She hugged me as if she had won the lottery.

Even with the royal city infiltrated with the throng of early morning trekkers, there were still many isolated and seemingly magical spots. Luckily, Vancho had convinced us to start early since the tour buses typically arrived around 8:00 a.m., transforming the sacred site into an overcrowded theme park.

With still so much of the citadel shrouded in mist, it was hard to get my bearings, so I headed toward the direction of the rising sun. Sitting on the edge of a dizzying drop, I gazed out over the *ceja de la selva*, the eyebrow of the jungle, which was what Vancho called the thick clouds that sat atop the dense rainforest.

I touched my Andean cross and crossed my legs, then dropped my hands to my knees and closed my eyes. After ten breaths, I could feel myself opening up to a palpable spiritual energy. Connecting to the apu of Machu Picchu and the energy of Pachamama, I released myself to the vibration. It felt that with every loud beat of my heart love was radiating. Images of people who had crossed my path in South America emerged in my mind's eye. Each time one surfaced, I would wrap him or her in a cloak of love and send out a twinkle of gratitude.

I thought of the kindhearted Don Rodrigo in Chile and his patriotic cheese. And Marisol, who was doing so much to help her son's vision by opening her home up to complete strangers. I thought of Kylie and the moment she appeared in the doorway when I was deathly ill and Dr. Torres, who rescued me from the depths of disease. There was Javier and his grandiose plans for helping as many kids as he could.

The faces of the children ran through my mind. I could visualize Daniela sitting in my lap, proudly wearing her glasses, and Tomás singing his meditation melody. I thought of all the little ones who had finally memorized "La capital de India es Nueva Delhi" and their impressive performance in front of the school. Tears gathered as I sent out a prayer for little, homeless Paula.

I thought of Pamela from the supply room and the three wise amigos. I could imagine Lupe still not tiring of reading *Green Eggs and Ham* and her mother and grandmother, who probably were. I sent good vibes to Dexter from the bus ride from hell and the crew from the Chichani expedition. I wondered if my doggy pal Colquita had found a new master. I relived the joy in Cesar's eyes when I gave him the kite on the island of Amantani in Lake Boobypoop. My heart warmed when I thought of the rotund Alfredo and his hearty laugh. I sent strength and love to Mayu and Joviana and prayed that they had found the courage to stay sober.

Although my eyes were closed, a warm sensation of sunlight splashed across my face. Deep gratitude swirled through me for each person in my current trekking group. By the time I had gone through each member of my own family and friends, it felt as if, were I to open my eyes, I would discover that I was levitating. My skin was tingling, and my breathing had slowed. I felt light, carefree, and entirely filled with pure love.

An all-encompassing realization washed over me and drowned my senses with clarity. This journey to Peru was to show me the way to my own heart. The beating source of Mother Earth—of Pachamama—was the common thread of the loving life force woven through all.

I exhaled and slowly separated my lashes. Once I opened my eyes, my mouth unhinged at what I saw. A panorama of sky-scraping peaks poked through the clouds with dozens of sunrays piercing the swirling mist. Dew reflected off trees from the distant mountainsides, creating an emerald-green landscape with diamond-like sparkles igniting the divinely majestic view. The distinctive Huayna Picchu mountain was perfectly visible, with tiny outlines of tourists making their way up the switchbacks.

Instead of running off to climb it, I found a secluded, grassy nook and leaned up against my backpack to reflect. Two hours later, I awoke to a fluffy-white llama chewing grass near my feet. Laughing to myself, I couldn't help but think about how I'd come all the way to Machu Picchu and didn't even climb the famous big green thumb of Huayna Picchu, but instead took a nap hidden away in the Palace of the Incas.

Feeling renewed, I ventured down to the Machu Picchu café, ordered a $15 cheeseburger, put my feet up, and finally started in on one of the three books I had brought. With Huayna Picchu jutting up in the distance, I bit into the juicy burger and groaned in sheer delight.

Aiden, Magnus, Carlitos (the dog), and I in front of Huayna Picchu.

46

THE LUCKY PAW

" ¿Más café?" asked the chirpy, round-faced waitress. I nodded for a refill and continued writing feverously in my journal. It had been three days since my return to Cuzco, and each morning had been spent at the same sunlit table, served by the same attentive server. One week was all that remained of my trip, and, based on my previous experience in the city, spending those days in Cuzco wasn't appealing.

After breakfast, an enthusiastic trekking company promoter invited me in to check out the adventures offered. A four-day canoe trip down the Amazon was his latest deal, but I didn't feel one prick of desire. I thanked the travel agent and went to visit Lupe instead.

Lupe and her mother, Teresa, greeted me like I was family. Lupe brought out her *Green Eggs and Ham* book and pleaded for me to read it with silly voices as I had done before.

"Pleeeease! No one in my family reads it like you," she begged.

After a few rounds of the story, I scanned through Teresa's glass cases of jewelry. Now that my trip was coming to a close, it would be a good time to make purchases for friends and family. Mesmerized, I stood before a necklace set with purple stones, silver swirls, and a delicate hummingbird. It was the style of jewelry that would make my mom swoon. Teresa gave me a price that seemed high, but there was no need to barter. The necklace was a gift for my mother, who had done so much to encourage me, and, in turn, the money from the purchase would help Teresa support her own daughter.

Teresa became emotional, hugging me repeatedly, and said, "That is my first sale in over two weeks."

Even though Christmas was a few months off, I figured it was a good time to take care of my list. I bought an assortment of dolls, purses, shawls, llama statues, and more jewelry. Waving good-bye, I promised to send Lupe and Teresa a care package at Christmas.

Early the next morning, the soft-spoken waitress brought my breakfast and coffee without me having to order it first. She had a gentle, childlike joy in her eyes and a dimpled smile that would charm any patron. Then it hit me. I still had a small collection of school supplies that I had reclaimed from the Arco Iris School. With the ever-expanding assortment of gifts and decorations for my classroom, there was little room for me to carry more.

Now on a first name basis with the waitress, I waved her to my table. "Clarabelle, can I ask you a personal question?"

"Sí, of course," she replied.

"Do you have children?"

She lit up. "Yes, Gonzo is ten, and my little angel, Rosa, is four."

"I have school supplies that I'd like to give your kids. If that's okay with you."

"¡Por supesto! Muchas gracias!" she said as tiny, grateful tears sprung up.

Quickly returning to my room, I brought back a bag full of treasures: crayons, construction paper, stickers, scissors, and a variety of books in Spanish. Clarabelle hugged me without hesitation and asked if I would meet her in the plaza that night after she got off work.

"Tonight? You work from now until then?" I asked, looking at my watch. It was 7:00 a.m.

"Yes. I work a twelve-hour shift—seven days a week," she said, slightly shaking her head but still smiling.

"No. Really? Seven days a week?" I said skeptically.

"Yes, but I'm very blessed to have this job," she said with sincerity.

I agreed to meet with her since nothing was on my agenda for the entire day, or the next few days, besides meeting up with the three amigos.

That evening, while I sat in the plaza waiting for Clarabelle, the street vendors swarmed. A hollow-cheeked boy with a rascally demeanor approached, selling finger puppets.

"Buy one, lady?" he said in English, then pointed at my stomach and added, "For your baby."

Luckily, I was feeling right-sized that day and didn't take offense, but I still advised him to try a new sales technique.

"Buy some for your grandchildren," he said with all seriousness. But then a smile spread across his face and we laughed together. Unable to resist his playful teasing, I handed over the money for a dozen puppets.

"Ana!" Clarabelle called from across the plaza.

Beaming, she stood in front of the plaza fountain proudly holding the hands of her two children. Rosa and Gonzo ran to me and jumped in my arms as if they had known me for years. They both handed me thank you cards designed with the materials I had given their mother earlier that day.

Rosa's long, black hair was perfectly woven into two braids that hung to her waist, and she wore bright pink overalls and corrective shoes. Her face was as precious as porcelain, with eyes to melt every heart they gazed into. Gonzo wore jeans a few sizes too small, and it looked as if he had outgrown his shoes long ago. Unconcerned, Gonzo chased the mass of pigeons gathering in the plaza. Rosa sat on my lap with her hand intertwined in mine.

Clarabelle turned and asked, "Would you like to come back to our home for a warm drink?"

A taxi took us up to the poor section of Cuzco. Although poor could pretty much describe most of the city, up in the mountainside was where compacted communities lived in nearly unbearable conditions. Clarabelle suddenly got embarrassed and told me it wasn't really a "home," but she did her best to make it one.

The taxi could only take us so far, since the rest of the way was on a steep, dirt road. Gonzo led as we climbed through an opening, breaching a metal fence, and moved down a dark passageway that smelled so pungent I had to cover my nose and mouth with my arm. My three hosts, unaffected by the stench, were in front and luckily didn't notice my reaction.

Next was a splintered, unsteady ladder that had to be climbed in order to reach the second level. Gonzo went first and sat at the top, stretching his hand down to help his sister. Rosa, in her bubble-gum-pink outfit, was a stark contrast to the dreariness of the worn-down building. The second story walkway cracked under my weight as I avoided gaping holes that opened directly to the cement below. The dark and solemn eyes of an elderly man watched me suspiciously as I passed by his open door.

My senses were on overload and a wave of anxiety took over. Where was Clarabelle taking me? Was I safe?

Rosa hopscotched her way down the passageway, avoiding the dangerous areas, which she seemed to know by heart. "¡Venga, Ana!" she motioned with a sweet little-girl giggle.

Hesitantly, I peeked my head into their home.

Inside, the three of them stood together with eager grins. My mouth just about dropped open in disbelief, but I maintained control of my expressions.

"Bienvenida a nuestra casa," said Gonzo. I thought I could sense a flash of shame in Clarabelle's eyes as I looked around.

It was a fifteen-by-fifteen-foot room for a family of four. There were two single beds head to head and a large box for a closet to keep their few possessions in. A dinner table took up most of the room, with a half fridge and a single camping burner for the kitchen. Since there was no running water, it was Gonzo's job to pump it into a rusty bucket from a spigot on the street, bring it up the ladder, and place it by the doorway.

Immediately, Gonzo dashed to the bed to grab his prized possession, the purple dinosaur Barney. The well-loved stuffed animal was splitting at the seams and had one eye. It was the only toy, and the two children shared it. That took a moment to digest as guilt stabbed.

As a child, not only did I have my own bedroom, which was the size of their home, but I also had two single beds. One for me—and one to display all my stuffed animals. I told Gonzo how I, too, loved dinosaurs, and described my childhood friend Topsy. Rosa was eager to hold Barney, and Gonzo handed it over to her tenderly, without protest.

Chilled to the bone, I sat with the kids and drew pictures with the supplies I had given them. Gonzo drilled me with endless questions: Are there parrots in Canada? Is Belgium near California? Can you draw a woolly mammoth? What do Nazis look like?

Clarabelle prepared a drink for me with hot water and quinoa grain. Rosa looked at the steaming cup hungrily and asked her mom for one. Clarabelle responded lovingly in Quechua, and although I didn't know the language, I could guess what she had said. The quinoa had been scooped from a large burlap sack that was nearly empty. There probably wasn't enough to go around, and since I was their guest, it was given to me. Understanding the unspoken rules of hospitality in Latin cultures, I drank my cup of the bland mush, although I wanted to insist that Rosa drink it instead.

Remembering our conversation from earlier that day, I probed Clarabelle about her job. "So do you really work seven days a week?"

She nodded.

"Do you get vacation time?" I asked.

She laughed, shaking her head. "No, no, Ana, no vacations."

"When do you get a break? What if you are sick?" My mind was whirling. It was hard to grasp. *No break— ever?*

"If I don't go, I will lose the job. But I am very lucky. At the restaurant, I'm making $125!"

A day? A week? Fortunately, I didn't ask. She made $125 a month, working twelve hours a day, seven days a week, with no benefits and no days off. Her husband, Manco, made $250 a month doing reconstruction on ancient Peruvian ruins like Machu Picchu. He was on-site during the week, but sometimes was able to come home on the weekends.

Feeling ashamed, I didn't know how to respond when she asked how much it cost to stay a night in a hostel. My stomach knotted remembering that I had spent over $100 that very day on a chessboard with hand-painted Incan warrior figurines facing off against Spanish conquistadors.

With obvious enthusiasm, she described how she made pies from the rotten fruit she collected from the trash. Gonzo and Rosa agreed they were the best pies in town, although it was rare that they actually got to eat one. Gonzo told how his mother sold these irresistible fruit-filled pastries door-to-door a few days a week after work, and although he and his sister always hoped she sold them all, they knew that if she didn't, they'd get one.

Something shifted for Clarabelle and she looked at me with piercing clarity and declared, "My children will get an education. I'll do *whatever* it takes. You probably have seen many kids working in the streets, but I will not let Rosa and Gonzo do that. They will never have a childhood like mine. If they go to school, they will have a better life."

A fiercely determined fire blazed from her eyes, and I knew without a shadow of a doubt that this woman was something remarkable. Then I made the mistake of asking my next question. "So what do Rosa and Gonzo do while you work?"

Instant emotion clouded her expression and she covered her face with her tiny hands. Wanting to rewind the moment and take back my question, I gently put my hand on her shoulder.

"Don't cry, Mama," Gonzo said, wrapping his arms around her. Rosa began crying too, reacting to her mother's sadness. Gonzo grabbed the Barney doll and gave Rosa kisses with its tattered nose. She giggled and he guided her over to the bed and began reading her one of their new books.

Because her husband was gone most of the time, Clarabelle explained, the responsibility of taking care of Rosa had fallen on the shoulders of ten-year-old

Gonzo. "I want to raise my children, but it's impossible. I have to work. So Gonzo is doing my job as a mother," she said, clearly devastated.

Clarabelle told me how Gonzo walked two miles each morning to drop Rosa off at daycare, took a bus to school across town, picked Rosa back up, made her dinner, played with her, and put her to bed—every day. On the weekends, it was his job to entertain her, unless their father was home. The neighborhood wasn't safe, so they remained inside the windowless room. Scanning the small area, I wondered what Gonzo did with all those hours cooped up with his sister. There was no television, radio, games, or toys. Only Barney and a few tattered books. At least now the treasure bag of imaginative goodies was available for entertainment.

Clarabelle wept, helplessly wracked with guilt as she looked over at her son fondly. From what I could see, Gonzo didn't complain but took on his responsibility with love and patience, unlike most boys his age. Not only that, Clarabelle told how he had encouraging words, drawings, songs, and smiles for her when she came home exhausted.

Rosa tugged on her mother's arm. "I want to go to the piñata, Mamá, please!"

Clarabelle explained that a piñata was what they called a birthday party. With noticeable grief, she sadly told me that she and her husband couldn't afford to have piñatas for Rosa and Gonzo—but they were currently saving money for Rosa's baptism.

I couldn't help but feel like I wanted to offer to pay for it all. The birthdays, the baptism, a babysitter, a

Sparkletts man to bring them jugs of fresh water, toys, sacks of quinoa grain, clothes that fit, and everything else a family should not have to worry about. Pausing for a moment, I listened to my intuition and then turned to my new friend.

"Five months ago I had a dream," I said. "I wanted to come to Peru and bring school supplies and help the children. It was not something easy to accomplish, but I believed in my heart it was what I was supposed to do. I did my best, and although it didn't turn out exactly as I expected, I feel like it made a difference."

I paused, not sure how to put into words my next statement.

"Clarabelle, is there something in your life that you dream about? Perhaps something you are passionate about but have not been able to do? Like an idea or a hope for something you'd like to make happen?"

Hesitantly, I sat back, not sure if I had made a mistake in opening my mouth. *Did I insult her? Clearly, there are a lot of things she could dream about making better. Was that inconsiderate to put on her my American faith in hopes and dreams?*

Her wheels were turning as Gonzo eyed her from the bed, obviously unable to keep his insatiably curious mind from eavesdropping.

Her cheeks became flush and I feared she might cry again. *Oh, dear, what have I done?*

The emotion cleared and she said, "Ana, we don't have time for dreaming. There is no chance for life to be different than what it is. Then I'd be sad because it could never come true."

Feeling immediate discomfort after my thoughtless inquiry, I started nervously digging in my purse for nothing in particular. Clarabelle jumped up and began tearing apart the bed frame, eventually coming to a black trash bag beneath. She presented me a beautifully hand-stitched llama purse she had made. I accepted it graciously and followed her out in the pitch black of night, cautiously stepping along the brittle balcony, down the ladder, and past the stinky pathway. She pointed out the public latrine, overflowing and more horrific than any toilet I had ever witnessed.

All of us walked Rosa to the piñata a few streets away. I stood in the doorway, transfixed by the bizarre entertainment. A clown with scary face paint and bloodshot eyes was dancing in front of the children. Rosa sat in the front row, hypnotized by the clown's creepy voice as he did hazardous magic tricks. First, he set his own hands on fire in the tiny room full of children, causing balloons near him to pop and streamers to catch fire. He belted out a disturbing cackle, then pulled a dirty, sickly bird out of his hat. I was so bewildered by the abnormal clown that I failed to notice the party guests turning away from his odd performance to stare at what they thought to be unusual—the tall, white *gringa* in their neighborhood.

Leaving Gonzo and Rosa at the piñata, Clarabelle and I walked to a street where I could catch a taxi. Suddenly, she let out a squeal, seeing something in the dirt. Her eyes widened in anticipation, turning the small, leather coin purse over in her hand. She held her breath as she opened it. *Please, let it be stuffed with cash!* I thought optimistically.

By the dim glow of a light nearby, she carefully pulled out the contents and gasped. Holding it up to the light, she revealed a petrified fox paw. Expecting something entirely different, I flinched from its curled claws and matted, reddish fur. She jumped up and down with so much excitement one would have thought she had a jackpot lottery ticket in hand.

"In my culture, this is very good luck. It is a sign from the gods that they will be sending me a miracle. And that miracle is you!"

47

CLARABELLE'S STORY

The taxi dropped me back at the Plaza de Armas. In spite of a few rowdy tourists crossing the grass toward the discotecas, it was strangely peaceful. The sensation was distinct from the daytime circus of tourists, vendors, dogs, parades, and protests. The plaza was neatly manicured and flower-lined, which was unlike any other area in Cuzco. Clearly, the city had spent a lot of effort to keep one square of area maintained for the flocks of tourists visiting Cuzco. I had usually blazed through the plaza as an efficient route from one side of the city center to the other but didn't take much notice of it—or its history. This was the very place where the Spanish conquistador Francisco Pizarro had laid claim to the city.

Turning to the mountain behind, the illuminated White Christ was glowing grandly in front of the black curtain of night. The stone block ruins of the fortress Sacsayhuaman lay scattered on the hillside next to El Cristo Blanco. Since it was difficult for foreigners to pronounce the name of the architectural wonder, it was simply called Sexy Woman. Sexy Woman was the site of the Incan warriors' last stand against Pizarro and his men. The ruins were held in great reverence, and the powerful energy of its importance was unmistakable.

The water from the fountain was off and the lights aglow on the two principal churches flanking the plaza. A wave of historical mysticism swirled thought the colonial stone archways. It was so quiet I could hear the rustle of feathers as pigeons sought out their nests tucked in the ornate façade of the baroque cathedral.

I sat on the exact bench where I had purchased the dozen finger puppets earlier that day. Only four hours had lapsed. The intensity of being with Clarabelle and her family had had such great impact, it felt as if I had suffered a severe head injury. My brain throbbed trying to digest the new data from my recent experience. It was hard to grasp how my new friend could have such a joyful sparkle in her eye when she lived in abject poverty stacked with insurmountable adversity.

How did she recharge? How could she go on day after day and still genuinely smile while serving breakfast? My stomach bottomed out with shame at how I recklessly spent money and took for granted my lifestyle full of vacations and flexibility to do exactly what I wanted, when I wanted. Since the first day of my arrival, I had witnessed enough gut-wrenching poverty to cause me to reflect deeply on my own life, but nothing had come close to what I felt after spending just four hours with Clarabelle.

Cynicism suddenly wormed its way into my thinking. *She just wants my money. I bet she told me that whole sob story to make me feel bad for her. And the lucky fox foot? I bet that was a setup.* I shook my head to rid the suspicious distrust from my thoughts. She just wanted someone to hear her. To know her story. To be her friend. Closing my eyes, I envisioned windshield wipers cleaning off the recycled filth of old beliefs from the window of my mind. It was time to see clearly by leading with my heart—like Clarabelle did.

My thoughts spun with ways I could help the family, but I had learned that this was a fragile line to tread. Flying in like Superwoman to save the day with a sum of money wasn't the solution. It would devalue the hard work Clarabelle put in daily. It was going to take some careful thought before I made any grand promises or generous offers. The profound words that our Machu Picchu guide, Vancho, had said about his mother echoed through my head, that female empowerment was the solution to poverty in third world countries.

Every evening for the next three days, Clarabelle and I met in the plaza and talked. She let me know that all her close friends called her Clara and invited me to do the same. Eager to tell me everything, she described the chocolates she sold at the Christmas fair and how Gonzo was getting bullied at school, about Rosa being pigeon-toed, her husband finding ancient treasures at Machu Picchu, and the many different jobs she had prior to being a server at the restaurant.

During one of our long chats, and with just a few days left before my departure, Clara unexpectedly announced, "Ana, I am ready to tell you about my life."

"Isn't that what you've been doing?" I asked in all sincerity.

"Oh, no. I have never told anyone *this* part. Not even my husband."

The plaza was bustling, so we moved in closer on the bench. With the first parting of her soft, pink lips, a pained, childlike moan escaped with her exhale. It was as if the seal had been broken and she'd made the conscious choice to release the memories that haunted her. The sun began its descent behind the hills as the last rays of light glittered off the splashing plaza fountain, reflecting her endless stream of tears.

Clara was one of eleven children born in a poor village deep in the Andes. With surprising awareness, she claimed that due to her parents' ignorance, they didn't know how to provide for the children they kept producing. After their father disappeared, her mother informed the children that he had died. Clara would never know the truth, but she was almost positive he had abandoned them.

Living below the poverty line, she went most nights without food. She suffered physical abuse at the hands of her uncle and was put to work at the age of six. Clara was responsible for collecting llama dung used for cooking fires.

After a few years of this daily task, she excitedly came upon an unlikely pile of wood. Although it was wet, she thought it might also be good for a cooking fire. Certain this discovery would please her mother and uncle, she skipped back home, having no idea that it was the last day that she'd ever see her family again. Furious that she had returned with wet wood instead of what was asked of her, she was beaten—and sold to a family in another village.

Her mother's last words to her were: "Maybe another family will find you useful, because you are useless to ours." Clara was only eight.

Unaffected by the constant stream of people around us in the plaza, I descended deeper into Clara's world, weeping along with her as she continued her story.

She was sent to work as a servant in a bigger village, never being allowed to visit her own family. I asked her if this family treated her well, but she covered her face and shook her head, shuddering with sobs. This portion of her story was so disturbing my throat constricted and I felt nauseous as she turned each devastating page of that chapter of her life.

I gave her my solemn promise that I would never recount to anyone what had happened to her during the time with this family. The quickness and intensity of her words made it seem like she believed the past might materialize if she were to hang on one word for too long. *Had she really never told anyone?* How could this woman possibly live with such joy without having had any example of love or tenderness, let alone not having anyone she could trust?

At eighteen, she ran away from her servitude and lived in the streets until she met Manco, her current husband. She got pregnant with Gonzo, and now, ten years later, they were still together, living in that tiny room with their two children.

"You see, Ana, I am free. I can work and make money. I can raise my children with love. I have a good life, and I feel very blessed," she said, concluding her story.

I had no words to respond. *Blessed? A good life?*

Perking up, she explained what her life had been like recently. Last year, she put herself through waitressing school and was able to get a restaurant job serving food. Transforming before my eyes, she noticeably sat up straighter and her sparkly eyes had even more shine. She let out a carefree giggle and said, "Mi amiga, I thought about what you asked me, about dreams."

Hardly able to control my excitement and relief that she wasn't offended by the original query, I took both of her hands in mine. "Tell me, Clara!"

"First, I want to be a chef. I don't want to serve food—I want to make it! At home, I don't have much to cook with, but I am creative with food and can make something good out of nothing!"

I laughed to myself; it was clear that her last statement was the metaphor for her life.

"And one more thing, Ana," she said. "I have a special idea—I think."

It was a secret design that she'd been harboring for years of a unique baby carrier that was comfortable and multifunctional and used exquisite indigenous cloth. She'd been afraid to market the carriers because there were no copyright laws for street vendors. A clever individual with more capital could copy an idea, mass-produce it, and then flood the market. Clara could only make one carrier at a time.

"I think it's a special idea," she said hopefully. "That's a hope or a dream, right? Like you were talking about?"

"Yes, that's a great idea," I told her. "I can't wait to see one! Bring it next time we meet."

I thanked her for sharing her story and we embraced. Pressing my palms to her back, I held her so close I could feel her heart beat. We made plans to meet up for our last time the next night, and I promised to take the family out for pizza afterward.

"Oh, Ana! The kids are going to be so excited! Thank you."

"No, Clara, thank you," I said, putting my palm across my chest in deep admiration.

* * *

My last night in Cuzco was a beautiful one. The sky was jumbled with billowing white clouds taking on various shapes. The air was dry and the temperature pleasant. Clara and I were silent, mesmerized by the character clouds, until she suddenly turned to face me with a serious expression and began her long, breathless request. "Ana, it would be an honor if you would be Rosa's *madrina*, her godmother. Will you come back in December when I save enough money for the celebration? I have never cut Rosa's hair and won't until the day of her baptism when her madrina will cut off a long braid. I want you to be the one who does this. Ana, I know in my heart you are the one."

My first thoughts were *Why me? She knows I'm leaving soon and can't be an active part of her life.* But then it came to me. Of course. She is taking out insurance for her daughter, securing Rosa's future. She was doing what a mother must to take care of her children. But what was admirable was that she hadn't asked for money at any point during all our conversations. She was a proud woman and was resourcefully creating ways to better her children's lives.

"I trust you," Clara went on. "And even though I've known you for only a week, it is destined to be. That's what God was telling me by giving me the fox paw."

Hmm, I didn't know God communicated through animal feet, I thought curiously. But I understood that she had seen a sign that, to her, meant I was the one to trust. I told her that although I wouldn't be back in December, I'd be honored to be Rosa's godmother. Deep relief swept across her, and she clasped her hands together and said a quick prayer.

"Oh, Ana! I brought the carrier!" she said. As Clara pulled it out of a trash bag, I saw for the first time the lovely, delicately sewn baby carrier made with brilliantly colored indigenous cloth. It was unlike anything I had seen before.

"Did you really make this?" I asked, stunned. "It's beautiful."

She beamed with pride.

"You're right, it *is* unique."

Turning the intricately handcrafted carrier in my lap, I ran my fingers along the colorful stitching. My brain spun at high velocity. I could hear a cacophony of voices in my head—but these weren't the Shit Birds squawking. They were the voices of reason, ingenuity, compassion, and possibility—all motivated to have a say in the master plan that was being conjured up.

"I've got some ideas, Clara," I said. "I'm not exactly sure what yet, but I'll figure it out by tomorrow." I gave her the address of my favorite pizzeria and asked her to bring the kids and meet me there later that night.

With the menu spread out before him, Gonzo couldn't seem to make a decision. He had nearly rocketed through the roof when I told him he was in charge of choosing the pizzas for all of us. Scouring over every option, he asked about each food item that wasn't familiar. What is a pineapple? Where is it grown? What does it taste like? Finally settling on a Hawaiian and pepperoni pizza, he popped up and down in his seat, unable to contain his enthusiasm, and shouted, "We have never been to a restaurant before!"

His eyes were wide with hungry anticipation as the cook pulled the bubbling pizza out of the adobe oven. Clara had positioned herself near the oven and had been carefully observing every step of the pizza-making process.

Rosa bounced on my lap, twirling my hair, when suddenly Clara dug in her purse and pulled out a pair of scissors. She leaned over and grabbed Rosa's long, snaking braid. "Ana, please," Clara said. "Even if you cannot come back in December for the ceremony, please do me the honor of being her godmother and cut her braid now before you leave."

Feeling put on the spot, I didn't know how to respond. Rosa's silky, black braid rested across Clara's palm. Did I really want to commit myself to this family? Taking a moment, I scanned the faces at the table. Gonzo, the brilliant young man thirsting for knowledge, who had to spend *all* his free time with a four-year-old. Rosa, the angel who whispered little girl secrets in my ears and drew pictures of me with wings.

And Clara, who'd survived a childhood that no girl should and who had dug deep to find courage in the face of great difficulty to bring love and values to her children. I believed in this woman, and I wanted to be a part of their lives.

I hesitantly took the scissors from Clara and asked Rosa if she was OK with me cutting her braid. "Sí, madrina. ¡Hágalo!" she said with an angelic smile. Yes, godmother. Do it!

The scissors made a crisp and decisive cut.

The thick, twisted lock of raven hair lay lifelessly in my hand. A pink rubber band held the braid together at one end. I smiled nervously as Rosa giggled and pulled me close. Cupping her little hands around her mouth, she whispered with tender maturity, "Madrina, always keep me in your heart."

* * *

The night seemed timeless as my mind tunneled its way to the golden-nugget idea trove. Sitting in meditative silence, I sent out nonstop prayers to be guided, and like a thunderbolt it struck me.

As Clara accompanied me to the airport early the next morning, I debriefed her on my plan. I told her what I was willing to do and what I expected her role to be. We shook on it and held each other tight.

"I'll contact you when I get back to the States, and we can start making this dream into reality! Are you ready, Clara?" I asked, feeling a rush of optimism.

"Sí, Ana. I have been waiting all my life for this chance."

48

INKA THREADS

A new school year began just days after my return to California. I shared with my new students inspiring stories, pictures, videos, and special mementos from my travels. My mini-documentary of the floating reed islands of Uros fascinated the kids to no end, along with my attempt to interview a llama who made Machu Picchu his home. I was back in the flow of my normal life, whereas a whole new chapter in Clara's life was just being written.

My proposal to Clara on that last day in Cuzco was unforgettable as two determined women came together with a dream—and put into motion something extraordinary. With her cheeks rosy and eyes sparkling, Clara had listened carefully as I laid out the details of my plan. If she was willing, I'd told her, I'd hire her for a three-month trial period to design baby carriers, paying her the same amount she was currently earning at the restaurant. This would allow her to sew from home and be the mother she so desperately wanted to be. Rosa wouldn't need daycare, and Gonzo could play with his friends after school.

Handing her an envelope with $150 to get started, I promised to provide a microloan once she had created a plan for production. The next stage was for her to assemble and sew these items and send the finished product to me so that I could sell them to Americans for five times what people would pay in Peru. The final phase would be to send Clara the profits.

It had all sounded promising as I'd explained it to her, but whether it would actualize as I had imagined remained to be seen. Feeling hopeful on that last morning together, we'd waved good-bye through the sliding glass doors at the airport.

With Clara being practically illiterate, there were going to be many unpredictable hurtles to overcome. Her first e-mail communication was practically illegible, and I was afraid she wasn't going to be able to read mine. All her messages were phonetically written, which I diligently decrypted using my experience with students who wrote Spanish essays in a similar style.

It was obvious when Gonzo transcribed the correspondence for his mother, and I insisted that he read mine to her so that my questions or responses were clear. Gonzo let me know he had been using the educational books I had sent him to help his mother learn to read. With Clara's skills and determination, and with Gonzo as our liaison, we began to lay the foundation of the business.

A fully functional workstation had been set up from her home after she bought a sewing machine, embroidery supplies, and bolts of material. Once she was in the swing of production, Clara informed me that she had used part of the loan to hire a group of her hardworking friends who lived in the same dreary predicament. She was adamant that the more families that benefited from her lucky opportunity the better. Then they would all share in the profits. She insisted that her new employees bring their children, and it soon became a community affair.

Upon the completion of three dozen baby carriers, I instructed her to send them to me in California, not considering that she had never mailed anything in her life, let alone a large quantity of goods to a foreign country. On my doorstep arrived a massive, transparent package fastened together haphazardly with clear tape. She had used a variety of plastic bags all taped together to make one. My name was written incorrectly, in nonpermanent marker, directly onto the see-through packaging. That it made that long journey to my doorstep and remained intact must have been due to Clara's persistent rubbing of the lucky fox paw.

Easily cutting through the thin wrapping, I reached our precious cargo. Each carrier had been carefully crafted using brilliant fabrics and with detailed, hand-stitched images of llamas, Incan crosses, and condors. They could be worn comfortably on the chest or the back and had a support belt that buckled at the waist. Each was truly a work of art. The royal blue and aquamarine designs were sure to be a hit, but I wasn't sure what to make of the half dozen fluorescent orange ones.

Calling my new small business Inka Threads, I began selling the carriers at fairs, parties, online, and by word-of-mouth. Soon enough, Clara was also designing diaper bags and beanies, which she learned to send in sturdy boxes with official packing tape. At the high school, the principal graciously allowed me to hold a Beanie Bonanza. During one thirty-minute lunch period, I sold more than one hundred stitched hats.

After I shared the story with my students, they decided to take matters into their own hands. Fundraisers were mounted, along with a clothing drive for the families of all the women sewing carriers. A fund was started for Rosa and Gonzo to have a piñata party for their next birthdays—hopefully without a dodgy clown. Students wrote Gonzo pen-pal letters to practice their Spanish, telling him interesting facts about California. One student was so touched by their story that she started a scholarship college fund for Gonzo and committed a donation of $50 for every semester of her high school career.

The bright orange carriers that never sold eventually found a welcoming home. After hearing the stories, Merit, another inspired student, started the Empowerment of Women Worldwide Club on campus. Her club raised awareness about the importance of empowering women in third world countries. Ultimately, Merit's group raised enough money to send one Cambodian girl to school for a year.

Merit asked if I'd be willing to donate the non-sellable carriers to a women's shelter where she volunteered. The facility provided the necessities for new mothers who lived in poverty. It was a beautiful solution—another wave from the ripple effect of Clara's dream.

Once Clara's loan was paid back, I was able to accumulate a hearty profit for her. Many restless nights were spent stewing over how I should turn over the money. My concern was that since she lived in daily survival mode, she wouldn't have a frame of reference for handling a surplus of money. How was she going to manage a sudden dramatic increase in her financial situation? What she had earned in two months of sewing was more than she and her husband made in a year combined.

Then I realized that it wasn't for me to decide. Up to this point, Clara had continually surprised me with her instinct, reliability, ingenuity, and focus. I was just going to have to trust that she would know what to do.

A few of Clarabelle's creations.

49

HE IS THE ONE

By the end of the first month of the school year, a satisfying rhythm to my life had taken shape. My time was divided into teaching Spanish, mentoring other sober women, and managing the Inka Threads business. My love life moved to the back burner. Friends encouraged me to dive back into the dating pool, hoping I'd finally find a good guy, but most likely they were eager for the next edition of my bad-date saga.

While scanning the Internet, a pop-up ad caught my eye for a singles camping trip on Catalina Island. It was slated as a twenties to thirties event for adventurous types to meet and participate in fun outdoor and social activities. At first glance, it seemed interesting, but I didn't click the link. But a few days later, something pulled at me to look into it further.

The second time around, the advertisement enticed me, and after careful consideration, I decided it was a great opportunity to meet an outdoorsy guy. Old-fashioned army tents that the Boy Scouts who often stayed on this particular part of the island used would be provided. The camp would be secluded on the northern cove and was accessible only by boat. So, with a burst of enthusiasm, I entered my personal information and clicked the submit button.

Optimistic and full of expectations, I boarded the boat for the adventurous singles three-day excursion. Lounging on the bow, I couldn't help feeling relaxed and hopeful as the sun shined and the wind whipped my hair. Laughing to myself, I revisited the fantasy I had created about the trip being overpopulated by dark-haired mountain men with scruffy beards who smelled like campfire.

Perhaps my luck had changed after taking a long break from all the disastrous dates prior to Peru. But I should have remembered my mom's theory that anticipation is always better than actualization. I fervently believed this philosophy referred only to risky online dating, but I was soon to discover that this singles outing also qualified.

Scanning the boat, I couldn't help but wonder if perhaps I was the only one headed to the event and the others were going somewhere else. They didn't look outdoorsy. Or adventurous. Or in their twenties and thirties. A woman in her fifties wearing fluorescent blue leggings and a leather vest passed out ginger to passengers, insisting they must eat it to evade seasickness.

Handing me a gooey, crystallized chunk, she parted bright pink lips in a smile that revealed a host of lipstick-smudged teeth, except for the front one she was missing. An overly tanned man clad in cowboy boots, surf shorts, and a tight white tank top flexed his bicep as he gladly accepted the ginger and then playfully slapped her backside.

"Excuse me," I asked the ginger lady, "are you going to the singles camping trip?"

"Yes, dear. We all are!" she said, making a wide arc with her arm toward the other travelers. My excitement instantly suspended into the arc she'd just wielded.

Closing my eyes, I tried to let the wind blow away the mounting judgment that clouded my thoughts. The fanciful and unrealistic expectation of the weekend began to swirl down the drain and bottomed out with a thud in my gut.

Once the two boats docked and the two hundred passengers disembarked, I witnessed the variety of unwoodsy characters that would be participating in the singles weekend. Right off the bat, I noticed that most were between thirty and sixty, with many having a definite social-misfit quality to them. Scanning the crowd, I couldn't spot one promising prospect. In a little pep talk with myself, I elicited some past examples of people I had misjudged only to later discover they were quality individuals.

Getting out of myself, I helped a tiny Japanese woman roll her gigantic suitcase over the wood-chip path. She wore a visor three times the size of her head, and the suitcase she pulled looked as if it was packed for an around the world tour instead of a three-day campout. The more I looked around, the more *I* felt like the misfit, and, worse, I was trapped until the boat returned in three days.

Standing still, I felt paralyzed amidst the mass of singles buzzing with anticipation. I felt no hope and my face clearly showed it. A tap on my shoulder startled me from my gloomy state, and a deep voice spoke to me from behind. "Well, hello, beautiful, why do you look soooo sad?"

Turning, I came face-to-face with Henry, a gray-haired man in his fifties with a neatly manicured mustache and goatee. His hand was wet when we shook.

"I like you," he said candidly with a wink. "I think we should be *special* friends this weekend."

Stunned, with teeth clenched, I turned my back and walked away.

A second older gentleman also propositioned me before I decided it was time to take refuge in my tent. Although it was suffocatingly hot in the canvas army tent, it felt safer than out with the others who had cheered when it was announced that the bar was open for business.

After reading for a while, I planned to explore the area near the camp and find a place to snorkel. As I put together a day bag, I heard a rustling in the bushes. Peeking out, I craned my neck from side to side, hoping to see a wild animal. Out popped a creepy stalker from behind a nearby tree with his arm awkwardly cocked behind his back.

"Ah-ha! I found you!"

"Why were you looking for me?" I said fearful of the response.

"It was really hard to find you with all these tents looking the same." He paused with a playful flicker in his eye. "So I was wondering…" He brought his arm out from behind his back. "Are these yours?"

He held a stick with a pair of dirty, little-boy underwear hanging on the end, probably left from the last Boy Scout camp. I said nothing in response, pulling the zipper closed on the tent door.

That afternoon, I braved the masses and set up my towel on the beach. I had brought my snorkel gear and knew that I would feel relief once I was out in the water and my internal mermaid was released. After chasing colorful fish around the bay, I was starting to feel more relaxed. But out of the depths, I saw something that made me gasp and swallow a mouthful of seawater. It was Mr. Let's Be *Special* Friends.

Henry was swimming below me on his back with a goofy grin—and waving. Slamming my fist into the surface of the water, I swam back to shore and returned directly to the confines of my tent.

That night, I emerged from my self-imposed prison to eat dinner but planned to make a quick return into hiding. Underwear-on-a-stick man waved from across the dining hall as it was announced that there'd be a salsa dance lesson directly following the meal. A few ladies approached and encouraged me to join in the activity since they had noticed how I kept separating myself from the group.

"I can see you're nervous. It'll be okay, sunshine," said Mary, a woman in a flowery muumuu and floppy straw hat. "We're all in this together."

It was impossible to wipe the dark misery off my face, but I softened up a bit with her genuine kindness.

When it was salsa time, the girls lined up on one side and the boys on the other, imbuing a junior high dance vibe. I could see Henry jostling for position, trying to line himself up with me. Instructed to take two large steps forward, I was soon facing my dance partner. Jerry was blond, grossly overweight, dripping with sweat, and had probably been drinking since the boat docked earlier that day. His bloodshot eyes widened when he saw that I was his partner, and he laughed nervously. Large drips of sweat splashed the floor and the rings under his arms were visibly getting wider.

The instructors demonstrated the sexy, swiveling moves we were supposed to emulate while pressing up against each other. Looking around for an escape route, I locked eyes with Mary, whose plump lips I could read from across the room. "It's okay. Relax."

Sulking, I turned back to Jerry, who was practicing the moves with an invisible woman while yelling the next steps to himself. My mind shouted, *No, no, no, no!*

I didn't want to dance with him, but I did. When it was all over. my front side was smeared with his sweat and my face felt layered with his intoxicating breath and spittle that flew from his mouth with each step he counted aloud.

That's it. I'm outta here! I thought with finality.

The next morning, after loading up my backpack, I set out. It was about twenty miles to Avalon, on the opposite end of the island, where I could catch a boat back to the mainland. It might take a few days and there might not be an easy route, but I was determined. I had walked across Spain by myself, I could certainly walk across a little island.

I was done with the singles event, done with dating, and I was certainly done with love. I would never need to calculate the score for one more guy on Dad's He's The One index. I could now officially wear the shirt Mom had given me with the skeleton saying, "Still waiting for the one." Only now, I planned to cross that out and write, "Will *never* find the one."

Trudging down a narrow, dusty road with my snorkel and flippers slapping the back of my pack, I shook my fist at the sky and kicked the dirt. After eight miles of angry marching, cussing, shouting at lizards, and winging rocks off the cliff, I finally reached Two Harbors.

Still pulsing with indignation, I surveyed the beach to calculate my next move. Then, something caught my eye. A woman with a golden tan lounging on the white sand with a frosty bottle of beer—and a lime wedged in the top. It looked like a scene staged for a Corona commercial. Suddenly, a villainous idea emerged. An ice-cold beer was the solution. *Maybe two! I had gone long enough without a drink, and it was such a hot day. I deserved it!*

The woman popped the lime in, licked her fingertip, and tilted the bottle up, taking a long, refreshing sip. She smiled contentedly, exhaled, and wiggled her pedicured toes in the sand. Instantly, my mind played out a feasible scenario where I would sprint past the woman, grab her beer, and swim on my back with it on my belly like a sea otter until I reached the dock in the harbor. Once there, I would lean back on the wood slats, swig down my prize, and wave at her—laughing. *Stop it!*

I thought, recognizing the absurd fantasy. *That's ridiculous!* Actually, all I have to do is walk into the bar—and order one myself!

The zing of my potential rebellion was instantly met with the familiar words of the serenity prayer booming in my mind. Guided by its own strength, the prayer repeated itself, but I was still unable to unlock my stare from the woman's seemingly idyllic life—where *she* could drink at leisure. Suddenly a child's high-pitch scream distracted my attention. A pig-tailed girl squealed as she licked the drips quickly melting from her ice-cream cone. Absorbing her uncorrupted, innocent delight I pursed my lips tight, and gasped with an immediate blast of relief. Clarity washed over me and I could see how The Shit Birds had landed while I was unsettled, and in a weakened state of mind. *Alcohol was not the solution. It was the problem,* I reminded myself. My life was infinitely better without it. Closing my eyes, and after taking a few deep inhalations I stood, turned away from the woman and her beer, and walked toward the ice-cream service window—and ordered a double scoop.

The friendly woman working the information booth tipped her sailor's cap at me as I sidestepped through the door with my backpack. She informed me there were no boats out of the harbor that day and I had missed the last bus to Avalon, so perhaps I wanted to camp there that night. Then she immediately recanted her offer. "Sorry, we're actually all booked up for tonight." Staring blankly out the window, my shoulders sagged in defeat. Camping sounded like a pleasant possibility, but now I was out of options. She grinned looking at the computer screen.

"It's your lucky day! We were full until about five minutes ago when someone cancelled an on-line reservation—at the best campsite in the harbor. So, it's all yours if you want it!"

With ice-cream dripping down my hand, I laughed and shook my head in delightful disbelief. "Yes! I want it!" It suddenly became crystal clear, that when I made good choices, and listened to my intuition the Universe conspired for my greatest good. I asked her if it would be warm enough to sleep outside since I had most of the camping gear I'd need, except for a tent.

"Seriously, you are blessed out today! Someone left a tent at a site this morning. I don't see why you can't use it," she said passing the nylon bag over the counter.

After purchasing a bundle of firewood, I lugged my gear to the tranquil campsite located just a few steps from the water, and set up the tent. The top of a picnic bench made the perfect spot to sit cross-legged and get centered. Soon I became present to the warm sunshine and the refreshing breeze that twirled through my senses. The smell of the salty ocean was soothing, and the view was that of true paradise. Nature was giving me every possible indication that it was time to let go of my frustrations and enjoy the moment. Connecting to Mother Earth was the solution.

Walking down to the cove, I sat at the shore and let the water lap my feet. With each rush of the water, the resentment washed away. My mind began to wander as I thought of my journey of finding love and all the personal growth along the way as an onion that had had its layers peeled. Especially evolving in sobriety and all the experiences in Peru, the Universe had certainly peeled me plenty. But why was the onion analogy so common? If one peels and peels away layers—then what? What was in the middle of an onion anyway?

The Andean cross from Peru rested heavily in the crux of my neck as I lay back, dragging my fingers through the sand. Maybe I shouldn't think of life as an onion—but more as an artichoke. The exterior layer was tough and had sharp points. But as the leaves were removed, they got softer and more pliant. Soon there was just the delicate, vulnerable heart within that had been protected by its outer shell. Maybe my own tough and pointy layers had blocked me from my intuition—the true callings of my heart.

Taking a few breaths, I could feel the resounding beat in my chest that seemed to synchronize with the incoming rushes of cool water washing up to my shins and then retreating. Exhaling with each receding wave, I surrendered to the soothing rhythm of my heart that was, and always had been, harmonized with Mother Earth—Pachamama.

Feeling refreshed, I walked into town that night for dinner at the only restaurant-bar in the small Two Harbors town. With just a few other patrons in the room, I positioned myself on a barstool, ordered a coffee, and lost myself in journal writing. With the singles camping fiasco fresh in my mind, I figured writing about it was a good way to spend the evening.

After describing in detail every twist of the previous day, I got to the part of the story about Jerry, my salsa dance partner. He reminded me of a beefy, loud comedian, but I couldn't remember his name. Turning to the guy a few stools down, I asked, "Hey, who was that funny fat guy from *Saturday Night Live* who died of a drug overdose?"

"Chris Farley?" he replied.

"Yeah, yeah, that's it! Thanks," I said, turning back to writing.

"Excuse me," he said with a grin. "That's kinda random. If you don't mind me asking, what are ya writing about that has to do with Chris Farley?"

Breaking the intensity of my journal-writing frenzy, I paused and looked over at the man sitting to my right. He had full-moon brown eyes, a stubbly beard, a dark tan, colorful tattoos on his upper arms—and he was wearing hiking gear. My heart stopped for a moment when he smiled.

Sam had been hiking by himself across Catalina Island, he told me, starting in Avalon and heading toward Parson's Landing, which was directly next to the Boy Scout camp I had just come from. Our paths had literally crisscrossed as I'd made my way to Avalon, with both of us making Two Harbors our midway stop. He was also camping by himself in the same cove where I was set up.

Moving onto the stool next to me, he showed me images on his camera of his recent solo adventure climbing mountains in the eastern Sierras. Even though we had just met, I invited him to continue our conversation back at my campsite. Sam exuded a gentle spirit, and I listened to my intuition and trusted it.

Sam built a roaring fire and we talked well into the night. Much to my delight, he playfully revealed that he carried sparklers in his backpack. He drew my name across the black backdrop of night with the illuminated sparkler and pointed out his favorite stars. Standing shoulder to shoulder with our faces tilted upward, we witnessed three consecutive shooting stars rip across the sky. My chest expanded in pure ecstasy of the moment with an eager desire for him to pull me close for a kiss. But he didn't. Instead, he thanked me for a wonderful night and went back to his tent.

Unable to sleep, I spent nearly the entire night fantasizing that he would tap on my tent and whisper my name. At one point, I eagerly unzipped the door, thinking I heard him, but I was greeted by the star-studded sky.

Sitting on the picnic bench alongside my tent, I wrote in my journal about the recent unexpected connection with this mystery man. "Why didn't he kiss me? He must have a girlfriend," I wrote with a twinge of disappointment.

"Hungry?" said a voice from behind, interrupting my writing. Sam held bananas, muffins, and a cup of coffee. My heart whirled.

"So I think you should call into work and get tomorrow off so we can kayak around the island. What do ya say?" he said expectantly.

I wanted to do cartwheels around the campsite and leap off the picnic table and shout, "Yes, yes, yes!"

But I kept my cool and said, "Yeah, I'd like that. I think I can swing a substitute for school."

Enthusiastically, we rented a double kayak and strapped both of our huge backpacks to the bow and stern of the boat. Paddling near the rocky cliffs, we were surrounded by crystal-clear waters dotted with bright orange garibaldi fish. Effortlessly, I became more and more enchanted with Sam as we shared stories about our lives and sang Jack Johnson and Bob Marley songs.

Seaweed anchored the kayak while we snorkeled and explored underwater caves. Pods of dolphins and playful seals accompanied us. Sunburned and caked with salty sweat, we pulled our vessel into the tiny boat-in-only campsite. It was secluded, pristine, and undeniably romantic.

That night, Sam built a fire with driftwood and I cooked mini grilled cheese sandwiches on his camp stove. Endless shooting stars saluted us as the night progressed, which I took to mean that I'd surely be getting a kiss. Consciously preparing for the moment our lips would connect, I huffed into my palm to check my breath and constantly moistened my lips with Chap-Stick.

But Sam kept his distance, making no indication that he had any interest in me other than being a fellow adventurer. With only one small tent for us to share, it was a tight squeeze, but he kept himself plastered to the nylon wall, not even once accidentally touching me.

By midafternoon the next day, we reached Avalon. Our connection was undeniable, but he seemed to have no romantic interest in me—at least from what

I could tell. Although elated about our recent spontaneous voyage, I was still a bit unsure of what our next step would be. A promise for another adventure? A wave good-bye and a "Thanks for the fun times!"? Or a friendly fist bump?

My brain chugged away with the options when suddenly he pulled me in his arms—and kissed me like I had never been kissed before. The rush was so intense it felt as if I had lost consciousness for a moment as my whole body tipped back and he scooped me up in a loving embrace.

"Whoa…" I said breathlessly. "I've been waiting for you to do that!"

Holding my cheeks in his palms, he pressed his lips gently to mine.

"Why didn't you do that before?" I asked. "Like when we saw all those shooting stars?"

He smiled, shaking his head. "The first minute I met you, you told me all about those guys who made you feel unsafe and uncomfortable. The last thing I wanted to do was to make you feel like that. We were isolated in that cove. What if I made a move and you didn't feel the same way? It would have put you in the same position, and I didn't want to take that chance. Plus it was already perfect—even without a kiss."

I couldn't believe my ears. "Pinch me," I said cautiously. "Are you for real?"

"Ann, I've wished on so many shooting stars then gone to sleep in my tent all alone, hoping to someday find a girl just like you. And here you are."

Nestling my face up to his bristly beard, I inhaled his scent of campfire and salty sea. Exhaling deeply, I knew with the purest clarity that he was The One.

Photo taken after knowing each
other just twelve hours.

50

CLARA'S TIME TO SHINE

Taking my spring break vacation as an opportunity to visit Clara again, I persuaded Sam to join me. Arriving in Cuzco in the early morning, we caught a taxi directly to the Plaza de Armas. Clara was waiting eagerly in front of the fountain with her children, Gonzo and Rosa.

Six months had passed since I had waved goodbye to her after the intense week we had spent together. Light emanated from Clara and the children, who, although usually content, now played with a distinct quality of joy. After blowing bubbles and feeding the birds, Clara grabbed my hand excitedly. "Ana, I have a surprise for you."

Pulling up to a park in a quiet neighborhood, Gonzo jumped out of the taxi before it had even come to a complete stop. He galloped around the grass like a wild stallion in its favorite pasture. Rosa immediately followed, clomping after him in her corrective shoes and the frilly pink dress I had sent for her birthday.

The two children dashed around the expanse of grass, picking a bouquet of wildflowers.

Distracted by the kids' carefree playing, I didn't notice that Clara had vanished. Rosa jumped up to my hip and handed me the flowers. "For you, madrina," she whispered, kissing my cheek delicately.

Sam wrapped his arm around my shoulder while Gonzo took Sam's free hand. Clara called my name in a singsong melody. Turning to her voice, I gasped at what I saw. She stood beaming in a double-breasted, long, white coat with her name embroidered in red. A black apron was tied around her waist, and a tall white chef's hat sat on her head. With her arms out in a welcoming gesture and tears rolling down her cheeks, she waved her arm toward the storefront behind her—a pizzeria!

Not only had she used the profits from the baby carriers to put a down payment on her own business, but she had moved her family to a better part of town, one block away from her new restaurant. The park in front of the pizzeria was a safe, clean place where Rosa and Gonzo played with kids from the neighborhood while she worked. She'd purchased bunk beds so the children no longer had to sleep together in the same single bed, and with the remaining money, she had bought her prized possession—a stovetop oven. Now she could make pizzas for her family in the adobe oven at work but also could design creative meals for them at home.

"You gave me the courage to dream, Ana!" Clara said.

We embraced, both crying with the profound gratitude we each felt for one another.

A month before I'd gone back to Cuzco, I had asked Clara what I could bring for her family when I returned. She didn't give me one hint about what she had been up to, and I was stunned when she'd told me that they didn't need *anything*. Proudly, she was taking a step back from any assistance, although she did make it very clear that she still wanted me to be a part of their lives.

"I'm able to support my own family in a way I never thought possible," Clara had told me. "We are healthy, happy, and have everything we could possibly need."

This statement had left me speechless, fully aware of my own insatiable desire to have more: a better car, a weekend getaway, a new bike, an expensive haircut. After my first trip to Peru, I'd taken a stand for frugality and had simplified my life by resisting material temptations. But inevitably the old way of spending money on a little retail therapy or a "well-deserved" trip had soon resurfaced. There was always something in the back of my mind that I wanted.

But Clara had been very clear that she was self-sufficient, no longer needed my help, and desired nothing more. This single act by Clara taught me volumes. "But there is something you can do," she'd added. "I would be very grateful if you'd help the children of the village where I was born. Used clothes would be best. Do you think your students could help like they did for the women who sewed the baby carriers? There's a school there too. They don't have much for the students. Can you help?"

"Don't worry, Clara," I'd said, bubbling with excitement. "That kind of request is right up my alley!"

Although Clara had never returned to her village, she had a deep longing to bring a spark of hope to the children who were raised in hopeless poverty. Clearly, she'd felt blessed by the opportunity that had been given to her and wanted to share the gift.

Now, sitting at the long, wooden table at the pizzeria, we dug into one of Clara's delicious creations. With the distinct adobe oven flavor, plus a dash of love and a whole cup of actualized dreams, the pizza was like no other.

Showing Clara the three suitcases of used clothing, children's books, and school supplies I had brought, we began making our plan. She explained that her deepest desire was to bring a piñata party to the children who never celebrated one. Giving her one hundred dollars, I told her to buy whatever she thought necessary to create the party she had in mind. She gasped, knowing that one hundred dollars would go a long way and in her hands was now the chance to create a fun-filled event that would bring joy to children who had so little.

At her suggestion, I rented a 4x4 minibus that could hold all the party supplies, the huge bags of used clothes, and enough animal crackers to feed a village—literally. Also packed in were two large piñatas, and, much to my surprise, a bigger-than-life-sized costume of a popular superhero that Clara had rented. The head of the beloved cartoon character was so immense that it had to be strapped to the roof. During a pit stop on the drive, I put on the head and jumped for a photo.

Along with her own family, Clara also invited half a dozen people from the village who'd never been able to afford a return trip. The route was difficult and a long distance from Cuzco, so she recommended I hire a driver who grew up in that village and knew the way. And we were off.

During the long drive, a thought struck and I turned to Clara. "Does your mom still live there?"

"Yes…She does," she replied.

"Really? Are you nervous? Are you mad? Have you forgiven her?"

Clara laughed, patting my leg. "Oh, Ana, you have to understand. My mother was ignorant and uneducated. She didn't know any better, and it was the best solution she could come up with. By selling me, she got the money to feed all her other children. I think she hoped it would give me a better chance at a life. What that family did to me wasn't *her* fault. My mother did the best she could."

Feeling a combination of discomfort and inspiration, I wanted to cry—but Clara didn't. It was the purest form of forgiveness I had ever witnessed and seemed light years beyond my own capacity to forgive. I rubbed my temples thinking of the trivial resentments that still frequently surfaced. I swallowed hard and looked out the window, wanting to hide my tears.

Clara tapped my thigh to get my attention. "But today I get to return to make my mom and the people of my village proud of what I've done with my life. This is a very special day for me, Ana, and I am forever grateful to you."

As soon as the van started its dusty descent over the mountain and into the valley where the village sat nestled on a stunning lake, we could see the local inhabitants beginning to gather. There had been no warning of our arrival since neither electricity nor mail service had yet reached the region. Cars were a rarity, so the large van with the cartoon head on the roof was quite a spectacle. Kids chased the car and Clara opened the side door so they had the chance to ride inside. Hearing a loud noise from the distance, I looked at Clara to see if she knew what it was.

"It's the village elder blowing the conch shell to let everyone know that something big is happening," she explained. "Watch what happens now!"

Flocks of locals headed toward the school playground where our bus parked and unloaded. Clara took charge, directing where food, drinks, and all the extra supplies should go. One of the boys traveling with us dressed up in the costume and walked around greeting the children, most of whom responded by crying and running away, having never been exposed to anything like it before.

Once the first piñata was cracked open, every single child within a one-mile radius piled in a wiggling heap, grabbing at the rare opportunity for the candy scattered below. All the children received half a cup of Coca-Cola and a handful of animal crackers, treats they had never experienced. Sam passed out lollipops, which the kids gladly put directly in their mouths, wrapper and all, uneducated in the logical steps of consuming a packaged sucker.

A line formed as Clara and I handed out one random piece of clothing per person from the bags of donations. The locals would later have to swap with one another to get the sizes needed. The ironic contrast of an indigenous woman clothed entirely in traditional attire holding up a pair of petite turquoise ski pants or a bright red USC sweatshirt was entertaining to no end. Socks seemed to be the golden commodity, and I noticed no one wore them over their black, cracked feet.

Sam and I kept catching each other's eye, shaking our heads in wondrous disbelief. An intense rush of love for him consumed me. A man who would travel to the far ends of the earth to help me—help someone else—realize a dream was definitely a keeper. That day in the village would be a special event in my life, but at long last, it wasn't just another wild, solo adventure documented in my journal or told to my family over dinner. It was an unforgettable experience shared with the man I loved.

Clara motioned us to follow her into the schoolroom and invited me to do an official book presentation. Sam and I pulled the books out one by one and laid them across the table. It was a vibrant display of every classic children's book translated into Spanish: *The Giving Tree*, *Goodnight Moon*, *The Very Hungry Caterpillar*, *Big Dog Little Dog*, and many more. Ten original books were hand-written and colorfully designed by my students in California.

It became a formal affair as the village elder wrote down this specific event in the annals of the village history record. The room was packed with locals all leaning in or standing on tiptoe to catch a glimpse of the unexpected addition to the school. For as long as anyone in the village could remember, there had been only a few tattered books for the kids to read.

The headmaster then declared that a library was to be created in my name. With more than fifty new books laid out before them, the kids stood in awe, nervous to touch the glossy covers. My hope was that—maybe, just maybe—with storybook inspirations to illuminate the minds of the children and adults alike, it might encourage others to dream big—like Clara dared to do.

After the book exchange concluded, Sam and I were asked to sign the official village registry, then we stepped back outside to the celebration. With so much stimulus, I had yet to take a moment to really absorb it all.

Leaning against a wall with two little girls attached to my legs, I observed the lively fiesta with a sea of delighted children surrounding tiny Clara who stood triumphantly in the heart of it all. Gonzo and Rosa were glued to her side, teeming with pride, as if they were making it clear for all the other kids, "This is *our* mother!"

From the corner of my eye, I glimpsed an older woman sitting on a low adobe wall. Round cheeks and light in her eyes, it was a face I faintly recognized. Her arthritic fingers lay clasped in her lap, and she seemed captivated by something as tears streaked her dark, leathered skin.

I followed her steady gaze to see what was moving this woman to tears. It was her daughter—the one she had sold many years before.

Clara's new pizzeria.

Sam and I present books to the head teacher.

Sam and Ann were married
on top of Mammoth Mountain
on July 15, 2012.

Resources

The following are websites and books I used for reference during the process of writing this book:

Websites

Pedro de Valdivia www.biographybase.com/biography/Valdivia_Pedro_de.html

Gabrial Mistral www.biographyonline.net/poets/gabriela_mistral.html

Isabel Allende www.isabelallende.com/ines_frame.htm

Pinochet www.nytimes.com/2006/12/11/world/americas/11pinochet.html

Bad drivers in Peru www.travel.state.gov/travel/cis_pa_tw/cis/cis_998.html

Inti Raymi Festival www.en.wikipedia.org/wiki/Inti_Raymi

Chasquis www.discover-peru.org/inca-roads-chasqui/

Flora and Fauna Arequipa www.incatourism.com/places-to-visit-in-peru/arequipa-tourism/flora-and-fauna/

Santa Catalina Convent www.perutravelling.com/arequipa_peru_santa_catalina_convent_arequipa.php

Lake Titicaca and Uros www.moon.com/destinations/
peru/lake-titicaca-and-canyon-country/lake-titicaca/
islas-uros

Books

Adams, Mark. *Turn Right at Machu Picchu: Rediscovering the Lost City One Step at a Time*. New York: Dutton, 2011.

Benson, Andrew, and Melissa Graham. *The Rough Guide to Chile*. New York: Rough Guides, 2006.

Blacker, Maryanne. *Eyewitness Travel: Peru*. London: Dorling Kindersley Limited, 2008.

Danbury, Richard. *The Inca Trail: Cuzco and Machu Picchu*. Surrey, UK: Trailblazer Publications, 1999.